OFF THE BEATEN PATH® SERIES

ELEVENTH EDITION

MINNESOTA

OFF THE BEATEN PATH®

MARK R. WEINBERGER

Globe
Pequot

Essex, Connecticut

All the information in this guidebook is subject to change. We recommend that you call ahead to obtain current information before traveling.

Globe Pequot

An imprint of Globe Pequot, the trade division of
The Rowman & Littlefield Publishing Group, Inc.
4501 Forbes Blvd., Ste. 200
Lanham, MD 20706
www.rowman.com

Distributed by NATIONAL BOOK NETWORK

ISSN 1542-4170

ISBN (paperback) 978-1-4930-7818-9 | 978-1-4930-7819-6 (epub)

∞™ The paper used in this publication meets the minimum requirements of American National Standard for Information Sciences—Permanence of Paper for Printed Library Materials, ANSI/NISO Z39.48-1992.

To my wife, Lisa, one of those rare spouses who is not afraid to be an honest editor. And to my children, Matthew and Alexandra, with whom I look forward to sharing many trips in the future.

About the Author

Mark Weinberger is a freelance writer who lives in White Bear Lake, Minnesota. His work has appeared in *Powder, Mountain Sports and Living, The Professional Skier,* and *Silent Sports.* He is also the author of *Short Bike Rides in Minnesota.*

Contents

RED RIVER
COUNTRY

■ Bemidji

ARROWHEAD

■ Moorhead

Duluth ■

HEADWATERS

Minneapolis ■ ★ St. Paul
TWIN
CITIES

PRAIRIELAND

Mankato ■

Rochester ■

BLUFFLAND

Introduction

Generally speaking, the interstate highway system has been good for our country. It has made motor vehicle travel faster, safer, and much easier for getting from point A to point B and beyond. It's scary to think of where our standard of living would be if we didn't have thousands of miles of interstate crisscrossing our country.

But we pay a price for all the convenience that interstates have brought us. As more miles of concrete sprang from the countryside, the travel habits of Americans changed. Instead of the leisurely trip where the drive was part of the experience, the multiple lanes of concrete caused us to begin treating the driving portion as strictly utilitarian. Got to get there as soon as possible, can't stop, got to make time.

As our travel habits changed, ubiquity became the feature most valued by travelers and truckers. McDonald's and Wendy's replaced Mom's Place and Al's Diner as the favorite haunts of hungry drivers, and generic convenience stores usurped the position occupied by the full service, get-your-oil-checked-and-windows-washed gas station.

Which brings us to *Minnesota Off the Beaten Path*. This book encourages the reader to turn off the impersonal interstates and travel the back roads that define our state. Leave the fast lanes to explore the rolling prairie country of the south and west where Plains American Indians and massive herds of buffalo once lived simultaneously. Take a two-lane ribbon of blacktop through lake country as it winds through tunnels of greenery and past thousands of large and small watery gems. Follow intimate country lanes in southeastern Minnesota through narrow ravines and around regal bluffs. Seek the unique in the Twin Cities of St. Paul and Minneapolis.

When you leave the interstates, time seems to slow, especially when you find yourself behind a piece of farm equipment. This slower pace provides the time to explore the lands of the Vikings, stoic Norwegian and German farmers, miners, lumberjacks, and fur traders. And though you can find some unique and even some undiscovered sites close to the interstates and major highways, to truly taste the local flavor of each region you must reach beyond and explore the minor highways and county roads.

Stray even slightly from the beaten path in such an environment and there's no telling where you might wind up. It could be in a squat canvas tent observing the bizarre courtship rituals of the prairie chicken. Or it could be enjoying an incomparable Mississippi River sunset from the roof of a chartered houseboat. But no matter how unexpected the turn of events, if the people around you are refreshingly civil and sometimes use quaint expressions like

"Uff-da" and "You betcha," know that you aren't really lost—you're just somewhere off the beaten path in Minnesota.

The more than three hundred destinations described in this book were selected following extensive firsthand field research. They reflect the breadth of attractions that Minnesota offers those travelers willing to venture down the back roads that radiate through our farmland and forests. There are sites of historical, geological, and archaeological interest; novel recreational opportunities; unusual restaurants, taverns, shops, and country inns; unique events and festivals; buildings of special architectural significance; compelling tours; fascinating museums and art galleries; and those occasional phenomena that refuse to be pigeonholed. As much as possible, these areas of interest have been represented equally in each region of the state. Consult the index if you are having trouble locating a specific destination in the text.

More than any state, Minnesota occupies a large geographical transition zone. From west to east, the landscape changes from prairie to hardwood forest. And from south to north it goes from prairie and hardwood forest to bogs and pine forest. Besides the obvious differences in landscape, the climate changes—often dramatically—along these lines of geographical demarcation.

Rainfall increases as you drive from west to east in Minnesota, which helps nurture the lush forests, streams, and lakes of this often ravine-riven landscape. While driving north, it's easy to see the effect of cooler temperatures and thinner soil as farms shrink in size, conifers become the dominant tree, and rock becomes an omnipresent feature of the topography. And to completely mix up the climatic equation, Lake Superior acts as a giant air conditioner in the summer, often causing dramatic temperature differences along its spectacular shores.

The Twin Cities region, which includes Minneapolis and St. Paul, occupies some choice Minnesota landscape. Located along the banks of the Mississippi, the state's largest cities also lie close to two other major rivers, the St. Croix and Minnesota. The region has many lakes, scenic parks bordering the rivers, and cultural attractions. Fun seekers could start their day canoeing the wild upper St. Croix and end it with a play at either the Guthrie or Ordway Theater. From nature lover to culture lover all in one day.

Bluffland runs southeast of the Twin Cities along the Mississippi and is a land of deep valleys, clear trout streams, and imposing limestone bluffs. Glaciers didn't scour this area as they did much of Minnesota. Instead of ice, torrents of meltwater from massive glacial lakes sculpted the broad Mississippi Valley, countless ravines, and caves. Small towns nestle between river and bluff, and picturesque views await the traveler around every curve or crest of a hill.

Prairieland covers a large chunk of southwestern and western Minnesota. This is the type of landscape many people drive through and call boring, and that's unfortunate. By putting on the blinders, these travelers miss the essence of this region. Rolling farm fields stretch around you for miles, oases of hardwoods provide shelter for wildlife during harsh winters and scorching summer days, and historical significance abounds in the settlement of the prairies. It's both a harsh region where winters are often brutal and a nurturing one where wildflowers and fields of small grain coexist under gentle summer breezes.

Red River Country includes the part of Minnesota once covered by Glacial Lake Agassiz, a body of water that at one time or another covered an area larger than all the Great Lakes combined. As you enter this region in northwestern Minnesota, you'll quickly see the legacy of this enormous lake—a landscape so flat that highway overpasses offer the only relief. As the lake receded, it also left behind incredibly rich soil that has led to this region becoming one of the most productive agricultural areas in the world. Featureless, prone to flooding because of the shallow river channels and tabletop-flat surroundings, and located in a region of harsh weather extremes, Red River Country has always exacted a toll on inhabitants lured by the promise of productive land.

In the form of lakes, rivers, swamps, and bogs, water best defines the Headwaters region. And though much of the region sports a thick carpet of pine forest, it's the lakes that draw people. Lake Itasca is perhaps the best-known body of water in this area because the Mississippi River begins its impressive journey from this humble lake. Besides this famous body of water, visitors to the area will find thousands of lakes dotted with hundreds of resorts. As you drive from south to north, the landscape changes gradually from sand plains and farmland with scattered lakes to sand, forest, and more lakes, and finally to peat and sand with thick forest and lakes and swamps around every curve in the road or clearing in the woods.

The Arrowhead region covers the northeastern part of Minnesota and is an area of vast forests, clear lakes, fast-flowing rivers, and the highest hills in the state. But the attraction that best defines this region and occupies a special place in the hearts of native Minnesotans lies in its farthest northeast corner. Lake Superior, with its 150 miles of Minnesota shoreline, dominates this part of the state. As the largest freshwater lake in the world, Superior exerts its influence over the north shore. During the summer, temperatures may run twenty to thirty degrees cooler along the lake than just a few miles inland, and in the winter the big lake helps keep the bitter cold from invading the shoreline. The soaring cliffs, rocky shore, and narrow canyons make this region the most unique landscape in Minnesota.

At the end of each chapter in this book, you will find phone numbers for chambers of commerce for most of the cities or towns featured in that chapter, websites where available, and a list of motels and restaurants. For general information on the state, or to receive an excellent travel guide, contact the Explore Minnesota tourism office at one of the following phone numbers: toll-free at (888) 847-4866, in the Twin Cities at (651) 556-8465, or TTY Relay Service for the Deaf at (800) 627-3529. The website is exploreminnesota.com and the e-mail address is explore@state.mn.us. The *Explore Minnesota Travel Guide* has an extensive listing of 151 chambers of commerce and good descriptions of each region in Minnesota.

Except where indicated otherwise, prices in the text are described in general terms according to these rough guidelines: Meals in restaurants are deemed inexpensive or modest if under $10, moderately priced if $10 to $20, and expensive if over $20. Accommodations are listed as modest or inexpensive if under $40, moderately priced if $40 to $100, and expensive if over $100. Admission prices are termed token, modest, or inexpensive if under $5; moderately priced if $5 to $20; and expensive if above $20.

At the end of each chapter, you will find a short list of scenic roads to try. While I have probably missed a few, some of those listed will take you even farther off the beaten path and may lead you to even more scenic routes through the ever-changing landscapes of Minnesota.

Climate

Minnesota has four distinct seasons. Summer highs average in the upper seventies to mid-eighties, with winter temperatures averaging from the low teens to twenties. The southern part of the state usually has about fifteen to twenty days of temperatures at or above ninety degrees, with the north rarely getting that warm. Winter can see temperatures as cold as thirty below zero, with several cold snaps of minus ten to minus twenty common throughout most of the state.

Autumn features cool mornings with warmer days and lower humidity than much of the summer. Spring features gradually warmer days and a dramatic growth of plants and trees. However, it has been known to snow in May.

Newspapers

St. Paul Pioneer Press
1 West Water St.
St. Paul, MN 55107
(651) 222-1111
twincities.com

Transition Zones

Besides having thousands of lakes and a landscape shaped by glaciers, Minnesota also has a geographic feature unique to this area. Unlike any other state, Minnesota straddles two transition zones: one that runs north and south, with another running east and west. The zone that runs north–south divides the state into prairie and forest, with the northern part of this line cutting through Red River Country.

Much of western Minnesota has the traits of the prairies, including few trees or lakes, less precipitation, and flat to gently rolling terrain. One area near Granite Falls in western Minnesota even has cactus. Moving east through the zone, rainfall increases, thick forest replaces grassland, river valleys get deeper, and lakes and wetlands begin to dominate the landscape.

On the Minnesota prairies, American Indians hunted buffalo and traveled by horse, while settlers built sod houses as they turned the fertile soil. In the forested eastern and northern parts of Minnesota, American Indians used canoes to travel through the labyrinth of lakes and rivers, while settlers exploited the vast tracts of huge white pine to form a lumber boom. Even today, the sizes of farms and cities reflect the type of geography, the amount of yearly precipitation, and the proximity of large rivers suitable for transportation.

Minneapolis Star Tribune
650 Third Ave. South, Suite 1300
Minneapolis, MN 55488
(612) 673-4000
startribune.com

Duluth News Tribune
424 West First St.
Duluth, MN 55802
(218) 723-5281
duluthnewstribune.com

Rochester Post Bulletin
1700 Greenview Dr. Southwest
Rochester, MN 55902
(507) 285-7600
postbulletin.com

For More Information

Explore Minnesota Tourism

121 Seventh Place East

Suite 360

St. Paul, MN 55101

(888) 847-4866

(651) 556-8465 in the Twin Cities area

exploreminnesota.com

Twin Cities

While most visitors to the Twin Cities area will not notice or care much about its geography, this part of Minnesota offers some striking contrasts. In a distance of about fifty miles, the landscape changes from rolling prairie now covered with subdivisions to shady ravines that cut through the steep, forested hills along the St. Croix River bordering Wisconsin.

In a state blessed with an abundance of lakes and rivers, it's no surprise that the Twin Cities area owes much of its existence to water. Both Minneapolis (known as the City of Lakes) and St. Paul sit on the Mississippi and evolved as grain-and-lumber milling centers. Between the two cities, the Minnesota River ends its journey from the South Dakota border and meets the Mississippi at historic Fort Snelling. Southeast of the Twin Cities the third major river of this region, the scenic St. Croix, joins the others near Hastings.

The rivers offer many options both in and away from the mainstream. In a day you could visit Fort Snelling, stroll or cycle along the popular River Road trails, and leave the cities behind to enjoy a quiet afternoon in the St. Croix River towns of Afton, Stillwater, Marine-on-St. Croix, or Taylors Falls.

N

0   20 mi
0   20 km

Taylors Falls
Center City
Lindstrom
Anoka
Buffalo
Marine-on-St. Croix
Stillwater
Minneapolis
St. Paul
Mendota
Afton
Hastings

Mississippi R.
Minnesota R.
St. Croix R.

WIS.
MINN.

The **St. Croix River National Scenic Waterway** lies only twenty-five miles from the Twin Cities. The lower section of the St. Croix, from Stillwater to its junction with the Mississippi River, is by far the busiest section of the river, especially on weekends when it seems as if every oversized yacht in the area is cruising the river. North of Stillwater the river is much shallower, and canoes outnumber powerboats by a large margin. The river flows through a varied landscape on its journey south, with the most spectacular features starting with a narrow canyon at Taylors Falls and continuing through tall, thickly forested bluffs to the Mississippi. After you spend some time visiting the lakes and rivers of the Twin Cities area, you'll quickly understand why residents have such an affinity with water.

Washington County

As the skinniest county in Minnesota, Washington County borders the St. Croix River for about forty miles, from the mouth at the Mississippi north to near Taylors Falls. Although the county is filling up as the Twin Cities expand eastward, it's still easy to find peaceful areas to visit, especially along the river. From St. Paul and Minneapolis, I-94 and MN 36 provide the most direct routes to the St. Croix, while MN 95 follows the river from its mouth at the Mississippi to Taylors Falls.

Afton, a quiet little river town only about thirty minutes from the Twin Cities, at times feels as if it's several hours removed from the city. If you're hungry while in Afton, **The Lumberyard Pub** is the place to go for a quick bite. It's located on the main street through town and a pleasant place to stop for a snack or lunch.

If you haven't stuffed yourself at The Lumberyard, walk the half block to **Selma's Ice Cream Shop**, which occupies the site of a Civil War arsenal. Selma's features exotic flavors for ice-cream connoisseurs and a wide variety of candy and other assorted sweets. The wood floor creaks as you walk about

AUTHOR'S FAVORITES

Afton State Park
(651) 436-5391

Historic Fort Snelling
St. Paul
(612) 726-1171

St. Croix River National Scenic Waterway
(Twin Cities region section runs from Taylors Falls to near Hastings)

perusing the sugary treats and hasn't received a coat of paint lately; the gaps in the planks make it look as if it hasn't changed in one hundred years. You may wish the walk was longer between the two eateries so you would have a chance of working off your lunch before tackling a double rocky road ice-cream cone.

During the summer, Afton is a popular destination for boaters who ply the river and bicyclists who cruise the quiet county roads. Although this area is scenic during the summer, it truly shows off its beauty during autumn, when the oaks and maples put on their best colors. The hills of Europe may have been alive with the sound of music, but the hills of the St. Croix Valley come alive with spectacular colors in the fall. Climbing south out of town, scenic CR 21 takes you to Afton State Park and the last section of the St. Croix River before it joins the Mississippi. Although it's only twenty miles from the Twin Cities, *Afton State Park* feels as if it's a hundred miles away from any metropolitan area. Located atop a bluff along the St. Croix River, the park has miles of hiking trails that wind and climb through thick stands of hardwood trees divided up by ravines and prairie. When the snow falls, the park grooms several miles of some of the most challenging cross-country ski trails in the area.

Driving north from Afton on MN 95 brings you to the historic river town of Stillwater, which hugs the St. Croix as it hangs from the steep hillsides and marks the line between the quiet upper and the busy lower St. Croix River. Although on summer weekends Stillwater may not seem off the beaten path, the scenic downtown has a totally different feel on quieter days. And compared to the suburban sprawl along MN 36 on the west side of town, the downtown is a step back in time.

We Speak for the Trees

The residents of Afton have a reputation for being protective of their turf. While some may call it a case of "not in my backyard," residents have passed tough zoning laws pertaining to residential and commercial development.

In a case that epitomizes their protectiveness, many years ago Washington County wanted to rebuild CR 21 south of Afton. While the narrow, winding road was due for some improvements, the county wanted to completely eliminate the curves and run it nearly ruler-straight from town to the state park. They also wanted to remove hundreds of gorgeous hardwoods that form a dense green canopy over the road.

Outsiders joined residents who lived along the road and those who didn't to fight the county. Hand-painted signs accusing county planners of a variety of sins, most to do with cutting down trees and ruining the character of the St. Croix Valley, appeared along the road. Eventually the county backed down, and though they widened the road and softened some of the sharpest curves, it retained much of its scenic quality. In this case the residents of Afton proved that sometimes you *can* fight city hall.

Turkey Sighting

Several years ago, while bicycling with friends along peaceful CR 21 near Afton, we saw a large dark object moving slowly across the road. Thinking it was a large cat or dog, we kept riding along.

As we closed in on the animal, it suddenly became apparent that this was no domesticated pet. In fact, it was a huge wild turkey ambling across the road, the first any of us had ever seen in the area. It surprised us to see one of these reclusive birds within minutes of the busy eastern suburbs of the Twin Cities.

Since that first sighting, I've found a small flock near Afton State Park and a large one in the northern part of the county. And every year I see more flocks of wild turkeys closer to populated areas. All my encounters with wild turkeys have come from the seat of a bicycle, reason enough to park the car and pedal along the quiet roads of eastern Washington County.

They say that Minnesota was born at the charming Washington County seat of **Stillwater**, where in 1848 a cadre of visionary pioneer settlers gathered to proclaim Minnesota's territorial status. Out of the wilderness they dispatched a fur trader named Henry Hastings Sibley to convince the US Congress of their legitimacy. The following year Sibley won official recognition on behalf of his group, and Minnesota was on the map.

More than a century and a half later, Stillwater persists as a living museum of nineteenth-century history and architecture blessed with one of the loveliest settings imaginable. Nestled in a pocket formed in the bluffs of the St. Croix River on the outside of a bend, the town centers on a commercial district of antiques shops, boutiques, and restaurants in historic buildings that line an attractive riverside park. The waterfront is alive with boat traffic spring through autumn, when, across the river, Wisconsin's undeveloped wooded shoreline explodes in fall color. Any one of the steep streets leading uphill from the center of town passes well-preserved residences, churches, and buildings representing numerous Victorian architectural styles. Call the convention and visitors bureau at (651) 351-1717 for information on **walking and auto tours** of Stillwater's historic buildings.

For those wishing to learn more about Stillwater's history, a visit is in order to the residence of the former warden's territorial prison, which now serves as the **Washington County Historical Society**. You'll find this 1850s-era stone structure at 602 North Main St., in a little canyon known as Battle Hollow; legend has it that two warring Dakota and Ojibway chiefs fought a duel to the death at this spot. Guides at the museum lead you through a variety of exhibits concerning Stillwater's early prominence as a lumber town, life in the penitentiary, and other aspects of county history. A small fee is charged for admission to the museum, which is open Tues, Thurs, Sat, and Sun, May through Oct, or by special arrangement. Call (651) 439-5956 for more information or visit wchsmn.org.

If several hours of wandering along Main Street in downtown Stillwater, especially if it's been a busy weekend day, has left you feeling some sensory overload, you may want to leave downtown and drive a few blocks west to **Meister's Bar and Grill**. This friendly neighborhood bar and grill, opened by Emmett James (Jim) Meister in 1948, is still owned and operated by the Meister family. In a town known for lots of restaurants, with many of them serving more unique fare that appeals to foodies, Meister's is a throwback to a time when bars with flattops and fryers often dominated the food landscape. You can't go wrong with a Burgermeister (crumbled bacon and American cheese), a side of hand-cut fries, and a cold beer. Meister's is open Mon through Sat, 11 a.m. to 11 p.m. Make sure you have cash because they do not take credit cards. Meister's is located at 901 Fourth St. South (651-439-9860; meistersstill water.com).

As MN 95 runs north out of Stillwater, it climbs a deep wooded ravine and follows the edge of the St. Croix Valley to the quiet little village of **Marine-on-St. Croix**. Like most towns along the river, Marine enjoyed early prosperity from the logging boom of the last half of the nineteenth century, resulting in the construction of a number of stately historic homes. Among them is one outstanding example of the Greek Revival style, a former bed-and-breakfast establishment named after its builder, Asa Parker, a founder of one of Marine's lumber mills. (Though now closed, you can still see the house on a hill from the road at 17500 St. Croix Trail North.) For those looking for a bed-and-breakfast to stay in, Stillwater (ten miles south of Marine) has a number of excellent options.

If you're driving through Marine and get a hunger knock or just want to stop at a unique place, you should visit the **Historic Marine General Store** at 101 Judd St. It's the oldest continuously operating general store in Minnesota, a full-service grocery store with a made-from-scratch deli, and is the heart and soul of the town.

Chisago County

From Stillwater, if you follow MN 95 north you'll gradually climb from the banks of the St. Croix and cross into Chisago County. Although the highway follows the St. Croix River to Taylors Falls, you won't see the river until you're on US 8 and dropping back into the valley. When you do see the St. Croix

In the Company of Eagles

One winter while driving along CR 16 north of Taylors Falls to Wild Mountain ski area early on a Sunday morning, for some reason I looked up and found myself rewarded with a clear view of a bald eagle perched near the top of a tree a few yards from the road. My tired brain suddenly sprang to life as the sight of the spectacular bird woke me up more than the cup of strong coffee I was working on. As usual I didn't have my camera, but the image of this majestic bird stayed with me as if I had snapped a photo of it. Upon reaching the ski area, my mood had brightened considerably from earlier in the morning as I shared my experience with some skiing companions. Although bald eagle sightings along the St. Croix River have become more common in recent years, seeing one in person still gets this city boy's adrenaline pumping.

again, you will know it was worth the wait. The road hugs a cliff high above the valley, and you'll have a spectacular view of the river and the impressive hills across the border in Wisconsin.

Although Chisago County is close to the Twin Cities, it shares characteristics with northern and southern Minnesota. Lakes dot the farmland that covers most of the county, and these pastoral scenes could pass for almost any county to the south. But this gently rolling landscape gives way to thick forest, steep hills, and exposed rock cliffs along the St. Croix River, giving the area a much more northern feel.

Minnesota's logging boom came early to the St. Croix River Valley. The grand bluffs and the valleys of the St. Croix's tributaries, thick with giant white and red pine, were the first areas in the state to suffer the effects of the sawyer's blade. By the mid-1850s, with each spring runoff the river became a highway of logs, each stamped with the distinctive mark of the company whose workers had felled it, all bound for the sawmills of Stillwater.

When these huge log booms reached **Taylors Falls**, however, they often ran into trouble. The river here enters the St. Croix Dalles, a constricted, steep-walled basalt canyon with a sharp ninety-degree bend at its center. The Dalles was the site of some truly spectacular logjams that kept river workers busy for weeks as they sought to keep the logs moving by whatever means necessary—including, at times, large charges of dynamite.

In an accommodating gesture to the boisterous loggers who frequented Taylors Falls each spring, the community erected a jail as one of the early public buildings. Built in 1856, this stone structure afforded an easy escape to anyone sober enough to climb over the top of the cell wall. The fact that it apparently served its function for twenty-nine years may be a testament to the sorry state of its occupants, but for whatever reason, in 1885 the town finally decided to invest $311 in the construction of a newer and more secure facility, now the *Historic Taylors Falls Jail.*

If you can swing a pass from the warden, you'll find plenty of engaging distractions in and around Taylors Falls. Just a block away from the jail is the entrance to *Interstate State Park*, where there are hiking trails through the Dalles, with its fantastic water-sculpted rock formations. Rock climbers from the Twin Cities frequent this area, as do kayakers who come to frolic in the rapids just downstream of the US 8 bridge. An excursion boat offers rides downstream in summer, and the park has a canoe rental facility as well.

To get a feel for the world inhabited by the town's early residents, you can tour the historic *W. H. C. Folsom House*, located just a block up Government Street from the jail. This 1855 Greek Revival home of a local logger, general-store owner, and state politician is the most significant building in the town's Angel Hill District, which has been listed in its entirety on the National Register of Historic Places. Almost all the furnishings in the house are original. The half-hour guided tour reveals many day-to-day details of the family's life while at the same time providing a glimpse into a particular point in history. The family was touched by the Civil War, as is evidenced by the displayed blue-and-gray uniform worn by William Folsom's son, Wyman. A local newspaper on a desk in the library interprets the significance of the assassination of President Lincoln. Tours are given daily, for a modest fee, from Memorial Day to mid-Oct; for more information call (651) 465-3125 or visit mnhs.org/folsomhouse.

Lava Flows and Glaciers Melt

Long before humans arrived in Chisago County, glacial activity shaped the landscape, leaving behind morainal hills, glacial outwash, and depressions that eventually became lakes. While the glaciers melted, the Glacial St. Croix River flowed through the region as it drained glacial lakes in the Lake Superior Basin. These torrents of meltwater carved out the St. Croix Dalles, now the site of Interstate State Park, the second Minnesota state park. As impressive a feat as this was, it's hard to imagine the event that preceded it.

Eons ago, a large fracture in the earth's crust developed across the central US, stretching from Kansas, through southeastern Minnesota, to Lake Superior and beyond. Thousands of individual flows of basalt lava streamed from this large crack to form a layer of rock more than twenty thousand feet thick. Today visitors can see a few of these lava flows at Interstate State Park, courtesy of the rivers that poured from the melting glaciers. For casual observers, it's easier to see the terraces carved into the cliffs by the ancient river and the abundant potholes scoured into the rock floor by pebbles and sand grains carried in the strong current.

Swedish Heritage

In a state known for its Scandinavian heritage, the Chisago Lakes towns of Lindstrom and Center City owe a large portion of their history to emigrants from Sweden. This area is the site of the first permanent Swedish settlement in Minnesota (Norbergs-holmen, now known by the prosaic name of Center City) and the setting for several historical novels. The emigrants traveled by boat up the St. Croix River to Taylors Falls and walked the final ten miles west to the lake district, where most started farming.

When historian and author Vilhelm Moberg used this region as a setting in four novels about Swedish migration to America, the area became famous in his homeland. His book, *The Emigrants*, created the local heroes Karl Oskar and Kristina Nilsson, and today these fictional characters stand as statues in downtown Lindstrom.

Other reminders of the area's Swedish ties include historical Glader Cemetery, the fictional burial place of Karl and Kristina, and their fictional home, the Nya Duvemala House. Both sites lie three miles south of Lindstrom off CR 25 on the shore of South Center Lake. The first pioneer was buried in Glader Cemetery in 1855, the last in 1916.

If you find yourself thirsty or craving a good cup of coffee after roaming around Taylors Falls, you won't have to go far. **Coffee Talk** (479 Bench St.; 651-465-6700) is a beautifully restored Victorian house on the main street on the northern edge of downtown. This cozy shop serves a wide variety of coffee drinks, from flavored lattes to a good strong cup of java, and has small tables strategically placed on both floors of this grand old house. It's a great place to kick back and read a book, talk, or just relax and stare out at the St. Croix River Valley.

As you drive west on US 8 and leave the St. Croix River Valley, you'll come to a group of small towns that sit on a chain of lakes. One large lake called Ki Chi Saga (now Chisago) by Ojibway originally covered this area, but railroad companies filled in some of the narrow and shallow places in the lake for rail beds, thereby forming the current group of lakes.

Today **Center City** stands out as perhaps the most historic of the Chisago Lakes towns. It is home to Chisago Lake Lutheran Church, which was organized as a congregation in 1854, and is one of the three oldest Lutheran churches in Minnesota. The congregation built the current church in 1889, and it sits on the site of the original one, which was built in 1856. From the church you can stroll along the Summit Avenue National Historic District, two blocks of distinctive late nineteenth- and early twentieth-century homes overlooking North Center Lake.

Center City doesn't have much of a downtown, but neighboring **Lindstrom** and **Chisago City** have more shops and restaurants. Chisago City, the smaller of the two, has several antiques shops and a mall area that contains, among other businesses, a coffee shop and a unique gift shop. Lindstrom has a more vibrant downtown and consequently a wider array of shops. Lake Boulevard, the main street through the heart of town, has enough shops to keep most power shoppers and browsers happy for several hours, including art galleries, a gift shop, and a bookstore. Lindstrom's water tower, painted to look like a giant teakettle, has become a tourist attraction. It's easy to find, and, of course, there's no charge for viewing it. For more information call the chamber of commerce at (651) 257-0620 or visit cityoflindstrom.us.

Ramsey County

St. Paul had its start as a ragged frontier settlement clustered about a tavern on the banks of the Mississippi. The proprietor of this saloon was a notoriously uncouth and licentious sixty-year-old ex-voyageur known as Pig's Eye Parrant. After one of his customers successfully used "Pig's Eye" as a return mailing address on a letter, this flattering name fell into use in reference to the settlement as a whole. Then in 1840 the Catholic Church sent a missionary to serve the needs of the area's settlers and the soldiers at nearby Fort Snelling. Father Lucian Galtier built a log chapel in honor of St. Paul near Parrant's saloon and eventually succeeded in promoting the use of this Christian name instead of the decidedly heathen one already in service.

From these humble beginnings, St. Paul's location at the head of navigation on the Mississippi River resulted in decades of explosive growth, as huge numbers of settlers streamed upriver from St. Louis to stake their claims on the northern frontier. Territorial status was achieved a mere nine years after Galtier's arrival, and Minnesota found itself under the leadership of a young Pennsylvanian named Alexander Ramsey, who served as Minnesota's first territorial governor and second state governor. Today the **Alexander Ramsey House** at 265 South Exchange St. provides some fascinating glimpses into this remarkable era of St. Paul's and Minnesota's infancy.

Your tour of the fifteen-room French Second Empire–style limestone mansion begins in the carriage house/gift shop with a video program on the governor's career. Then a costumed guide leads you into the outer parlor, where, had you been a female acquaintance of Mrs. (Anna) Ramsey and of proper standing, you might have paid a highly ritualized "call." Staying no more than fifteen to twenty minutes and being careful to discuss only the appropriate topics (politics and religion were taboo), you would then have been free to proceed to your next stop confident that Minnesota's first lady was obliged to return the favor of your visit. The governor, however, dispensed with this formality by ushering his male guests via a side door to his second-floor office, where you can bet that discussions of politics and other contentious subjects were the rule.

The exquisitely preserved house, which remained within the family until it was willed to the Minnesota Historical Society in the 1960s, retains almost all of its original furnishings and many of the innovations (such as running hot water upstairs) that made it a noteworthy structure in its time. Tours last an hour and operate the first Sat of the month for a small fee. For more information call (651) 296-8760 or visit mnhs.org/ramseyhouse.

After absorbing some early history of Minnesota and St. Paul, take a short walk to Italy in the form of *Cossetta Alimentari*. This well-known Italian eatery may not be off the beaten path but it's worth visiting even if you don't plan to do a full sit-down meal. You can pick up an authentic Italian pastry, gelato, or espresso at the Pasticceria, grab some groceries for your own pantry at the Italian Market, stop for a quick bite at Frank's Levee Tavern, or go for the full dinner option at Louis Ristorante and Bar. But if you want to experience the essence of what Cossetta's is, you have to stop at their Eatery and Pizzeria. Reminiscent of the trattorias of Napoli, this bustling part of Cossetta's opened in 1911 and formed the foundation for the other venues that followed. Come to think of it, Cossetta's opened just fifty three years after Minnesota became a state, so you could almost say it's part of the early history of the state. Cossetta's is located at 211 Seventh St. West. For more information call (651) 222-3476 or visit cossettas.com.

In the very early 1900s, St. Paul police chief John O'Connor set up a system that provided a safe haven for criminals of all types, provided they obeyed the laws while in the city. Though O'Connor stepped down from his post in 1920, his system remained in place. The result was that, from the late twenties to mid-thirties, during the heyday of Prohibition and the Depression, St. Paul served as "home safe home" to some of the most notorious gangsters of the twentieth century.

The *Wabasha Street Caves* at 215 Wabasha St. South (651-224-1191; wabashacaves.com) is located on the site of the famous underground nightclub, The Castle Royal. This event center offers *Down in History Tours* (the St. Paul Gangster Tours, the Historic Cave Tour, the Ghosts and Graves Tour, the Mill City Mobs Tour, the Twin Town Tacky Tour, and the Rivers and Roots Tour), swing dance music nights, and seasonal theater.

As one of the more popular activities, *St. Paul Gangster Tours* provide an outstanding way to learn about this era. A couple of costumed guides host the two-hour tour to the city's most famous gangster hangouts and hideaways. You'll see the apartment complex where John Dillinger shot it out with St. Paul's finest and the sites of the Hamm and Bremer kidnappings. You'll also visit the post office where the Barker Gang pulled off the Swift Payroll Robbery. All the while your guides will regale you with stories about the likes of "Baby Face" Nelson, "Machine Gun" Kelly, and Alvin "Creepy" Karpis.

The Memorial Concourse of the **St. Paul City Hall** and **Ramsey County Courthouse** has been well preserved as an art deco masterpiece and as one of the capital city's most noted architectural landmarks. Entering the narrow three-story room feels a little like entering a hallowed chamber in the city of Oz. Very dark blue Belgian marble on the walls creates a mysteriously somber atmosphere. A mirrored ceiling reflects your every move and lends even greater apparent stature to the *Vision of Peace* statue that stands at the far end of the room. Made of sixty tons of luminous white onyx by Swedish sculptor Carl Milles, the thirty-six-foot statue depicts five American Indians in a spiritual ceremony, with a common godlike vision—of Peace—rising among them. The St. Paul City Hall and Ramsey County Courthouse, 15 West Kellogg Ave. in downtown St. Paul, is open to the public, free of charge.

Learning through hands-on exploration of some of the most unlikely objects is the key to fun at the **Children's Museum,** situated in downtown St. Paul. Don't be fooled by the name of this place, either—many adults, as well as kids, will enjoy filming one another in a television studio with real video cameras or operating a large electromagnetic crane.

The Children's Museum regularly holds special events involving its own theatrical troupe and in cooperation with other arts and educational programs in the Twin Cities. There is also a gift shop full of creative surprises. The museum is open Tues through Sun year-round, plus Mon from Memorial Day through Labor Day only, for a modest admission fee. It is located at 10 West Seventh St. For information on special events, call (651) 225-6000 or visit mcm.org.

If you had a model railroad as a child, or even if you didn't, the **Twin City Model Railroad Museum** should make it on your list of sites to visit in St. Paul. Visitors will find a three-thousand-square-foot O-scale operating model of railroads in Minnesota during the 1930s to 1950s, a collection of railroad art, and a history wall. The museum is located at 668 Transfer Rd., Suite 8 (651-647-9628, tcmrm.org).

For those who like their trains life-size as well as pint-size, the **Minnesota Transportation Museum**, 193 Pennsylvania Ave. East (651-228-0263, transportationmuseum.org), is another fun place to visit. Besides a restored roundhouse at this location, the museum also has steam- and diesel-powered trains in Osceola, Wisconsin (thirty-five miles northeast of St. Paul), and vintage streetcars at Lake Harriet in Minneapolis.

Sadly, the Russian Piroshki and Teahouse closed in 2019, so if you're craving Russian cuisine in St. Paul, *Moscow on the Hill* is the place to go.

Located at 371 Selby Ave. in what was once one of the toughest parts of town, Moscow on the Hill serves a variety of Russian dishes in a cozy, historic building. Selby Avenue became gentrified over the past twenty-five years, but it's still not as well-known or popular as it's more famous neighbor, Grand Avenue. Although Moscow on the Hill isn't as off the beaten path as the Russian Piroshki and Teahouse, it's a unique restaurant in a historic part of St. Paul. For more information call (651) 291-1236 or visit moscowonthehill.com.

Another slice of regional history has been well preserved on the grounds of the Luther Seminary in the quiet neighborhood of St. Anthony Park. Here, tucked behind several classroom and administration buildings on top of a hill, is an attractive log building, the *Old Muskego Church*, which stands as a living monument to the first organized Norwegian Lutheran congregation in the New World.

As the door to the lovely old church swings open, there is an aroma of aged red oak and walnut that is as strong as frankincense. One's attention is drawn immediately to the front of the chancel, where, in simplicity and grace,

TOP ANNUAL EVENTS IN THE TWIN CITIES

JANUARY

St. Paul Winter Carnival
St. Paul, late Jan
(651) 223-7400
wintercarnival.com

JUNE

Grand Old Day
St. Paul, early June
(651) 699-0029
grandave.com

JULY

Karl Oskar Days
Lindstrom, early July
(651) 257-0620
cityoflindstrom.us

Wannigan Days
Taylor Falls, mid-July
(651) 465-5133
tfwannigandays.com

Rivertown Days
Hastings, mid-July
(651) 437-6775
rivertowndaysmn.com

Aquatennial
Minneapolis, late July
(612) 376-7669
aquatennial.com

Lumberjack Days
Stillwater, late July
lumberjackdays.com

a solid walnut five-sided altar sits below a turret-shaped pulpit, whose prominence in the building reflects the importance of the spoken Word in the worship of the day. The straight-backed pews, the rough-hewn benches on the balcony, and the grim portraits of some of the early pastors convey something of the life these settlers led. Having chosen a swampy site for their community near Milwaukee, Wisconsin, the settlers experienced a staggering incidence of death by cholera during the first few years (1843 to 1847). But the settlement finally prospered, producing the country's first two Norwegian newspapers, the first elected officials of Norwegian descent, and even a Civil War hero. The church was moved to its present site in 1904 and was added to the National Register of Historic Places in 1974. The building is open for self-guided tours daily, requiring only that you check in at the Seminary Information Desk in the Olson Campus Center on the southeast corner of Hendon Avenue and Fulham Street. For Olson Campus Center hours call (651) 641-3456 or visit luthersem .edu/campus/map/campus-buildings.

The St. Paul campus of the University of Minnesota was developed originally as a "farm school," and the study of agricultural science is still a primary activity there. But within the School of Home Economics in the attractive McNeal Hall, 1985 Buford Ave., is an unusual exhibition dedicated to common objects of human design—clothing, textiles, household items, and decorative arts. Exhibits at the small **Goldstein Gallery** change every two to three months and cover a broad range of themes, from underwear making to the history of inventions by women. The gallery is open daily, free of charge; for information on current exhibits, call (612) 624-7434 or visit design.umn.edu /goldstein-museum-design.

As the expanding populations of the Twin Cities pushed the city limits ever closer to each other around the turn of the twentieth century, the Herman Gibbs family on the northern perimeter of this "interurban zone" adapted their farming practices to the growing urban market. By planting a greater variety of fruits and vegetables and by rushing their fresh produce to the farmers' market each day, they joined ranks with a little-known agricultural tradition called the urban-fringe farm. The farmhouse, with its original furnishings, and the outbuildings used by the Gibbs family have been preserved as the **Gibbs Farm Museum**, located at Larpenteur and Cleveland Avenues in Falcon Heights, where the clock has been set back to 1901.

Guided tours of the farm begin with a short slide show and then lead through a one-room schoolhouse, two barns, and the house, where something's frequently cooking on the woodstove in the summer kitchen. On Sunday, staff and volunteers in period dress provide demonstrations of such tasks as candle dipping, butter churning, doll making, and quilting, to name only a few. The educational practices of the time are explained by a teacher holding forth at the blackboard. And during special festivals it's not unheard of for staff and volunteers to kick up their heels and dance or to compete in such contests as seeing who can produce the most attractive shawl starting with a mass of uncarded wool. The museum charges a small fee and is open Tues through Sun, planting time through harvest. Call (651) 646-8629 for more information or go to rchs.com/gibbs-farm.

"From Urban Places to Country Spaces" is the motto of the **Gateway Trail**, an old rail trail that connects St. Paul to Stillwater, and it couldn't be more accurate. The trail runs for a little bit over seventeen miles from Arlington Avenue in St. Paul to Pine Point Park, five miles north of Stillwater. For its first few miles, the trail provides a nice alternative to busy highways as it passes through the communities of East St. Paul, Maplewood, and North St. Paul.

Then, after passing beneath I-694, the Gateway Trail becomes decidedly pastoral as it meanders past many ponds, barns, and marshes in a gently rolling landscape. The primary trail is paved, providing an ideal surface for bicycles and in-line skates. A gravel trail, which can be used by horses and mountain bikes, runs beside it. Steep grades are few and access points many, making the Gateway Trail quite user-friendly. For maps and more information, contact the Minnesota Department of Natural Resources Information Center at (651) 296-6157 or dnr.state.mn.us.

healthyrivalry

Although Minneapolis can easily lay claim to being the bigger and more cosmopolitan of the Twin Cities, it still takes every opportunity to kick sand in the face of St. Paul. When St. Paul received a pro hockey franchise, it didn't take long for Minneapolis to try to lure the team across the river to play in their arena. If the capital city lures a business away from Minneapolis, the bigger city cries foul and carries on about how perpetual underdog St. Paul stole the company.

If you are one of the many poor souls allergic to domed stadiums and plastic grass, a visit to a **St. Paul Saints** baseball game could be just what the doctor ordered. The Saints, who play forty home games a year at CHS Stadium (in the lowertown area of St. Paul), are members of the Northern League, a six-team independent league whose teams aren't affiliated with Major League parent clubs. The play is not quite of Major League caliber, but the games are fast paced, and the between-innings entertainment is at least half the fun. Tickets are inexpensively to moderately priced. For reservations or information call (651) 644-6659 or visit saintsbaseball.com.

Dakota County

The same glacial river that carved out the impressive river valleys of the Twin Cities region also shaped the landscape of Dakota County. Outwash, layers of sand and gravel deposited by glacial meltwater, formed the gentle hills of this fertile county that sits south of St. Paul and Minneapolis. The glacial streams deposited mostly sand to the west, forming the Anoka Sandplain, an area of dunes and sparse vegetation. The difference in terrain between the two counties provides evidence of the unbelievable power of ice and water.

The geographical hub around which much of Minnesota's history has revolved is the confluence of the Minnesota and Mississippi Rivers. In 1805, two years after the Louisiana Purchase gave the US access to the Mississippi watershed, the territory surrounding this strategic junction of Minnesota's two largest rivers was obtained through treaty from the Dakota for sixty gallons of whiskey and $2,000 worth of trade goods. The land wasn't occupied by its new owners, however, until fourteen years later, when two hundred soldiers spent a miserable winter (forty of them died of scurvy) camped near the site of what was to become Fort Snelling, Minnesota's first military outpost and the Northwest's remotest fort for thirty years (see Hennepin County later in this chapter).

Eventually the Twin Cities sprang up in proximity to this spot—St. Paul a few miles downstream, at the head of navigation on the Mississippi, and Minneapolis at a roughly equal distance upstream on the same river, where the once-magnificent St. Anthony Falls produced waterpower for early industry. But well before either city was established, Minnesota's first permanent white settlement took root in Fort Snelling's protective shadow on the southern banks of the Minnesota–Mississippi confluence.

Mendota (from the Dakota word for "where the waters mingle"), as the town is called now, grew around a fur trading post run by Henry Hastings Sibley of the American Fur Company. A visit to the **Sibley House**, a historic site operated by the Daughters of the American Revolution, reveals much about this pioneer statesman and the era in which he lived.

A year after his arrival in 1834, Sibley and a group of fellow traders and local Dakota built the handsome limestone dwelling as a home and business center. As you step into its large entry, a glass wall panel reveals an innovative building process: The interior walls combined river mud, sand, and clay with a latticework of grass and woven willow branches. But despite the primitive materials used in its construction, the Sibley House was an oasis of civility on the frontier. Tasteful period furnishings in every room suggest how lucrative the fur trade was, while providing insight into the lifestyle of the Victorian society to which the Sibleys aspired. A "fainting couch" placed at the top of the stairs was available for tightly corseted ladies who may have arrived upstairs short of breath. In Mrs. Sibley's bedroom a bootjack features a decorative panel positioned so as to have prevented anyone present from glimpsing her emerging ankle.

The Sibley House is adjacent to the **Faribault House**, built by the fur trader Jean Baptiste Faribault and operated now as a museum, with exhibits on the fur trade and the Dakota and Ojibway cultures.

Both houses are open Tues through Sun for a small fee from May through Oct; they are also open weekends in Oct, when they are decorated for Christmas. Living-history demonstrations are scheduled occasionally. Both are located along MN 13 on the west end of the town of Mendota. For more information call (651) 452-1596 or go to mnhs.org.

Hastings—located about twenty miles downstream of Mendota at the junction of the Mississippi, St. Croix, and Vermillion Rivers—is another community that owes its early existence to the flowing waters at its doorstep. This Dakota County seat of twenty-two thousand retains much charm from its heyday in the second half of the nineteenth century, when water-powered grain mills made the city one of the greatest wheat markets of the Northwest. A drive down the old main street, Second Avenue, reveals many original storefronts still intact.

Another way to enjoy Hastings's rich architectural heritage is to take a self-guided **front-porch tour** of the historic district, following directions in a brochure available from the chamber of commerce at 314 Vermillion St.

Hastings was founded in 1857, and this river town works hard to preserve its history. The town is known for its Victorian architecture and has sixty-two buildings on the National Historic Register. The list includes thirty-three commercial buildings, twenty-eight private homes, and two churches, one of which is a building designed by Frank Lloyd Wright. Visitors can find a map of the **Historic Hastings Walking Tour** on the back of the city street map, available from the chamber of commerce tourism office.

What else is there to do in Hastings? The **LeDuc–Simmons Mansion**, one of the few remaining nineteenth-century Hudson River Gothic Revival dwellings in the country, is worth a stroll by its address at 1629 Vermillion St. Farther south on Vermillion Street, you will cross the Vermillion River, where just to the east is the beginning of a lovely park around a dramatic waterfall. The ruins of the **Ramsey Mill** can be explored downstream where the river rounds a bend.

Continuing out of town south on US 61, in one mile you'll see signs for Minnesota's first full-fledged vineyard, planted in 1973. The approach to the production facilities of **Alexis Bailly Vineyard** is through a field of more than six thousand hybrid grapevines that are especially well-suited to Minnesota's harsh winter climate. The wine these grapes produce has received national recognition for its excellence. Visitors are welcome to taste the Bailly wines and to observe the fermenting process. The vineyard is open free of charge year-round, Fri through Sun afternoons. For more information call (651) 437-1413 or visit abvwines.com.

As you continue south along US 61 past the vineyard, you'll come to the small town of Miesville, population 126. Though barely a blip along the busy highway, Miesville has an outsized reputation for great baseball and amazing burgers. The local amateur baseball team, the *Miesville Mudhens*, plays in Class B of the Minnesota Baseball Association. They are a six-time Class B champion team. Home games are at Jack Ruhr Stadium, which is regarded as one of the best ballparks in Minnesota. For more information go to miesville mudhens.com.

After watching a game, or if you're just hungry for a great hamburger, you can either walk across the highway to *King's Bar and Grill*, or stop while passing through. Built in 1874, King's began as a saloon, restaurant, and board-inghouse to serve people traveling between Hastings and Red Wing by horse and buggy. In 1888 the building became a grocery, saloon, and post office, and withstood two floods and two tornadoes before the current owners bought the business in 1984. The restaurant features over fifty burgers and staff is always coming up with new combinations. Prices at this family-friendly establishment are reasonable, the service is friendly, and the burgers are well worth the drive. For more information call (651) 437-1418 or visit kingsplacebar.com.

Hennepin County

By the late nineteenth century, Minneapolis's flour mills had earned the city a reputation as the flour capital of the world, a reputation dependent on the tremendous waterpower generated by the Falls of St. Anthony. By far the largest drop in the Mississippi's 2,348-mile run to the sea, the falls, with their unstable limestone base, have precipitated some extensive engineering projects over the years. Today they are covered with concrete, and two locks—one fifty and the other twenty-five feet deep—provide passage for barges, pleasure boats, and an occasional canoe. An observation deck at the *Upper St. Anthony Falls Lock and Dam*, with displays and brochures explaining the operation of the lock and the history of the falls area, is open daily Apr through Nov (a parking area is located near the corner of Portland and Washington Avenues). For information call (651) 293-0200.

Art on Ice

Unique to any part of the county where lakes freeze over for a few months a year, ice shanties (or icehouses, shelters, etc.) allow die-hard anglers to keep fishing year-round. Shanties vary in size from the most basic two-person models that only offer shelter from the elements to elaborate models with TVs (satellite nonetheless), stoves, refrigerators, beds, and most of the comforts of home.

In what has to be an "only in Minnesota" occurrence, ice shanties have also become the centerpiece of a type of art gallery on ice. *Art Shanty Projects* is a display of decorated ice shanties that runs for three weeks every year from the middle of January to early February. Artists set up their shanties on Medicine Lake in the Minneapolis suburb of Plymouth for this celebration of winter, and designs change each year. You may find a taxi shanty, a library shanty, or a science shanty among the approximately twenty different shanties on the ice. For more information go to art shantyprojects.org.

Built between 1819 and 1825 as Minnesota's first permanent structure, *Historic Fort Snelling* still dominates the confluence of the Mississippi and Minnesota Rivers from a prominent bluff several miles downstream of St. Anthony Falls. The fort has been restored to its original appearance and is superbly managed by the Minnesota Historical Society as a popular interpretive center and living-history site. Daily, from May through Oct, a contingent of soldiers in heavy wool uniforms reenacts with humor and robust spirit the highly regimented and often tedious life led by the early occupants of this military outpost, which, for all its apparent might, has never seen a moment of fighting. Look for the fort at the junction of MN 5 and MN 55 (there are signs on both highways, but don't confuse the historic fort with Fort Snelling State Park, also close by). A small fee is charged for admission to the fort but not to the adjacent interpretive center, where an excellent exhibit space, film-viewing area, and gift shop are open whenever the fort is and on weekdays the rest of the year. For more information, call (612) 726-1171 or visit mnhs.org/fortsnelling.

the "minneapple"

While Minneapolis has many attributes, including several beautiful urban lakes surrounded by parks and a vibrant downtown, for some reason certain residents and city government officials seem to harbor feelings of insecurity. In an attempt to align their city with New York City, Minneapolis advertised itself in the early 1990s as the "Minne Apple," apparently in an attempt to be recognized as the Midwest version of the Big Apple. Go figure. In staying its usual steady course, St. Paul responded by calling itself St. Paul.

Though he never traveled to the northwestern wilderness, Henry Wadsworth Longfellow helped create in the nation's imagination a highly romantic impression of the Minnesota frontier through his epic 1855 poem, *The Song of Hiawatha*. In particular the story of Hiawatha's courtship of Minnehaha endowed two landmarks with mythical significance: the "shining Big-Sea-Water" of "Gitche Gumee" (Lake Superior) and a waterfall along a small Minneapolis creek from which the lovely maiden received her identity. "From the waterfall he named her, / Minnehaha, Laughing Water," wrote Longfellow, and ***Minnehaha Falls*** hasn't been the same since. Visitors to the burgeoning metropolis during Longfellow's time flocked to see Minnehaha's laughing waters, which are just as inspiring today, as you can discover for yourself by heading a couple of blocks east on Minnehaha Parkway from the intersection of (what else?) Hiawatha Avenue.

Given what you can see of the ***Minneapolis*** skyline from afar, you might easily suspect that the entire city has been built since 1980. While it's true that most buildings with enough stature to be seen from any distance away are new and reflect an innovative variety of current architectural tastes, there is still one remnant of earlier times that now reaches only chest height of its taller neighbors. This is the ***Foshay Tower***, an obelisk design inspired by the Washington Monument and built as an ostentatious monument to prosperity on the verge of the stock market crash of 1929 by one of the city's more interesting public figures.

Wilber Foshay, a newly rich utility company owner, spent almost $4 million in the construction of this first skyscraper west of Chicago and then took the trouble to seek two patents on its design so that it would never be duplicated elsewhere. He planned to install himself in a lavish penthouse suite that complemented the building's art deco styling with a vaulted entry, rich woodwork, and gold-plated faucets.

For the grand opening of his tower, Foshay invited President Hoover (the war secretary came in his stead), along with every state governor in the country. He also commissioned John Philip Sousa to write a march in honor of the occasion, a work the celebrated composer directed in person.

Two months later Foshay's entire dream crumbled around him in the wake of Black Thursday's stock market plunge. Not only was he unable to pay the bills for the lavish party he had thrown; he was also indicted for mail fraud by the federal government. Foshay spent some time in Leavenworth Prison before being pardoned by President Roosevelt in 1935. He died in a Twin Cities nursing home in 1957, leaving his monument behind for us to visit today. Self-guided tours of the observation deck, which has outstanding views of the cityscape and surrounding countryside, and a small museum devoted to the building's history are available during business hours and on Sat for a small fee. You'll find the Foshay Tower by tracing its unmistakable shape to its foundation at 821 Marquette Ave. Call (612) 215-3783 for more information.

Another less-celebrated monument to posterity is found in Minneapolis's **American Swedish Institute** at 2600 Park Ave., which helped inspire a movement to preserve Swedish culture that was initiated by the building's first owner, Swan J. Turnblad. This Swedish-born businessman built a thirty-three-room Romanesque château–style castle for himself that was financed by his success as a publisher of America's largest Swedish newspaper, the *Svenska Amerikanska Posten*. He lived in his early twentieth-century mansion only a relatively short time, donating the building and his collection of Swedish art and historic artifacts to the institute in 1929.

It is an amazing building. The elaborate turrets and carvings of the limestone exterior only half prepare you for the incredible woodwork and rich ornamentation found inside. Eighteen craftspeople worked for two years to complete the intricately carved statues, panels, and banisters—all made of exotic woods—that you continue to discover throughout your tour. There are eleven unique *kakelugnar* Swedish stoves made of porcelain tile. And at the first-floor stair landing is a grand stained-glass window based on a historic painting that depicts, of all things, the ransom of a Swedish community by a Danish king.

Rooms on three floors of the Institute are dedicated to exhibits on contemporary and historic Swedish artists and to the immigration experience. Perhaps the most unusual item on display is a pre-Viking glass beaker dating from the fifth century and believed to be among the earliest glass objects in the world. The institute also frequently shows films and has public programs related to Swedish culture. The building is open for tours Tues through Sun, year-round, for a small fee. For more information call (612) 871-4907 or visit asimn.org.

On an obscure side street near the western shore of Lake Calhoun, one of Minneapolis's lovely urban lakes, is a singularly fascinating museum and library dedicated to the role electricity has played in our science and culture. Upon entering the 1920s English Tudor–style mansion that houses the **Bakken Library and Museum**, you are confronted with several aquariums of electricity-producing fish. Such fish were used by the Romans as early as the first century in the treatment of arthritis. The afflicted patient was directed to go to the ocean shore and stand with one foot in the water and the other on top of one of these slithering fish, whose sensible response was to blast the offending foot with as much juice as it could muster.

The Bakken self-guided tour moves quickly from ancient times to displays of eighteenth-century devices and procedural drawings that illustrate the first

Twin Cities Gorge?

Most visitors to the Twin Cities don't know about it, and for that matter, most residents probably don't either. But thanks to a soft layer of St. Peter sandstone lying beneath hard Platteville limestone and a torrent of meltwater from Glacial Lake Agassiz, the only gorge on the Mississippi River sits between St. Paul and Minneapolis.

Although this gorge isn't in the same league as the great canyons of the western US, it is still impressive. Unlike the other canyons, however, the Mississippi River gorge lies right in the middle of a metropolitan area of more than two million people. This landmark is ringed by two scenic parkways and pedestrian paths that offer great views of this large gash in the Midwest landscape.

Unlike the bluffs south of the Twin Cities that overlook the Mississippi across an often broad floodplain, the river runs close to the base of the cliffs through this canyon. The gorge is beautiful any time of year, but autumn is the best time to visit when the thick stands of hardwood trees that line the edge explode into a mix of red, yellow, and orange.

You can view the gorge and access the paths from any overlook along East River Road in St. Paul, or from West River Road in Minneapolis. You can also see it from the Ford Parkway bridge or the Lake Street/Marshall Avenue bridge.

widespread use of electricity for public entertainment and in medicine. Electric "showers," in which a simple static generator produced a mild current, or "fluid," which was allowed to flow through the body, were thought to have an invigorating influence on the subject's health. More powerful localized applications via the "method of sparks" or, stronger still, the often painful "electric commotions" were used to cure anything from "hysteria" and other complaints thought to afflict only women to states of "suspended animation" resulting from drowning or heart failure.

In another room a series of nineteenth-century photographs reveals the results of an experiment in which the electrical stimulation of specific facial muscles was shown to produce in the same subject strained expressions covering the full spectrum of human emotion. A number of early X-ray machines are displayed, as is a picture of Alexander Graham Bell using an early electric metal detector to find a bullet in the body of President Garfield. If you feel the need, you can even get a charge yourself and watch your hair stand on end by placing a hand on an eighteenth-century Ramsden generator. One of the exhibits, *Frankenstein: Mary Shelley's Dream*, is a multimedia exploration of the history and science of *Frankenstein*. The exhibit includes artifact photos with links to information about the science, literature, and life experiences that inspired Mary Shelley to write *Frankenstein*.

The Bakken Museum and twelve-thousand-volume reference library were established in 1976 by Earl Bakken, the inventor of the first wearable cardiac pacemaker. The Bakken has switched from guided to self-guided tours. Contact the museum at (612) 926-3878 or thebakken.org.

The invention of the telegraph by Samuel Morse in 1835 portended great things for human communication. With the telegraph, for the first time in the history of the planet, people could send messages halfway across the country in a matter of seconds. The only problem was that if the wires that carried these signals became damaged—as they frequently did in wild expanses of the largely unsettled North American continent—no message could be sent. So in 1895, after a series of experiments, Thomas Edison applied for a patent for his "wireless telegraph." With this device messages could be sent through the air via radio waves, and thus the age of radio was born.

From these forgotten beginnings the ***Pavek Museum of Broadcasting*** in suburban St. Louis Park traces the growth of radio and broadcasting in a most delightful manner. Founded by radio collector and enthusiast Joseph Pavek in 1988, the museum houses an impressive collection of radios, phonographs, tape recorders, and other equipment. Bing Crosby sounds remarkably good crooning on a recording made on one of the very first tape recorders. The museum also has a working ham-radio center and a 1960s-vintage recording studio, often used by schoolchildren on field trips to write and produce their own radio programs.

The whole place takes you back to a simpler time, when families used to gather in living rooms—Mom and Dad in their favorite chairs, the kids lying on the floor with their heads propped on their hands—to listen to the radio. Nowhere is this innocence better illustrated than in the Minnesota Room's collection of paraphernalia from the state's radio past. Hidden in one of the display cases is a membership card to the Cowboy Bill Club (Cowboy Bill hosted a children's radio program in the 1930s and 1940s). Printed on the card are Cowboy Bill's Rules for Success:

> OBEY YOUR PARENTS.
> BE CHEERFUL.
> KEEP CLEAN.
> SAVE YOUR MONEY.

Ah, the good old days.

The Pavek Museum of Broadcasting, 3517 Raleigh Ave., St. Louis Park, is open Wed through Sat, year-round. Admission is inexpensive. Call (952) 926-8198 for group reservations, or check out their website at pavekmuseum.org.

Are you someone who was convinced at one time or another that being a firefighter is life's highest calling? If so, you might enjoy a visit to the *Firefighters Hall and Museum*, in northeast Minneapolis near the northwest corner of Broadway and Central, where you can indulge in the fantasy once again. From a 1796-vintage hand-drawn water pump to the 1940s engine that roars in and out of the building, siren wailing, loaded with kids for a ride through the neighborhood, there are dozens of fire engines and plenty of firefighting memorabilia to spark your childhood recollections or generate some new ones. Modern trucks from the 1940s, 1950s, and 1960s dominate one part of the museum, whereas a second area is dedicated to horse- and hand-drawn pumps. There are big-billed firefighters' hard hats and rubberized coats to try on for photographs (bring your own camera), pictures of historic Twin Cities fires in progress, and models of various firehouses. The museum is open the second and fourth Sat of every month and charges a small fee. It is located at 664 Twenty-Second Ave. Northeast. If you get lost, listen for sirens or call (612) 623-3817. The website is minnesotafiremuseum.org

If you escaped childhood without ever having dreamed of being a firefighter, then perhaps the *Wings of the North Air Museum*, the successor to the Planes of Fame War Birds Air Museum, would be to your liking. Occupying space at Flying Cloud Airport in Eden Prairie, Wings of the North Air Museum is a much smaller version of the previous museum, but in a few years it's possible that they'll have a larger collection of airplanes to view. There is a modest admission charge at the museum, which is open limited hours on weekends and is located at 10100 Flying Cloud Dr. Go to wotn.org for more information.

There's no better way to soothe your shattered nerves than to leisurely stroll through the *Normandale Japanese Gardens* at Normandale Community College in Bloomington. Created by Tokyo designer Takao Watanabe, the garden's large waterfall and creek, three arch bridges, lagoon, and shrine exude serenity. A self-guided tour booklet is available for a small fee, and guided tours can be arranged for groups of ten or more. To find the garden, look for signs at the entrance to the college at 9700 France Ave. South, Bloomington, or call (952) 358-8145. The garden is always open, though the waterfall is turned off Oct through May. Sunsets are lovely.

Places to Stay in the Twin Cities Region

AFTON

Afton House Inn
3291 St. Croix Trail
(651) 436-8883
aftonhouseinn.com

CHISAGO LAKES AREA

Country Bed & Breakfast
17038 320th St.
Shafer
(651) 257-4773
countrybedandbreakfast.us

Amerivu Inn and Suites
29579 Sportsmen Dr.
Chisago City
(651) 213-3400
amerivuinn.com

HASTINGS

Nichols Inn of Hastings
2400 Vermillion St.
(651) 437-8877
nicholsinn.com

Hastings Country Inn
300 Thirty-third St.
(651) 437-8870
hastingscountryinn.net

MINNEAPOLIS

Comfort Inn
Bloomington Airport
1321 East Seventy-eighth
St.
Bloomington
(952) 854-3400
choicehotels.com

Embassy Suites Airport
7901 Thirty-fourth Ave.
South
Bloomington
(952) 854-1000
hilton.com

Loews Minneapolis Hotel
601 First Ave. North
(612) 677-1100
loewshotels.com

**Hampton Inn
Bloomington West**
5400 American Blvd. West
(952) 905-2950
hilton.com

Nicollet Island Inn
95 Merriam St.
(612) 331-1800
nicolletislandinn.com

STILLWATER

Grand Stay Hotel and Suites
2200 West Frontage Rd.
(651) 430-2699
grandstayhospitality.com

Lowell Inn
102 North Second St.
(651) 439-1100
lowellinn.com

Water Street Inn
101 Water St. South
(651) 439-6000
waterstreetinn.us

Stillwater has five bed-and-breakfast inns and an excellent convention and visitors bureau website (discoverstillwater.com).

ST. PAUL

Doubletree by Hilton
411 Minnesota St.
(651) 291-8800
hilton.com

Covington Inn Bed & Breakfast
100 Harriet Island Rd. B3
(651) 292-1411
covingtoninn.com

Embassy Suites
175 East Tenth St.
(651) 224-5400
hilton.com

Holiday Inn Express & Suites
9840 Norma Ln.
Woodbury
(651) 702-0200
ihg.com

The Saint Paul Hotel
350 Market St.
(651) 292-9292
saintpaulhotel.com

TAYLORS FALLS

Wannigan Point Cabins
150 Maple St.
(651) 465-3247
wanniganpointcabins.com

Note: St. Croix Falls, WI, which is located across the river from Taylors Falls, has several lodging options.

Places to Eat in the Twin Cities Region

AFTON

Afton House
(American)
3291 St. Croix Trail
(651) 436-8883
aftonhouse.com

The Lumberyard Pub
3121 St. Croix Trail South
(651) 691-9140
lumberyardpubmn.com

CHISAGO LAKES AREA

Anderson's Ice Cream Shoppe
12710 Lake Blvd.
Lindstrom
(651) 401-5394
andersonsicecreamshoppe
.com

Gustaf's on Main Eatery
13045 Lake Blvd.
Lindstrom
(651) 263-0737
gustafseatery.com

Swedish Inn
(American)
12678 Lake Blvd.
Lindstrom
(651) 257-2571
theswedishinn.com

Northwoods Roasterie Coffee
12710 Lake Blvd.
Lindstrom
(651) 257-5240
northwoodsroasterie.com

The Stone Inn
(American)
10805 Lake Blvd.
Chisago City
(651) 213-3178
stoneinnchisago.com

HASTINGS

Dunn Brothers
(coffee)
919 Vermillion St., Suite 140
(651) 438-9297
dunnbrothers.com

Lock and Dam Eatery
(American)
101 Second St. East
(651) 319-0906
lockanddameatery.com

El Mexican
119 East Second St. East
(651) 437-5002
elmexicanrestaurantsmn
.com

The Busted Nut Bar and Grill
(American)
118 Second St. East
(651) 438-6887
thebustednut.com

MARINE-ON-ST. CROIX

Brookside Bar and Grill
140 Judd St.
(651) 433-1112
brooksidebarandgrill.com

Marine Landing B.O.T.M.
(American)
10 Elm St.
(651) 433-4577
Open summer only

Nita Mae's Scoop
(ice cream)
101 Judd St.
(651) 433-0137
nitamaes.com
Open summer only

MINNEAPOLIS

Brit's Pub & Eating Establishment
(eclectic)
1110 Nicollet Mall
(612) 332-3908
britspub.com

Bryant Lake Bowl
(American)
810 West Lake St.
(612) 825-3737
bryantlakebowl.com

Buca
(Italian)
1204 Harmon Place
(612) 288-0138
bucadibeppo.com

Key's Cafe
(American)
114 South Ninth St.
(612) 339-6399
keyscafe.com

Pizza Luce
119 North Fourth St.
(612) 333-7359
pizzaluce.com

Surly Brewing Company
(eclectic)
520 Malcolm Ave. SE
(763) 999-4040
surlybrewing.com

STILLWATER

Brian's Restaurant
(American)
219 South Main St.
(651) 571-3132
briansstillwater.com

Daily Grind
Espresso Cafe
(coffee)
217 North Main St.
(651) 430-3207

Leo's Grill and Malt Shop
131 South Main St.
(651) 351-3943
leosgrill.com

Lowell Inn
(full-course dining)
102 North Second St.
(651) 439-1100
lowellinn.com

Main Cafe
(American)
108 North Main St.
(651) 430-2319
themaincafe.wixsite.com
/maincafe

Meisters Bar and Grill
901 South Fourth St.
(651) 439-9860
meistersstillwater.com

Phil's Tara Hideaway
(American)
15021 Sixtieth St. North
(651) 439-9850
tarahideaway.com

Victoriano's New York
Style Pizza
(Italian)
402 North Main St.
(651) 430-3700
victorianosmn.com

ST. PAUL

Boca Chica Restaurante
(Mexican)
11 Cesar Chavez St.
(651) 222-8499
bocachicarestaurant.com

Café Latte
(American)
850 Grand Ave.
(651) 224-5687
cafelatte.com

Cecil's Deli & Restaurant
(American)
651 Cleveland Ave. South
(651) 698-0334
cecilsdeli.com

Cosetta's Italian Market
& Pizzeria
211 West Seventh St.
(651) 222-3476
cossettas.com

Dunn Brothers
(coffee)
1569 Grand Ave.
(651) 698-0618
dunnbrothers.com

Key's Restaurant
(American)
504 North Robert St.
(651) 222-4083
keyscafe.com

TAYLORS FALLS

Juneberry Café
(sandwiches and coffee)
360 Bench St.
(651) 240-0105
juneberrycafe.com

SELECTED WEBSITES IN THE TWIN CITIES

Chisago Lakes Area
Chamber of Commerce
(651) 257-1177
chisagolakeschamber.com

Hastings Area Chamber of Commerce
and Tourism Bureau
(651) 437-6775
visithastingsmn.org

Minneapolis Convention and
Visitors Association
(888) 676-6757
minneapolis.org

Stillwater Area Convention
and Visitors Bureau
(651) 351-1717
discoverstillwater.com

St. Paul Convention and
Visitors Bureau
(800) 627-6101
visitsaintpaul.com

Taylors Falls Chamber of Commerce
(715) 483-3580
fallschamber.org

Coffee Talk
479 Bench St.
(651) 465-6700

The Drive-In
(American)
572 Bench St.
(651) 465-7831
taylorfallsdrivein.com
Summer only

Schooney's Malt Shop
384 Bench St.
(651) 465-3222

Bluffland

When driving into the southeastern corner of Minnesota, visitors will find a startling landscape not found anywhere else in the state. Along the Mississippi River, limestone bluffs tower above the valley floor, looking like sentinels that seem to guide the river on its journey south. Much of this land resembles parts of the Appalachians or Ozarks, and it has a more southern climate than any other area in Minnesota. The western edge of Bluffland is flat to mildly rolling farm country, and as you drive east to the Mississippi River, the landscape becomes much more rugged and dramatic.

Bluffland lies in the driftless area, a region of rocky uplands that covers ten thousand square miles in Minnesota, Wisconsin, Iowa, and Illinois. The last glaciers didn't cover this area, which left a landscape of rolling plains. Over time, rivers have carved spectacular valleys in this region, leaving behind gentle hills interrupted by these gashes. Since the underlying limestone is soluble, caves formed here but nowhere else in Minnesota. Because of this dramatic landscape, this region has become a favorite destination for weekend visitors who come to hike, bike, or just relax while staying in one of the scenic towns nestled among the hills. One of the defining features of

Bluffland is the beautiful valley carved out by the Mississippi River. A drive on **US 61** is one of the best ways to see the valley and the great river towns along it.

Goodhue County

When you enter the picturesque Mississippi River town of Red Wing, it's hard to not notice **Barn Bluff**, an oblong mountain that abruptly rises three hundred feet above the heart of the business district like the back of some great subterranean elephant. Thousands of years ago this protrusion of ancient sandstone was an island surrounded by a much larger and glacial Mississippi River. Today Barn Bluff offers hikers the same grand views of the city and river environment as it did when Henry David Thoreau climbed to its peak in 1861.

Several hiking trails begin at the base of the mountain near the east end of Fifth Street. One trail winds through an old sandstone quarry that overlooks the river, while another passes near the remains of a large limestone kiln that was used in the late nineteenth century. A third trail ascends to the crest of the mountain and follows its ridge from one end to the other, offering great vistas of the town on one side and the wooded channels of the Mississippi on the other. Still another trail follows the southern side of Barn Bluff and allows hikers to peer into backyards all over town.

At about the time of Thoreau's visit, **Red Wing** was well on its way to becoming the world's largest primary wheat market. This economic activity drew businessmen from all over the country, prompting local boosters in 1875 to build a monument to the town's prosperity in the form of a first-class hotel and restaurant. Thanks to an extensive and faithful restoration effort in 1979, the **St. James Hotel** (406 Main St.) today offers the same luxurious accommodations and excellent dining that it did more than a hundred years ago, when the *Minneapolis Mail* proclaimed that the hotel was "second to none in the state, in arrangement, elegance of furniture and general appointment."

AUTHOR'S FAVORITES

Cannon Valley Trail and Root River State Trail

Towns along the Root River (Lanesboro, Harmony, Preston)

The drive on US 61 along the Mississippi River

whygoatprairies?

As you drive through the magnificent Mississippi River Valley between Red Wing and Winona, the mighty river competes with the towering bluffs for your attention. From a distance, the vegetation that covers the sides of the bluffs looks unremarkable. Known as *goat prairies*, the bluffs harbor several varieties of vegetation unique to this area of southeastern Minnesota. But the most important question remains. Why call them goat prairies? The name refers to the steep angle of the slopes because "only goats can graze it."

Graciously decorated and spacious guest rooms—many offering fine views of the river—are furnished with Victorian-era antiques and antique reproductions. There are two restaurants in the hotel; *The Port* in the lower level, where cozy candlelight meals are served surrounded by the building's original rough limestone walls, and *Scarlet Kitchen and Bar*. Rooms and meals at the St. James are moderately to expensively priced. For reservations or more information call (651) 388-2846 or visit st-james-hotel .com.

Although the St. James is certainly a fine place to stay, to keep with the theme of getting off the beaten path, you really should stay at one of the unique bed-and-breakfast inns located in or near town. At last count Red Wing had at least six such establishments, most of which occupy restored homes in this historic river town. Accommodations range from an 1880 Queen Anne home with two guest rooms to a large home that housed three Red Wing Shoe Company presidents to a couple of inns located in the rolling countryside outside of town.

A second industry that drew national attention to Red Wing beginning in the late nineteenth century was the production of durable and attractive stoneware under the Red Wing label. Early in the 1880s three small stoneware manufacturing companies banded together to form the Red Wing Union and began nationwide distribution of their distinctive ceramic water jars, jugs, pitchers, crocks, and dinnerware, all of which were made from local clays. Until it was eclipsed by more economical glass production techniques in the 1940s, the Red Wing Union's pottery was in such demand that at one point the company was the largest stoneware manufacturer in the US.

Today there are several sites in town that give visitors a glimpse into the Red Wing pottery tradition. *Pottery Place* (2000 Old West Main St.; 651-388-1161; potteryplaceredwing.com), a large brick complex at the west end of town, was the center of stoneware production from the time of the building's construction in 1885. Now the complex is home to a series of factory-outlet retail stores, though photographs and displays offer some insight into the Red Wing Union and its operation. This building was also the site of the world's first tunnel kiln, and a small section of one of these kilns is on display to the south of the main entrance. In the **Pottery Salesroom**, located next door to Pottery Place, some of the original Red Wing pottery is sold, along with a large selection of glassware.

Besides pottery and stoneware, Red Wing is also home to the Red Wing Shoe Company. If you love shoes, or just enjoy seeing unique places, the **Red Wing Shoe Museum** is a fun place to visit. Exhibits include a display on how the company makes shoes, firsthand "shoe" tales, and a station for visitors to try their hands at assembling a boot. You won't find any footwear from the closets of Imelda Marcos, but you will see interesting exhibits on shoes of a more utilitarian function. The museum is located next to La Grange Park at 315 Main St. in the Riverfront Center in downtown. For more information call the Red Wing Convention and Visitors Bureau at (651) 385-5934 or the museum at (651) 388-6233.

If you find yourself enjoying Red Wing and maybe looking for a few other attractions to visit, you should check out a couple of unique places you won't find anywhere else. **Stoney End Harps**, which is located just west of Red Wing at 920 Hwy. 19, welcomes visitors to their workshop. They've been making traditional folk lever harps for twenty-five years, and also make banjos, mountain dulcimers, and bodhrans. To check on a guided tour or to find out when the next live musical performance is, call them at (651) 388-8400 or visit stoneyend.com.

For those with even a casual interest in snow sports, the **American Ski Jumping Museum and Hall of Fame** is worth visiting. Ski jumping has a long history in Minnesota, and the first recorded tournament in the US was held in 1887 at Red Wing. The museum is located in the mezzanine of the St. James Hotel in downtown Red Wing, and has a collection of ski jumping memorabilia from the beginning of the sport in this country. For more information go to intergarten.com/asjx.

If you ride a bicycle and happen to be in Red Wing, make sure you allow time for a trip on the **Cannon Valley Trail**. This paved trail runs 19.7 miles from Red Wing to Cannon Falls through a tunnel of trees beneath the bluffs formed by the Cannon River. A perfect trip starts in Red Wing and goes uphill (don't worry, it's a gentle railroad grade) to the halfway point in Welch, before turning around for the return cruise to Red Wing.

The drive west from Red Wing up and over the wooded bluffs and through a pastoral landscape of gentle hills dissected by an occasional river valley is a pleasant one. The same journey five hundred million years ago, however, would have required a submarine, for at that time all of southern Minnesota was covered by what geologists call the Ordovician Sea—a warm, shallow ocean that stretched all the way south to what is now the Gulf of Mexico. Today, evidence of the primitive marine life that thrived in that body of water can be found all over southeastern Minnesota, wherever selected layers of limestone bedrock have been exposed to view.

One such site for collecting **Ordovician fossils** is located in a roadside cut along Goodhue CR 8, less than a half mile north of CR 9 and seven miles west of the town of Goodhue. Park your car on the shoulder of the road, and with a good guidebook in hand, such as *Constance Sansome's Minnesota Underfoot*, start sifting through the gray-green rock fragments collected at the base of the exposed rock face on either side of the road. What you'll find without much effort will be fossilized remains of corals, sponges, and other long-extinct species of organisms. Some of these—such as clams or snails—will look familiar, whereas others will send your imagination reeling in unexpected directions, trying to recognize familiarity in their shapes.

In the nearby community of Zumbrota, you will find a historic landmark preserved from a far more recent era. Just north of town, in the center of a city park on MN 58, sits Minnesota's last **covered bridge**. From its construction in 1869 until 1932, the 120-foot wooden structure, which is listed on the National Register of Historic Places, carried traffic over the Zumbro River. The bridge originally was part of the stagecoach route from St. Paul to Dubuque, Iowa. Perhaps harried stagecoach drivers were the target of the sign above the bridge's entrance that reads: $10 FINE FOR DRIVING FASTER THAN A WALK ACROSS THIS BRIDGE.

Wabasha County

It was a hot, hazy day in **Lake City** during the summer of 1922, when eighteen-year-old Ralph Samuelson walked down to Lake Pepin, strapped a couple of nine-foot-long wooden planks to his feet, and shouted the immortal words, "Hit it!" With that, the sport of waterskiing was born. Waterskiing has obviously grown by leaps and bounds since that fateful summer day, but its humble beginnings are still marked by Ralph's original pair of skis, mounted on the wall at the Lake City Area Tourism Bureau (100 East Lyon Ave.).

A favorite Lake City eatery is the **Chickadee Cottage Cafe**, 317 North Lakeshore Dr. (US 61). Modeled after a traditional English teahouse, Chickadee Cottage offers a delicious assortment of lighter fare for breakfast and lunch, including omelets, sandwiches, salads, and cheese plates. An afternoon tea, including scones, tea sandwiches, and various sweets, is served daily 3 to 5 p.m. All-you-can-eat family breakfasts are offered Sun 8 a.m. to 1 p.m. Call (651) 345-5155 or visit chickadeecottagecafe.com.

A beautiful bed-and-breakfast in Lake City offers a healthy dose of Victorian charm. *The Frog & Bear*, at 411 West Center St. (651-345-2122), is located in the heart of Lake City, within walking distance of Lake Pepin.

Driving east on MN 60 from Zumbrota through Wabasha County is a great way to appreciate the special geology of the bluff country. Tight, winding canyons with walls of crumbling limestone and sandstone alternate with straight stretches of road that offer sweeping views of the pastoral landscape. As the Mississippi River approaches, the valley widens, the bluffs become more pronounced, and hillsides are covered with hardwood forest.

gimmetheskinny

What must be one of the skinniest attractions in the world runs through Bluffland. The *Upper Mississippi River National Wildlife and Fish Refuge* begins above Wabasha, Minnesota, and runs to Rock Island, Illinois. It measures more than 260 miles in length and up to 3 miles at its widest point. Covering more than 200,000 acres, it provides habitat for 292 species of birds, 57 species of mammals, 45 species of amphibians and reptiles, and 118 species of fish.

After driving inland from Lake City to get a different taste of the scenery in Bluffland, those interested in a more intimate exploration of the Mississippi should plan on circling back to the river and booking a kayak trip with *Broken Paddle Guiding in Wabasha* (213 Main St. West). Nothing beats being in a kayak for an up-close and personal view of the Mississippi, and taking the Flooded Forest tour with Broken Paddle will take you away from the sometimes busy main channel of the mighty river and into the quiet and at times eerie backwaters. You will paddle under a thick canopy of trees and through some of the most remote channels and meanders on the river. Participants spend 90 percent of the tour in the smooth and shallow river channels. Broken Paddle also offers raptor and sunset tours that end with a stop at a local brewery. Open early May through late Oct. For more information, call (651) 955-2222 or visit brokenpaddleguiding.com.

Capitalizing on the success of *Grumpy Old Men*, the 1993 hit movie starring Jack Lemmon and Walter Matthau, which was based in Wabasha (but filmed in Faribault), Wabasha now stages the *Grumpy Old Men Festival*, the highlight of which is an ice-fishing contest. For information regarding this event, which takes place in late February, contact the Wabasha-Kellogg Chamber of Commerce (651-565-4158) or visit wabashamn.org/grumpyoldmenfest.

Wabasha is also home to a large bald eagle population, prompting volunteers to set up *Eagle Watch*. Every Sun between 1 and 3 p.m., from Nov

A New/Old Era of Travel

The powerful tow boats, large cabin cruisers, and fast fishing boats that ply the Mississippi River today are far different from the simple boats used by American Indians and early explorers and settlers. For many years the bark canoe served as the main mode of transportation on the big river and its tributaries. Portable and easy to build, canoes were used by American Indians, explorers, and trappers for hauling supplies as well as for transportation.

As more people started arriving in the region, the need to haul larger loads not only down the river but back up led to the development of the keelboat. First used on the upper Mississippi by the French in 1751, keelboats could haul large loads of cargo, and the flat bottoms made them useful for navigating in even shallow water. Although crews could move keelboats upstream, it was hard work done by poling or tying ropes to tree stumps on shore and pulling the boats along. Despite the manual labor involved, keelboats could go eight to twelve miles upstream per day.

In 1823 the first steamboat to visit Minnesota docked at Fort Snelling and started a new era of river travel. Soon thereafter, as the lumber industry began along the upper Mississippi in the mid-1800s, a boat called a flatboat or broadhorn became a popular vessel. Made of lumber and logs, the sixty-foot-long by twenty-foot-wide boats that evolved from simple rafts floated downriver with lumber and other products from the northwoods. After reaching their destination, the boats were torn apart and sold piece by piece along with the cargo.

The only way the often rough crews could return upriver was to catch a ride on a steamboat. It must have been a funny sight to see these hardworking (and hard-drinking) river men riding a fancy steamboat with the more refined passengers. Although romanticized in stories, steamboats faced many hazards, including snags, boiler explosions, collisions with other boats, log rafts, ice, and floating trees. By 1915 the banner days of the fancy river steamboats had ended, with the surviving ones tied up at river towns as tourist attractions.

through Mar, volunteers from town set up telescopes and binoculars so visitors can catch a glimpse of these majestic avians, once on the brink of extinction but now making a strong comeback in these parts. Call the Wabasha-Kellogg Chamber of Commerce at (651) 565-4158 for more information. You can also contact *The National Eagle Center* at (651) 565-4989 or nationaleaglecenter.org.

Cruise six miles south of Wabasha just off US 61 and you will enter the magic kingdom of L.A.R.K. Toys. Opened in 1986 by Donn and Sarah Kreofsky, and now owned by the Gray family, *L.A.R.K. Toys* is a haven for lovers of the handmade wooden toys of yesteryear. The ever-expanding L.A.R.K. Toys compound currently includes an office building, factory building, gift shop, toy museum, bookstore, and a gigantic carousel.

The highly entertaining gift shop offers an impressive collection of imported Christmas toys, tin toys, nesting dolls, handmade pull toys, books, and games. What's more, look carefully about this whimsical place and you may find trolls hidden in the rafters and large slingshots mounted here and there (used to propel the trolls on their nightly travels); there are even little mouseholes carved into the baseboards.

The toy factory is also a delight to behold, for it is here that the hand-carved characters for the carousel were made. Sure, we've all ridden a horse on a merry-go-round, but who among us has ever ridden a dinosaur? Or a moose? Or a fish?

L.A.R.K. Toys may not be the Fountain of Youth, but odds are you'll feel just a little bit younger by the end of your visit. Catalog and ordering information are available by calling (507) 767-3387 or by visiting larktoys.com.

For many people the Mississippi River flowing slowly southward is an irresistible attraction. If you're such a person—someone fascinated with the incredibly rich history associated with the river, a lover of waterfowl, an angler, or a river rat in the Huck Finn tradition—stop in at **Great River Houseboats at Alma Marina**, located just across the river in Alma, Wisconsin. Alma Marina does not rent houseboats anymore, but they still rent twelve- or fourteen-person pontoon boats. This is one of the few places in the state where you can rent a boat. Depending on group size and boat, prices are inexpensive to moderate. Reservations should be made well in advance by contacting Alma Marina at (608) 685-3333 or almamarina.net.

Olmsted County

The city of **Rochester** repeatedly finds its way into the nation's headlines because of the **Mayo Clinic**—the world's first and largest private practice medical facility and the city's largest employer. Perhaps it should be no surprise that most attractions in and around this city of 93,000 have something to do with the Mayo family, medicine, or both.

A tour of downtown Rochester's main attractions should leave no doubts as to the influence of the Mayo family on the world of medicine. But a visit to **Mayowood**—the family's sprawling country estate, just west of town—reveals a flip side to the same coin that is just as interesting. This forty-room mansion, built into a wooded hillside above the Zumbro River, is a testament to the great wealth and social influence that resulted from the Mayos' successes in the medical field.

Mayowood lies at the heart of what was once a 3,300-acre estate of rolling hardwood forest purchased by Dr. Charles H. Mayo at the turn of the twentieth

Saving the Wetlands

When the first settlers arrived in southeastern Minnesota, they must have felt as if they had landed in paradise. Clear streams flowed through heavily forested hills, and fertile soil covered the valley floors. They soon set to work planting crops, cutting trees for lumber, and grazing cattle on the steep hillsides. But exploitation of the land eventually led to serious erosion of the rich topsoil that fouled streams and forced people to leave the area.

Looking at the neat farms, prosperous towns, and heavily forested hills of southeastern Minnesota today, it doesn't seem possible that much of this region lay in ruin in the early 1900s. Minnesotans owe a debt of gratitude to Richard J. Dorer, who through his work for the Minnesota Department of Conservation and Bureau of Game surely saved this spectacular area. He appealed to and worked with many groups, from hunters and anglers to garden clubs and the Izaak Walton League to make changes for the better.

He shared his love of the land with others through his poetry and children's books, and he initiated the "Save the Wetlands" movement, a Minnesota program now spreading throughout the world. Today the *Richard J. Dorer Memorial Forest* covers a large section of southeastern Minnesota and has become a rich habitat for wild turkey and trout and supports a booming tourism industry.

century. The stone-and-poured-concrete mansion, built in 1910 and 1911, was largely designed by its owner, who also had the Zumbro dammed as a power source for Mayowood and to form a private lake.

The Mayo family presence is almost palpable in the mansion today. Among the numerous personal effects and furnishings is a collection of signed photographs and framed letters from former guests at the estate, and in these the Mayos' considerable social influence can be gauged. Just consider these players on the world scene: Franklin Roosevelt, Dwight Eisenhower, Lyndon Johnson, the king and queen of Nepal, Emperor Haile Selassie of Ethiopia, and King Faisal of Saudi Arabia.

Mayowood can be rented for special events, and scheduled tours are offered Tues through Sun from Apr through Oct for a modest fee by the Olmsted County Historical Center. For information and tour reservations, call (507) 282-9447 or visit olmstedhistory.com.

Tucked away in a beautiful wooded valley west of Rochester, near the town of Byron, are a county park, nature center, and zoo unlike any other in the state. *Oxbow Park* (5731 CR 105 Northwest) is situated on 572 acres of an old farmstead around an oxbow bend of the Zumbro River. Ten kilometers of hiking and cross-country skiing trails meander among the dense maples on the surrounding bluffs. The zoo, focusing on native Minnesota wildlife, doubles as a shelter for injured or orphaned animals, and the twenty-five species exhibited in tasteful displays include bison (buffalo), elk, wolves, a pair of playful otters, and an impressive group of owls, hawks, and eagles. Oxbow Park has picnic and camping facilities, too.

On weekends staff at the nature center offer hands-on educational programs covering a wide range of topics. Each March, for example, there's the A to Z of maple syrup production, whereas in the fall you can learn everything you'd ever want to know about how to tan deer hides by using the animal's brains. Special events are held on major holidays, too. The park, which is open daily, can be found three miles north of Byron and US 14 on CR 105 (the route from Byron is well marked). Admission is free. For more information call (507) 328-7340.

Dodge County

There is probably no town in Minnesota where the late nineteenth century is as alive and healthy as it is in *Mantorville*, the Dodge County seat. This unpretentious little community of 750 has been named to the National Register of Historic Places. The reason? Virtually every commercial building to be found, and many residential ones as well, has been preserved and maintained in the spirit of the town's past.

A good place to begin a walking tour of Mantorville is the *Dodge County Courthouse*. Like many buildings in town, the courthouse, ca. 1865, was constructed of Mantorville limestone—the industry largely responsible for having kept the community afloat since its founding in 1854. But unlike those of any other structure, the courthouse's walls are a full forty inches thick. Perhaps this ample use of Mantorville's greatest natural and economic resource accounts for the building's survival as the oldest working courthouse in the state and the only remaining one built in the Greek Revival style. For more information call Mantorville Regional Welcome Center at (507) 635-5170, or visit mantorville .com.

Mantorville's other most famous landmark is the *Hubbell House*. This fine restaurant, which was also built of native limestone, has been in continuous operation since its establishment in 1854. The original Hubbell House served as a hotel for travelers who were passing from the Mississippi River to St. Peter. The guest lists reads like an eclectic who's who of American society: Dwight D. Eisenhower and Ulysses S. Grant represent past presidents; Senator Alexander Ramsey, two Drs. Mayo from Rochester, and Bishop H. P. Whipple hold up Minnesota's historical tradition; and from the sports and entertainment world hail Mickey Mantle, Roy Rogers, and the Ringling Brothers, among others. The guest register is prominently displayed, along with many photographs and documents of historical interest. What's more, the American-style food is good and moderately priced. For reservations call (507) 635-2331 or visit hubbell houserestaurant.com.

Winona County

The county seat of **Winona** is a classic Mississippi River town—rich with history and graced with natural beauty—that has grown into a city. From the lookout at **Garvin Heights Park**, perched atop the limestone bluff five hundred feet immediately above the city, many of Winona's outstanding architectural attractions are visible against the backdrop of the twisting channels of the river and the Wisconsin shoreline beyond.

Among the most noteworthy buildings in Winona are two banks: the **Merchant's National Bank** and the **Winona National Savings Bank**. The ornately detailed, somewhat boxlike Merchant's Bank, built on the corner of Third Street and Lafayette in 1911 by Purcell, Feick, and Elmslie, is considered one of the state's greatest examples of the Prairie School tradition. The National Savings Bank, with its huge pair of granite pillars looming skyward before the entry, is a fine example of the Egyptian Revival style. It was built by George Maher in 1914 at Fourth Street West and Main and, like the Merchant's Bank, boasts extremely beautiful stained-glass windows and skylights. The National Savings Bank also has an extensive collection of mounted African game animals that were hunted by a bank manager in the 1920s.

Although several interesting museums in town document Winona's booming development as a riverboat and lumbering community in the latter part of the nineteenth century, perhaps the most unusual among them is the **Polish Museum**, located in a former lumber warehouse at 102 Liberty St. The museum claims to house the country's largest collection of objects from the Kashubian region of northwestern Poland—a contention supported by the fact that historically about one-third of the town's residents were from that part of the country. Poles who settled in Winona were largely members of the working class, and items in the museum document their lifestyle through examples of clothing, household objects, and photographs of laborers, fishermen, and housewives going about their daily tasks. A Winona Wagon Works wagon recalls the westward treks once made by settlers arriving by riverboat. Also, the museum's close association with St. Stanislaus Catholic Church is revealed in the many religious articles on display. The museum is open several days each week free of charge (donations accepted) from May through Oct and is a site of great festivity each Apr for the Polish Heritage Days and in Oct for the Polish Apple Festival celebration. For more information call (507) 454-3431 or visit polishmuseumwinona.org.

One of Winona's less well-known claims to fame is that of being the "Stained Glass Capital of the United States." The nation's two largest art-glass companies, along with another smaller studio, are located in this town of thirty thousand. **Cathedral Crafts** offers tours of its operation at 730 Fifty-fourth Ave. In the shop you can see artists designing windows for churches and other institutions and workers scoring and breaking glass to fit the designs and then piecing the rich colors together with sections of lead channels soldered at each joint. Cathedral Crafts also works with the much-thicker slab glass and does a limited amount of glass etching using sandblasting equipment. Viewing the entire production process takes forty minutes to an hour. Visitors should call (507) 454-4079 or visit cathedralcrafts.com to arrange for tours.

A visit to the **Bunnell House**, which commands a good view of the river five miles south of Winona on US 61, in the little town of Homer, provides some rare insights into the lives of several of the area's earliest pioneers. This Gothic Revival–style three-story structure—whose white-pine, board-and-batten exterior has never been painted—was built in the late 1850s by Willard Bradley Bunnell and his family, the first permanent settlers of Winona County. The house is well appointed with period furniture, suggesting a simple but comfortable lifestyle for the Bunnells and their children. But more interesting still are the lessons to be learned about its original inhabitants.

Willard was a Great Lakes steamboat captain and fur trader who apparently was on good terms with Dakota chief Wapasha, who gave him permission to build his home in Homer. Willard's wife, Matilda, was described by one contemporary as a model pioneer woman who spoke French, English, Ojibway, Winnebago, and Dakota, as well as several other American Indian dialects. She was also a capable markswoman and canoeist, while remaining "lady-like and modestly feminine."

The Bunnell House is open for tours Memorial Day through Labor Day (call 507-454-2723 or visit winonahistory.org for hours). A modest fee is charged.

Another historic site of special interest is found ten miles south of Winona, along a tributary of Big Trout Creek on CR 7 at the tiny town of Pickwick. Here in a lovely narrow valley dominated by steep limestone bluffs is the **Pickwick Mill**, 26421 CR 7. When built in 1854, it was one of the first industrial sites in Minnesota. The mill is an imposing seven-story native limestone building constructed with such fortitude that it has withstood a tornado and a major flood. These facts are even more remarkable considering there isn't a single nail to be found in the structure's beams, rafters, and floor columns—they are held

Fun Facts about Winona

- Winona is the only place in Minnesota where you face north when looking at Wisconsin, a neat trick since the Mississippi River flows north to south. A jog that causes the river to flow briefly from west to east creates this geographic anomaly.

- Actress Winona Ryder was born Winona Laura Horowitz on October 29, 1971, in Winona.

- The dentist who invented the formula for concentrated grape juice lived in Winona from 1858 to 1868. His name? Dr. Thomas Welch.

- William Windom of Winona is the only person from Minnesota to have appeared on US currency. Windom was a congressman, senator, twice secretary of the treasury, and leading contender for the Republican nomination for president in 1880. He appeared briefly on two-dollar bills.

in place by weight alone. Flour from the mill helped feed troops of the Union army during the Civil War; in the years that followed, Pickwick flour was also shipped to destinations worldwide. The mill is open weekends only. For information call (507) 457-0499 or visit pickwickmill.org.

Fillmore County

It seems impossible, but of the ten thousand plus lakes located in Minnesota, Fillmore County contains exactly . . . none. That doesn't mean, however, that there's no fishing in this part of the state. In fact the area's cold-water streams support native trout populations that attract anglers from throughout the region. A good way to find your way to the area's hot fishing spots is to call **Root River Rod Company** at (507) 467-2101 or visit rootriverrodco.com. They're located in Lanesboro at 116 Parkway Ave. North and offer guided trips and plenty of fly fishing gear.

The Root River, which flows west to east through the heart of Fillmore County, is one of the region's waterways deserving special note. The valley it has carved is deep—up to three hundred feet in some places—and forested with remnants of the Big Woods that once blanketed much of the southeastern part of the state. Wild turkey, eagles, osprey, and deer abound. And the towns the river passes along the way—Chatfield, Lanesboro, Rushford—are charming and steeped in history.

Depending on the time of year and personal predilection, there are several ways to take in the splendors of this river valley. MN 16 follows the river from

Lanesboro nearby to its confluence with the Mississippi River and is a lovely drive any time of year. In warmer months the Department of Natural Resources–designated **Root River Canoe Route**, which begins just downstream of Chatfield and runs for ninety miles to the Mississippi, is excellent for swimming and canoeing. **Root River Outfitters**, located in Lanesboro, rents canoes, kayaks, and tubes. Contact them at (507) 467-3400 or visit rootriveroutfitters.net.

Bicyclists and hikers can follow the thirty-five-mile **Root River State Trail**—an old railroad grade that has been converted to a multiple-use recreational trail—along its gentle downhill course from Fountain (nine miles west of Lanesboro on CR 8) to Rushford. The same trail is groomed for cross-country skiers in winter.

Regardless of your mode of travel, picturesque Lanesboro is a great place to begin or end any adventure in the valley. The **Lanesboro Trail Center**, in the lower level of the **Lanesboro Historical Museum** at 105 Parkway South, has maps and information about local canoe and bicycle rentals. History buffs can acquaint themselves with the town's past by perusing the two floors of exhibits upstairs.

With twelve bed-and-breakfasts in town, Lanesboro isn't lacking in interesting places to stay, either. The flavor of a small late nineteenth-century hotel has been lovingly re-created at **Hotel Lanesboro** (507-323-3239; hotellanesboro

Karst Topography

While the lack of recent glaciations in the driftless region of southeastern Minnesota resulted in a scenic landscape of gently rolling highlands carved up by deep ravines, another less obvious geologic feature exists. A good example of karst topography runs through Fillmore County, and a short drive on MN 80 from Fountain to Wykoff provides good views of this unique geology. In fact, Fountain has claimed the title of "Sink Hole Capital of the U.S.A."

Along this route, fields of corn and soybeans are pitted with small round tree islands. These small circles are steep rocky holes and from a distance look just like unplowed parts of a field. They range from 30 to 150 feet in diameter and may be up to 30 feet deep. While generally dry, they will fill with water during heavy rainstorms but will drain in a few hours or days.

Karst topography exists in other parts of the world, but in Minnesota only in a few southeastern counties. Fillmore County has the most sinks, with an estimated 5,750 dotting the landscape. The karst sinks resemble potholes in some respects but are formed much differently. Sinks form when rain causes limestone to dissolve; potholes form in solid rock at the base of waterfalls or where sand and gravel are spun around in a stream.

.com), though the building, ca. 1872, was originally used by an undertaker and furniture maker.

There are two destinations just outside Lanesboro that outdoors enthusiasts will find interesting. The **Lanesboro State Fish Hatchery**, built around a freshwater spring at the site of an old mill just south of town on MN 16, produces two million trout annually—nearly half the trout stocked in Minnesota waters. An educational slide show and self-guided tours are available free of charge.

Three miles north of Lanesboro on MN 250, signs point the way to the **Eagle Bluff Environmental Learning Center** (28097 Goodview Dr.). This small nonprofit environmental education center sits in the middle of nine hundred acres of state forest on top of a spectacularly steep bluff overlooking the Root River. Excellent skiing and hiking trails radiate from the main lodge, which also serves as a great site for observing golden and bald eagles (up to twenty of the latter have been spotted in a single autumn day), wild turkey, and osprey. A tunnel, dug decades ago beneath the bluff to power a now-defunct hydro plant, has become home for the largest known wintering population of pipstrel bats. More accessible to visitors is a bat condominium, located at the center's main facility, which houses up to three thousand of the fascinating nocturnal creatures. Also, tours are given of the country's largest shiitake mushroom-growing operation—the center's main demonstration project and source of

TOP ANNUAL EVENTS IN BLUFFLAND

FEBRUARY

Grumpy Old Men Festival
Wabasha, late Feb
(651) 565-4158
wabashamn.org/grumpyoldmenfest

MAY

**Sykkle Tur Bike Ride on
the Norsk Riviera**
Fountain, mid-May
(507) 268-4923

JUNE

Steamboat Days
Winona, late June to early July
(507) 452-2278
winonasteamboatdays.com

JULY

Cedar River Days/SPAM Jamboree
Austin, early July
(507) 437-4563

SEPTEMBER

Fall Foliage Fest
Harmony, late Sept
(507) 886-2469

Three Rivers Rendezvous
Rochester, late Sept
(507) 282-9447

NOVEMBER

Swan Watch Weekend
Winona, early Nov
(507) 494-6229
friendsoftherefugeheadwaters.org

income; the delicious mushrooms are sold here, too. The center is open year-round. For program information call (507) 467-2437 or visit eagle-bluff.org.

Upstream from Lanesboro a few miles along the banks of the Root River is the town of **Preston**, where many years ago a group of desperate prisoners tried to escape the Fillmore County Jail by tunneling out with their spoons. Although their laborious plan failed, today you would never be driven to such desperation—you wouldn't even *want* to escape from the place—because the old Fillmore County Jail has been transformed into the **JailHouse Inn**, a charming and most unusual bed-and-breakfast located at 109 Houston St. Northwest in Preston. Through much sweat and finance, the building has been restored to its original Victorian architectural style and graciously appointed, with breathtaking results.

There are twelve beautiful guest rooms, some with fireplaces, some with whirlpool tubs, all decorated with exquisite taste. From the hand-tiled bathrooms to the ornate wallpapers to the authentic antique furnishings, each room has its own distinct flavor. Some are named for their original function (the Sheriff's Quarters, the Drunk Tank, to name two), whereas others are named after their decor (the Oriental Room, the Amish Room, etc.). Perhaps most interesting of all is the Cell Block, which contains two queen-size beds, a shower, a bath, and the original iron jail bars.

Breakfast, every bit as tasty as the scrumptious accoutrements would lead you to expect, is served in a bright and sunny modern dining room. The entire premises can be rented, space permitting, for company retreats and other group lockups. Call the inn at (507) 765-2181, or visit jailhouseinn.com.

Those seeking a more traditional incarceration experience may want to consider doing time at the **Historic Wykoff Jail Haus**. Located just ten miles west of Preston, the Jail Haus was an abandoned one-room jail scheduled for demolition. A group of concerned citizens realized that this would be a waste of a charming brick structure, so they decided to refurbish it and turn it into a bed-and-breakfast.

Touted as the smallest B&B in Minnesota, the Jail Haus accommodates just one couple per night, but guests have free rein over the entire structure. This consists of a combination sitting-sleeping room, a modern bathroom, and a "cell room," complete with the original iron bars and narrow bunk beds. The bunk beds have been fitted with cushy new mattresses, which, had they been in place one hundred years ago, might have made the area's more notorious hombres—folks such as Jesse James—a lot less ornery. Breakfast is served up the block at the **Gateway Inn** restaurant. For reservations or more information, call the Bank Gift Haus at (507) 352-4205.

harmony

The Bluffland town of Harmony got its name accidentally. The village started as a railroad stop, and during a heated discussion of what to name the new town, one resident who had grown tired of the arguing stood and exclaimed, "Let us have harmony in here!" The surprised group stopped fighting, thought about the statement, and decided that Harmony would make a good name.

Harmony, a sleepy little town a few miles north of the Iowa border, is unquestionably in the heart of farm country, and an unusual opportunity to visit Amish farms is made possible through ***Amish Tours of Harmony***. Some farmsteads are historic and furnished with antiques, others are clean and modern, but all offer a taste of farm life and afford a glimpse into the lifestyle of Minnesota's largest Amish colony. Prices are modest. For more information, call (507) 696-1354 or visit amish-tours .com.

A few miles south of Harmony is a hole in the ground that has been swallowing up visitors for decades. The ***Niagara Cave*** used to rate right up there with Wall Drug and Reptile Gardens as one of the most heavily advertised tourist attractions in the country, as a result of an extensive billboard and bumper sticker campaign (the attraction used to have three kids working full-time on bumper sticker detail). But highway-beautification laws in the 1960s changed all that, and now Niagara Cave draws a relatively modest stream of visitors who seek it out because they know what they're looking for.

The hour-long tour begins in the basement of the entrance building and quickly descends to a series of well-lit horizontal passages that were cut into the ancient limestone bedrock by seeping underground streams. One of these waterways still courses through sections of the cave and in one place forms an impressive sixty-foot waterfall that visitors can view from a suspended platform projecting past the brink of the falls.

In the cave, too, are many other interesting formations—deposits of colorful minerals, numerous fossils, impressive stalactites, and unusual eroded limestone shapes, some of which have been given cute names and labeled with placards by the cave's managers. There is also a damp little "wedding chapel" that, believe it or not, has been the site of more than two hundred weddings. The entire round-trip hike is a mile in length and represents only half of the known extent of the cave. At its deepest point, more than two hundred feet below the surface, the stream briefly reemerges into view in a room adorned with a fine collection of still-growing stalactites.

A modest fee is charged for the guided tour, which is offered on weekends during Apr and Oct and daily from May through Sept. The cave is closed

Nov through Mar except by special arrangement (507-886–6606 or niagaracave .com). Niagara Cave can be found just south of Harmony and west of MN 139 on CR 30.

Southeast of Spring Valley is a second cave system open to public tours. The **Mystery Cave** has known passages that total twelve miles in length. Tours highlighting the natural history of the cave are staffed by naturalists at nearby **Forestville State Park**, which now owns and manages the cave system.

One tour begins along the banks of the Root River at a spot where a portion of the river disappears underground—a common occurrence in this region of the state. Most of this cave is in the four-hundred-million-year-old Dubuque limestone layer, a formation of huge blocks that results in square-shaped passages and large rooms. A second tour, starting at the Minnesota Caverns entrance, is mostly in the five-hundred-million-year-old Galena limestone layer, which is characterized by high, narrow, irregularly shaped passages. In the Mystery Cave system are two brilliant turquoise lakes, as well as dramatic and colorful collections of stalactites, stalagmites, and flowstones (all of which are formed by water-deposited calcite). The Mystery Cave is maintained in its natural state (neither placards naming formations after familiar shapes nor wedding chapels are to be found), and the inexpensive tours, which begin at the state park, have a strong natural-history focus.

Thomas Meighen's Farm Village, also part of Forestville State Park, offers an immersion experience of a different sort. Park your car and cross the bridge to the farm village and you will be magically transported to the year 1899. The "locals" (costumed interpreters portraying Forestville residents) are likely to strike up a conversation about the politics of the day or perhaps the bright future of the railroad industry. They will then lead you on an informal tour of the village, which includes a general store, a barn, a gristmill, an herb garden, and a homestead, complete with office, parlor, and kitchen. Not only can you talk with the laborers as they go about their daily chores, you may even be asked to help with a little cooking, grinding, or gardening. If you're lucky, they may even offer you the going wage (about twenty-five cents a day).

The original community of Forestville died out because the railroad went to Wykoff instead. **Historic Forestville**, on the other hand, is alive and well and lots of fun. Admission is free, but a state park vehicle permit is required. For more information on cave tours and park programs, call (507) 765-2785 for Historic Forestville, (507) 352-5111 for the main park, (507) 937-3251 for Mystery Cave or visit dnr.state.mn.us and click on state parks.

For several decades around the turn of the twentieth century, farms in southern Minnesota were worked by teams of farmers using gigantic steam-powered engines. This tradition is proudly celebrated today in the little town of Mabel.

Since 1960 **Mabel** has been the annual site of the **Steam Engine Days** festival, which each year draws some thirty-five thousand people to town the first weekend after Labor Day. Because of the widespread interest in this event, in 1988 a **Steam Engine Museum** was established on the Steam Engine Days festival grounds. From May to Sept visitors can see various models of these huge iron workhorses, as well as classic and antique tractors, early gasoline engines, and several different evolutions of the threshing machine. Call (507) 493-5350 for museum times and for information on the annual Steam Engine Days celebration or go to steamenginedays.com.

Should you happen to pass through the small town of **Wykoff**, and the timing is right, you may want to stop at **Ed's Museum**. Longtime resident Ed Krueger owned the Jack Sprat Food Store for many years and never threw anything away. When Ed died, he left his store and the accumulated trappings of his life to the town, with the stipulation that the store become a museum. The ladies of the Wykoff Progress Club took on the job of cleaning and organizing fifty years of stuff. The results are a collection of everyday items, much of it items that most people would have thrown out, including his cat that died in 1986 and is stored in a box. The museum also houses a large collection of toys.

Ed's Museum is located in downtown Wykoff at 100 Gold St. (MN 5) in the old Jack Sprat Food Store. It is open from Memorial Day weekend to the last weekend of Sept, 1 to 4 p.m. on Sat and Sun, or by appointment. Call (507) 352-4205 for more information.

Houston County

In the heart of Houston County, three miles west of the county seat of Caledonia, is a lovely pocket of wilderness encompassing a series of steep wooded ravines that dissect the valley of Beaver Creek, a tributary of the Root River. **Beaver Creek Valley State Park** (15954 CR 1), as the area is known, has fine hiking trails, trout fishing, camping, and weekend interpretive programs in the summer (for information on park programs, call 507-724-2107). The park also has within its boundaries a unique anachronism: the only unadulterated, fully functional water-powered gristmill in the state.

Though it's within the boundaries of the park, **Schech's Mill** is actually situated on the working farm of Edward Krugmire, who still uses the original machinery to custom-grind feed for his livestock. The facility has been operating in this lovely little valley since the mill's completion, in 1876, by Bavarian master miller Michael J. Schech.

When visitors step inside the building's two-foot-thick native limestone walls, Edward briefly explains the history of the mill and sends visitors on a self-guided tour of the mill's upper two levels. Then everyone gathers around the millstones on the main floor, and Edward sets the turbines in motion to demonstrate the "new process" milling technique.

As the floodgates are opened and the heavy grindstones start to spin, the entire interior of the solidly constructed building—from the maple flooring to the heavy fir timbers far below—is sent into a shudder. Thick leather belts that run through the floor to connect wheels, axles, and wooden gears on different levels of the mill whir into motion. And the kernels of dried corn that trickle into a hole in the center of the twenty-two-inch Diamond Buhr millstone are ground into a coarse powder. Tours are given for a small fee on weekends from Apr through Oct; call (507) 896-3481 for more information or visit schechsmill.com.

Rice County

The exterior limestone wall of the building housing the **Northfield Historical Society**—a building that originally served this Cannon River town as the First National Bank—has the kind of rough and weathered look you'd expect of a structure that's more than a century old. But closer inspection reveals some telling pockmarks that, to the residents of **Northfield**, carry a special significance, for it was here, on an autumn day in 1876, that one of the most famous bank robberies in Minnesota history was thwarted by a group of uncommonly brave citizens.

A visit inside the museum reveals the whole story. With its teller windows, vault, and account books open on the tables, the scene looks just as it did on that fateful September Thursday when three members of the notorious James–Younger gang strolled through the door to make an unauthorized withdrawal. Five more robbers, all wearing the gang's characteristic knee-length linen "dusters" to conceal their weapons, were stationed in the street outside.

Although the gang was accustomed to carrying out an operation like the Northfield raid without encountering significant resistance, on this occasion it was in for a surprise. Two citizens on the street who detected what was afoot gave out a call to arms, while inside the bank the acting cashier, Joseph Lee Heywood, refused to open the vault (which was actually unlocked). After a second bank employee escaped out the back door, taking a bullet in his shoulder as he went, the robbers decided to abort the raid. One of them paused long enough while exiting the bank to end Heywood's life with a shot to the head. Meanwhile, outside, a street battle was blazing.

In the end two townsfolk were killed in the fight, as were two of the outlaws. Several days later four of the remaining six bandits, who had fled westward, were captured or killed, leaving only Jesse and Frank James as fugitives.

Visitors to Northfield the first weekend after Labor Day can witness a reenactment of this event in the annual *Defeat of Jesse James Days* celebration. During the rest of the year, exhibits and a videotape at the historical society tell the tale. The museum, open daily, is at the corner of Division and Fourth Streets; call (507) 645-9268 for hours or visit northfieldhistory.org.

Though Northfield has calmed down considerably since the James–Younger boys were driven from town, there are still many interesting attractions for curious and adventuresome visitors. However, if, for whatever reason, you find yourself beating a hasty retreat from Northfield into the sunset, you may want to do what the fleeing James-Younger gang did—stop in at the *Millersburg Store*. What was at that time a general store down the block from a hotel used by several members of the gang the night before the bank raid is now a lively saloon and restaurant run by Rose Hanzel. A few historical pictures on the walls recall the store's earlier incarnation, but the main attractions are the outlaw-size hamburgers, criminally delicious ice-cream drinks, and the sprawling beer garden out back, which is replete with a horseshoe pit. The store is located in the heart of tiny Millersburg, two miles west of I-35 on Rice CR 1.

In 1826, knowing a good thing when he saw it, a French Canadian fur trader named Alexander Faribault set up a trading post for the American Fur Company below a rampart of high bluffs where the waters of the Straight River joined the larger-flowing Cannon. Business with the neighboring Dakota was good, and Faribault eventually decided to settle at this picturesque spot permanently, building in 1853 the *Alexander Faribault House*, a Greek Revival design that stands today as the first frame house built in Rice County. Two years later the town of Faribault was named after its founder. Public tours of the completely restored Alexander Faribault House, located at 12 First Ave. Northeast, are given for a modest fee May 1 through Oct 1. Call the Rice County Historical Society at (507) 332-2121 for times and prices of tours; rchistory.org.

Soon to follow Faribault's example was a German cabinetmaker named Carl H. Klemer, who in 1865 established a woolen mill on the banks of the Cannon River. Though in Klemer's time woolen mills were common enough in river communities like Faribault—his was one of eight hundred in the country—today the *Faribault Mill* exists as only one of three such operations nationwide and produces more than half of all wool blankets made in the US.

Tours of the old mill are offered on weekdays at Faribault Woolen Mill (1500 Second Ave. Northwest; 507-412-5534; faribaultmill.com) and allow visitors to witness the entire manufacturing process—from the cleaning of raw wool stock from all over the world to the dyeing of fibers in huge basement vats to the now-mechanized weaving process in a large room full of clattering electronic looms. The Faribault Woolens Factory Store (on Second Avenue just across the river), which offers blankets at discounted prices, is open every day except holidays.

In the heart of Faribault's downtown Heritage Preservation District, which includes two fine examples of art deco–influenced architecture in the *Rice County Courthouse* and the *Thomas Scott Buckham Memorial Library*, are several other destinations worthy of a visit. Woodcarver *Ivan Whillock's studio* is located at 122 First Ave. Northeast just a couple of doors away from the Alexander Faribault House. Since 1962, when Ivan established his studio in Faribault, he has been upholding the Classical Spanish style of craftsmanship by working exclusively with chisels, gouges, and other hand tools to produce a variety of religious images for churches throughout the region. He also creates secular pieces, such as landscapes and wildlife scenes that reveal the visual perspectives gained by the artist during his early work as a painter.

The *Cathedral of our Merciful Saviour*, at 515 Second Ave. Northwest, holds special interest from an architectural and historical perspective. Hailed

What's in a Name?

In the case of the rivers that flow through Bluffland, many of the current names have come from the American Indians or French and were loosely or inaccurately translated into English. Like many rivers in other parts of Minnesota, various tribes named them for the most prominent feature or characteristic.

Cannon River: A loose or inaccurate English translation of the French name *Riviere aux Canots* or "Canoe River." The French and American Indians cached their canoes at the mouth of the river while hunting buffalo on the eastern edge of the prairie.

Zumbro River: Again a loose translation of French, in this case *Riviere des Embarras,* which meant an obstruction by logjams or driftwood, a common feature of the lower part of this river.

Whitewater River: From the Sioux name, *ska* for "white" and *mini* for "water."

Root River: Derived from a Sioux name for the river, possibly referring to tree roots exposed after floods. *Hokah* or *hutkam* was the Sioux word for "root," and the Houston County town of Hokah came from this word.

Mississippi River: This name originated in Minnesota, not the South as some believe. The Chippewa called it *Mee-zeeseepee,* or *Messipi,* and other tribes used *Mesesebe, Missicipy,* or *Meschasipi.* Finally, *Mississippi* became the name, which means "Big River" or "Father of Waters." Enough said.

by architectural historians as one of the most impressive English Gothic–style churches in Minnesota, it was completed in 1869 as the first cathedral in the American Episcopal Church. Moreover, the structure, with its high vaulted ceilings, was home to one of the most important religious figures in Minnesota history—the Reverend Henry Benjamin Whipple, the state's first bishop. Whipple, whose crypt is in the basement of the cathedral, was a great advocate of American Indian rights. As a result of his intercession with President Lincoln on behalf of some three hundred Dakota who were held responsible for deaths in the great Dakota conflict in 1862, 262 of the Dakota were spared.

Another highlight of a visit to the cathedral (tours can be arranged by calling 507-334-7732) is the lever-operated bell chimes, ca. 1903, in the bell tower. Visitors are given an opportunity to try their hands ringing out a tune for the benefit of the long-suffering residents who live close by.

Steele County

Legend says that during the worst winter in memory, Owatonna, the daughter of Chief Wabena, became gravely ill. Desperate to save her, he moved his village from the Minnesota River area to a place where the endless prairie started changing into the hardwood forest of southeastern Minnesota. They ended up finding a place where a spring known as a *minnewaucan* ("curing water") flowed from the earth. Owatonna recovered after drinking the water, and today the town of the same name occupies this place.

Except for the likes of Jesse James, most people aren't inclined to go far out of their way to investigate a bank that holds none of their money. The **Wells Fargo Bank** at 101 Cedar St. North in **Owatonna**, however, is one such institution that cries out to be visited. Completed in 1908 as the National Farmers Bank, this nationally acclaimed architectural treasure represents the most celebrated work of one of America's outstanding architects, Louis H. Sullivan. The cubelike shape of the building's exterior, adorned with huge arched windows of stained glass by Louis Millet, quickly earned the building widespread recognition as, according to one historian, "a jewel box set down in a prairie town."

Entering the bank through the low-hung entry, one is suddenly overwhelmed by the beauty of the interior. The arched shapes of the resplendent windows are repeated in lovely pastoral murals on two walls, whose earth tones blend harmoniously with the surrounding terra-cotta and cast-iron ornamentation that was built by the country's best craftsmen of the time. Though the building has undergone several renovations since its completion, these have been undertaken with a dedication to preserving the spirit and many of

West Hills Museum

The topic of orphans and neglected children is one that most people try to avoid. It's a subject sure to evoke strong feelings and opinions among others and has become news again as some politicians have talked about reviving orphanages as a way to take care of neglected children. For anyone interested in an honest and detailed look at the history of orphanages, the **West Hills Museum** at 540 West Hills Dr. in Owatonna is a must to visit.

Created in 1886, the Minnesota State Public School for Dependent and Neglected Children provided education and housing for twenty thousand children over sixty years. Besides a school, hospital, gymnasium, and assorted other buildings, the orphanage had its own power plant, greenhouse, icehouse, cemetery, and farm. It eventually expanded to 329 acres, 42 for the buildings and 287 for crops, and became virtually self-sufficient.

Today the main building, which made the National Register of Historic Places in 1975, also houses the Owatonna city administrative offices. The museum provides a compelling look at how the state cared for dependent children through displays of pictures, artifacts, personal stories, and movies. For more information call the Owatonna Visitors and Convention Bureau at (507) 451-7970.

the details of Sullivan's original masterpiece. Brochures explaining the history of the bank are available, as are brief tours by bank personnel.

Another interesting historic site in Owatonna can be seen on the grounds of the Owatonna Tool Company, located at 655 Eisenhower Dr. Resting on a short stretch of tracks next to the old Owatonna Railroad Depot sits *Engine 201*, a steam locomotive that happens to have been the first engine ever driven by railroad legend Casey Jones. Tours of the engine for groups of five or more can be arranged by calling (507) 455-7000. Also, a booklet describing the history of the engine and the story of Casey Jones is available.

Waseca County

Before it was extensively developed for agricultural purposes, the heart of Waseca County used to represent the dividing line between the Big Woods to the east and the prairies that stretched for hundreds of miles westward. Today at this historic ecological junction is an institution that enables visitors to contemplate the changes that have taken place since the plows of the first settlers left their marks.

Farmamerica is an interpretive center that chronicles the evolution of the Minnesota farm from the late 1850s until the present. Visitors make this historic journey by exploring three different farmsteads: an 1850s settlement farm, a 1920s dairy farm, and a contemporary farm operation. There are also a prairie restoration area, a historic one-room schoolhouse, a blacksmith shop, and a church. From June to Oct, when Farmamerica is open each weekend for a small fee, interpretive volunteers occupy each farm site and illustrate historic farming activities. Festivals are held the second Sun each month. Farmamerica is located four miles west of the town of Waseca on CR 2. For more information call (507) 835-2052 or visit farmamerica.org.

Freeborn County

Ever since humans first occupied the prairies of southern Minnesota, Albert Lea Lake, just east of the city of **Albert Lea**, has been a busy place. Following the retreat of the last glacier some ten thousand years ago, the shores of the lake were frequented by hunters surviving on large game animals. In the ensuing millennia the area's rich natural resources continued to support groups of nomadic small-game hunters and fishermen as well as more sedentary, village-dwelling prehistoric farmers.

Those who would like to learn more about how these early Native Americans adapted to southern Minnesota's changing environment over the centuries would do well to visit **Myre-Big Island State Park**, just east of Albert Lea at exit 11 on I-35 (19499 780th Ave.). Within this beautiful sixteen-hundred-acre sanctuary, three natural communities characteristic of the region during late prehistoric times—oak savanna, wetlands, and northern hardwood forests—can be explored firsthand. Also, the close proximity of these different natural environments creates a lush habitat for wildlife. Deer, several species of birds of prey, waterfowl, and white pelicans are plentiful, especially during fall migration.

Prehistory buffs will want to spend some time at the park's Owen Johnson Interpretive Center, where exhibits from a collection of thirty thousand local prehistoric stone artifacts (one of the state's largest private collections) provide insight into past cultures. From the big-game hunters' exquisitely crafted large spear points to the hand-carved fishhooks of a later time, one can gain real respect for the ingenuity and craftsmanship of those whose technology depended on stone, clay, wood, and bone. Some of the stone knives on display reputedly hold an edge to leather better than any modern metallic blade. For more information about the park, call (507) 668-7060 or visit dnr.state.mn.us /state_parks.

Each autumn Bancroft–Bay Park in Albert Lea is the site of the **Big Island Rendezvous**, a gathering of groups dedicated to celebrating the lifestyle of the fur trade. Highlights of this event, which is held in early Oct, include a black-powder shoot, tomahawk- and knife-throwing contests, dancing and crafts displays, and a tepee village and trading post. For more information call (507) 402-6371 or visit bigislandfestivalandbbq.org.

Places to Stay in the Bluffland

ALBERT LEA

AmericInn
811 East Plaza St.
(507) 373-4324
wyndhamhotels.com

Comfort Inn
810 Happy Trails Ln.
(507) 377-1100
choicehotels.com

Country Inn and Suites
2214 East Main St.
(507) 373-5513
choicehotels.com

Holiday Inn Express
77820 East Main St.
(507) 473-2300
ihg.com

FARIBAULT

Boarders Inn and Suites
1801 Lavender Dr.
(507) 334-9464
staycobblestone.com

Days Inn
1920 Cardinal Ln.
(507) 334-6835
wyndhamhotels.com

Grandstay Hotel
1500 Twentieth St. Northwest
(507) 334-2888
grandstayhospitality.com

Historic Hutch House
305 Second St. Northwest
(507) 323-8107
historichutchhouse.com

HARMONY/LANESBORO

Country Lodge Inn
525 Main Ave. North
Harmony
(507) 886-2515
www.countrylodgeinn
harmonymn.com

Green Gables Inn
303 Sheridan St. West
Lanesboro
(507) 467-2936
greengablesinn.biz

**Historic Scanlon House
Bed & Breakfast**
708 Parkway Ave. South
Lanesboro
(507) 467-2158
scanlanhouse.com

Lanesboro has too many B&Bs to list here. Check out lanesboro.com *for a complete list.*

LA CRESCENT

**Brickmakers Bed
& Breakfast**
234 North First St.
(608) 792-1966

Most lodging for the La Crescent area is across the river in LaCrosse, Wisconsin.

LAKE CITY

AmericInn
1615 Lakeshore Dr.
(651) 345-5611
wyndhamhotels.com

Willows on the River
100 Central Point Rd.
(651) 345-9900
willowsontheriver.com

NORTHFIELD

Fairfield Inn and Suites
114 Second St. West.
(507) 366-5000
marriott.com

**Contented Cottage
Bed and Breakfast**
5 Walden Place
(507) 301-3787
contentedcottage.com

Country Inn & Suites
300 Hwy. 3 South
(507) 645-2286
choicehotels.com

The Magic Door Bed & Breakfast
818 Division St. South
(507) 581-0445
magicdoorbb.com

AmericInn Lodge and Suites
1320 Bollenbacher Dr.
(507) 645-7761
wyndhamhotels.com

OWATONNA

Baymont Inn & Suites
245 Florence Ave.
(507) 413-7715
wyndhamhotels.com

Comfort Inn
2345 Forty-Third St. Northwest
(507) 444-0818
choicehotels.com

Country Inn & Suites
130 Allan Ave. Southwest
(507) 455-9295
choicehotels.com

Northrop–Oftedahl House Bed & Breakfast
358 East Main St.
(507) 451-4040

RED WING

AmericInn
1819 Old West Main St.
(651) 347-1031
wyndhamhotels.com

Country Inn & Suites
4275 Hwy. 61 West
(651) 388-9000
choicehotels.com

Pratt-Taber Inn
706 West Third St.
(651) 388-7392
pratttaber.com

Nichols Inn and Suites
1819 Old West Main St.
(651) 388-6633
nicholsinn.com

Moondance Inn
1105 West Fourth St.
(651) 212-6305
moondanceinn.com

St. James Hotel
406 Main St.
(651) 388-2846
st-james-hotel.com

Red Wing has two additional bed-and-breakfasts.

ROCHESTER

Country Inn & Suites
4323 West Frontage Rd. Northwest
(507) 218-9559
choicehotels.com

Fairfield Inn and Suites
470 Seventeenth Ave. Northwest
(507) 258-7300
marriott.com

Hampton Inn
1755 South Broadway
(507) 287-9050
hilton.com

LaQuinta Inn
4353 Canal Place Southeast
(507) 289-4200
wyndhamhotels.com

Springhill Suites by Marriott
1125 Second St. Southwest
(507) 281-5455
marriott.com

WABASHA

AmericInn Lodge & Suites
150 Commerce St.
(651) 565-5366
wyndhamhotels.com

Anderson House Hotel
333 West Main St.
(651) 565-2500
theandersonhousehotel .com

Eagles on the River Rentals
152 West Main St.
(651) 565-3509

The River Nest B&B
20073 CR 77
Reads Landing
(651) 560-4077
therivernest.com

Turning Waters Bed & Breakfast
136 Bridge St.
(651) 564-1568
turningwatersbandb.com

WASECA

Grandstay Inn & Suites
2201 North State St.
(507) 835-0022
grandstayhospitality.com

Miller Armstrong Bed & Breakfast
204 Second St. Southwest
(507) 835-1146
millerarmstrong.com

Pine Gardens Bed & Breakfast
522 Second Ave. Northeast
(507) 204-3379
wasecabedandbreakfast .com

WINONA

**Alexander Mansion
Bed & Breakfast**
274 East Broadway
(507) 474-4224
alexandermansionbb.com

**Carriage House Bed
& Breakfast**
420 Main St.
(507) 452-8256
chbb.com

Holiday Inn Express
1128 Homer Rd.
(507) 474-1700
ihg.com

Plaza Hotel & Suites
1025 Hwy. 61 East
(507) 453-0303
plazawlnona.com

**Riverport Inn
Express Suites**
900 Bruski Dr.
(507) 452-0606
riverportinn.com

Places to Eat
in the Bluffland

ALBERT LEA

Casa Zamora
(Mexican)
2006 East Main St.
(507) 373-6475

China Restaurant
(Chinese, Vietnamese)
805 East Main St.
(507) 377-8888
chinarestaurantal.com

Elbow Room
(American)
310 East Eighth St.
(507) 373-1836

Jake's Pizza
126 West Clark St.
(507) 373-7350

Trumbles 2.OH
(American)
1811 East Main
(507) 369-5258
trumbles2oh.com

112 on Broadway
(American)
112 South Broadway Ave.
(507) 373-3000

FARIBAULT

A & W Family Restaurant
(American)
404 Wilson Ave.
(507) 334-9379
awrestaurants.com

Boonies Bar and Grill
(American)
3301 Millersburg Blvd.
(507) 645-6424
booniesgrill.com

Basilleo's Pizza
108 Fourth St. Northwest
(507) 332-6701
basilleospizza.com

Janna's Market Grill
129 Central Ave. North
(507) 334-7476
jannasmarketgrill.com

Good Day Coffee
313 North Central Ave.
(507) 581-7538

Depot Bar & Grill
311 Heritage Place
(507) 332-2825
faribaultdepotbarandgrill
.com

**El Tequila Mexican
Restaurant**
951 Faribault Rd.
(507) 332-7490
eltequilamexican.com

Mizuki Fusion Restaurant
(Asian)
609 Fourth St. Northwest
(507) 323-8111
mizukifusionfaribault.org

HARMONY/LANESBORO

Estelle's Eatery and Bar
(eclectic)
121 Main Ave. North
Harmony
(507) 886-1234
estelleseatery.com

Clara's Eatery
111 Parkway Ave. North
Lanesboro
(507) 467-2200
claraseatery.com

Breakers
(American)
94 Second St. Northwest
Harmony
(507) 886-7263

Pedal Pushers Café
(American)
121 Parkway Ave. North
Lanesboro
(507) 467-1050
pedalpusherscafe.com

Old Barn Restaurant
(American)
downtown Preston
(507) 467-2512
barnresort.com

On the Crunchy Side
(American)
31 Main Ave. North
Harmony
(507) 886-5560

LA CRESCENT

Corky's Pizza & Ice Cream
25 South Walnut St.
(507) 895-6996
corkyspizza.net

Kaddy's Kafe
(breakfast and lunch)
236 Main St.
(507) 895-2900
sites.google.com/view
/kaddys-kafe-la-crescent

LAKE CITY

Cheung's Garden
220 South Washington St.
(651) 345-3818

Chickadee Cottage Cafe
(American)
317 North Lakeshore Dr.
(651) 345-5155
chickadeecottagecafe.com

Fiesta Jalisco Restaurante
117 South Lakeshore Dr.
(651) 345-2216
fiestajalisco-lakecity.com

Marien's Deli
716 West Lyon Ave.
(651) 345-2526

Papa Tronnio's Pizza
124 South Washington St.
(651) 345-3540
papatronnioslakecity.com

Heidi's Huggamug Café
220 East Chestnut St.
(507) 226-3036

NORTHFIELD

Basil's Pizza
301 Water St. South
(507) 663-1248
basilspizza.net

The HideAway Coffeehouse and Wine Bar
421 Division St.
(507) 664-0400
thehideawaynorthfield.com

El Tequila Mexican Grill
1010 Hwy. 3
(507) 664-9139
eltequilamexican.com

Goodbye Blue Monday Coffeehouse
310 Division St.
(507) 663-6188
gbmcoffee.com

Hogan Brothers Cafe
(American)
415 Division St.
(507) 645-6653
hoganbros.com

Mandarin Garden Restaurant
107 East Fourth St.
(507) 645-7101
mandaringardennorthfield
.com

Ole Store Restaurant
(American)
1011 Saint Olaf Ave.
(507) 786-9400
olestorerestaurant.com

Cakewalk Dessert Bar
303 Division St.
(507) 786-9255
cakewalknorthfield.com

Quarterback Club
116 West Third St.
(507) 645-7886
quarterbackclubrestaurant
.com

OWATONNA

Asian Kitchen
641 West Bridge St.
(507) 446-8800

A Taste of the Big Apple
(delicatessen)
104 West Broadway
(507) 455-3633
atasteofthebigapple.
business.site

Central Park Coffee Co.
113 North Ceder Ave.
(507) 451-4242
centralparkcoffeeco.com

Foremost Brewing Cooperative
131 West Broadway
(507) 214-3462
foremost.coop

Grace's Tex Mex
1170 Twelfth Ave.
Northwest
(507) 451-1908

The Kitchen
(American)
329 Cedar Ave. North
(507) 451-9991

RED WING

Bev's Cafe
221 Bush St.
(651) 388-5227
bevscafe.com

Fiesta Mexicana
2918 North Service Dr.
(651) 385-8939
fiestamexicanaredwing.com

Wisteria Twig Tea Room and Café
1920 Old West Main St.
(651) 276-4616
wisteria-twig-tea-room.
square.site

Mandy's Coffee & Cafe
419 West Third St.
(651) 800-2026
mandyscafe.com

Hay Creek Saloon
(American)
31655 Hwy. 58
(651) 388-3998
haycreekcampground.com

Red Wing Brewery
1411 Old West Main St.
(651) 327-2200
redwingbrewing.com

Staghead
219 Bush St.
(651) 212-6494
thestaghead.com

Hanisch Bakery and
Coffee Shop
410 West Third St.
(651) 388-1589
hanischbakery.com

The Bleu Dog Café
14689 Welch Trail
Welch
(651) 388-7494
thebleudogcafe.com

ROCHESTER

Fiesta Cafe & Bar
1645 Broadway North
(507) 288-1116
orderfiestacafebar.com

Foragor Brewery
1005 Sixth St. Northwest
(507) 258-7490
foragerbrewery.com

India Garden
1107 North Broadway Ave.
(507) 288-6280
indiagarden.us

Opa! Opa! Greek
Restaurant
1106 Fifteenth Ave.
Southeast
(507) 282-1212
opaoparochester.com

Five West
(American)
1991 Commerce Dr.
Northwest
(507) 361-5555
fivewestrochester.com

PI Wood-Fired Pizza
3932 Marketplace Dr.
Northwest
(507) 424-3885
live4pi.com

Wong's Cafe
4180 Eighteenth Ave.
Northwest
(507) 288-3730
wongscafemenu.com

WABASHA

Eagle Valley Cafe
(American)
1130 Hiawatha Dr. East
(651) 565-2040

Reads Landing
Brewing Company
70555 202nd Street
Reads Landing
(651) 560-4777
rlbrewingco.com

Silver Star Saloon
and Grill
170 Pembroke Ave.
(651) 565-2800
silverstarsaloongrill.com

Hoppy Girl Brewing
136 Bridge Ave.
(651) 564-1568
hoppygirlbrewing.com

WASECA

Jonnie Beans
Coffeehouse
204 Second St. Southwest
(507) 833-7540

El Molino
(Mexican)
214 North State St.
(507) 835-4223
elmolinowaseca.com

Tasty House
Chinese Restaurant
105 Seventeenth Ave.
Northeast
(507) 835-2699

Pizza Ranch
212 Seventeenth Ave.
Northeast
(507) 833-9080
pizzaranch.com

Pleasant Grove
Pizza Farm
41142 160th St.
(715) 523-0857
pleasantgrovepizzafarm
.com

Starfire Grill
(American)
204 Second St. Southwest
(507) 833-8756

Yellow Mushroom/
Bridgeman's
(American, ice cream)
1208 South State St.
(507) 835-5000
yellowmushroompizza
minnesota.net

WINONA

Acoustic Cafe
(American, coffee)
Second and Lafayette
(507) 453-0394
acousticcafewinona.com

The Blue Heron
Coffeehouse
162 West Second St.
(507) 452-7020
blueheroncoffeehouse.com

SELECTED WEBSITES IN THE BLUFFLAND

Albert Lea Convention and Visitors
Bureau
(507) 373-2316
explorealbertlea.com

Austin Convention and Visitors
Bureau
(507) 437-4563
austinmn.com

Faribault Area Chamber of Commerce
(507) 334-4381
faribaultmn.org

Harmony Tourist Information
(507) 886-8122
www.harmony.mn.us

Historic Bluff Country
(507) 886-2230
visitbluffcountry.com

La Crescent Area Chamber of
Commerce & Tourism
(507) 895-2800
explorelacrescent.com

Lake City Area Tourism Bureau
(651) 345-4123
visitlakecity.org

Lanesboro Office of Tourism
(507) 467-2696
lanesboro.com

Northfield Area Chamber of
Commerce
(507) 645-5604
northfieldchamber.com

Owatonna Convention and Visitors
Bureau
(507) 451-7970
visitowatonna.org

Red Wing Convention and Visitors
Bureau
(651) 385-5934
redwing.org

Rochester Convention and Visitors
Bureau
(507) 288-4331
experiencerochestermn.com

Wabasha–Kellogg Chamber of
Commerce
(651) 565-4158
wabashamn.org

Waseca Area Chamber of Commerce
(507) 835-3260
wasecachamber.com

Winona Convention and Visitors
Bureau
(507) 452-0735
visitwinona.com

El Patron Mexican Grill
1415 West Service Dr.
(507) 961-0241
elpatronofwinona.com

Golden China
411 Cottonwood Dr.
(507) 454-4261
goldenchinawinona.com

Lakeview Drive Inn
(American)
610 East Sarnia
(507) 454-3723
lakeviewdriveinn.com

Pickwick Inn Restaurant
(American)
24731 CR 7
(507) 474-2044

Rocco's Pub & Pizza
5242 West Fifth St.
(507) 454-3360
roccospubandpizza.com

Wellington's Pub & Grill
1429 Service Dr.
(507) 452-2103
wellingtons-pubandgrill
.com

Prairieland

In a state known for thousands of lakes, countless miles of streams and rivers, and thousands of acres of wetlands, this region of Minnesota presents to travelers an anomalous landscape. Resembling the great open spaces of the Dakotas more than the forested hills of eastern Minnesota, it doesn't seem as if Prairieland belongs to the state. Prairieland covers southwestern and west-central Minnesota and contains the headwaters of the Minnesota River and some of the most intensively farmed land in the state.

Visitors to this region will find panoramic views of fields of row crops stretching to all four horizons. Broken only by the occasional farm with its silos or island of trees, this vast landscape exists in an area where nature can be both cruel and kind. While enough rain usually falls to ensure a good crop, Prairieland is drier than eastern Minnesota, which can make for stressful times for the stoic farmers of the region.

Although it is now a land of agricultural bounty, we can only imagine what this region looked like to the American Indians and first European settlers. Historical records show us a scenic land of dry prairies, wetlands, and shallow lakes, all set among rolling hills. Bison, elk, and antelope lived on the fertile

grasslands, while the marshes and creeks supported populations of waterfowl that at times darkened the sky. Unfortunately the conversion to intensive farming led to the draining of wetlands and straightening of countless creeks, which forever altered the landscape.

Meeker County

When the first railroad train steamed across the Meeker County line on its way westward from the bustling Twin Cities in 1869, the first town it encountered was **Dassel**, east of Litchfield on US 12. The train screeched to a stop at a small wooden station, disgorged a few passengers and some freight, and then slowly chugged its way back up to speed, leaving a cloud of black smoke and ash in its wake.

In those bygone days—when huge steam-powered machines were transforming American life and half the North American continent seemed to many to be crying out for settlement—the railroad and accompanying telegraph service were the primary lifelines connecting little towns like Dassel with the rest of the civilized world. Today in this community of one thousand, there is a museum dedicated to the role the iron horse has played in the history of many a Minnesota small town.

Originally, Dassel's **Old Depot Museum** stood in nearby Cokato. In 1985 the building was moved six miles west to its present site on the north side of US 12 in "downtown" Dassel. Parked out front of the well-maintained wooden structure is a 1922-vintage wooden caboose that's been restored with such details as a coal-fired stove, a spring-mounted kerosene wall lamp, a real icebox, and a primitive "flush" toilet that could be operated in good conscience only when the train was at least a mile from the nearest town.

Inside the depot is a gallery of paintings and prints by Currier and Ives, Norman Rockwell, and others that capture the incomparable mystique of

AUTHOR'S FAVORITES

Blue Mounds State Park
Luverne
(507) 283-6050

Camden State Park
Lynd
(507) 872-7031

Lower Sioux Interpretive Center
Redwood Falls
(507) 697-8674

Pipestone National Monument
Pipestone
(507) 825-5464

traveling by train to exotic locations. Another room contains collections of such railroad artifacts and memorabilia as railroad lanterns, signs, buttons, playing cards, uniforms, and dining-car china. There are also two delightful vehicles formerly used by track and telegraph-line workers: a velocipede—an odd-looking three-wheeled-bicyclelike contraption that reached speeds of twenty miles per hour by means of a two-handled push-pull stick—and another one-person scooter, with bicycle handlebars, that was actually pedaled along the tracks. The museum is open daily Memorial Day through Sept; a small fee is charged.

A few miles farther down the line, in the even-smaller hamlet of Darwin (population 282 by last count), there stands what is indisputably Minnesota's greatest monument to the archetypal human urge to collect: the **World's Largest Ball of Twine**.

The ball of twine is only one of many achievements realized by Francis A. Johnson, who passed away in 1989 at the end of a long life of collection. During odd moments in his career as a farmer, he claimed to have squirreled away some five thousand pencils, two hundred feed caps, and untold numbers of wooden ice-cream containers and paddle locks. Still, it was The Ball that elevated him to such heights of notoriety as being listed in the *Guinness Book of World Records* (which officially lists The Ball's weight as a staggering ten thousand pounds), *Ripley's Believe It or Not*, and Charles Kuralt's *On the Road*. Drive into Darwin on Meeker CR 11 and see The Ball for yourself—it is slowly rotting beneath the water tower.

Among the cultivated fields near Litchfield, there's one farm that warrants closer inspection. Prefabricated metal sheds and modern field equipment are nowhere in sight, and without them the neat red-and-white barn and outbuildings, old cement silo, and turn-of-the-twentieth-century farmhouse create the image of a farm perhaps from an earlier time. That's exactly the effect that Don and Sonja Nelson had in mind when they began offering **Experience Agriculture** tours of their farmstead in 1987.

Don, whose farming career has included work as an agriculture teacher, saw the need to educate the public about the importance of agriculture and the dying institution of the family farm. Accordingly, he and his family restored their farmyard to its original appearance. The Nelsons usually only conduct farm tours for groups such as school field trips and family reunions. But for six weeks in Sept and Oct, they have a pumpkin festival that is open to the public.

Visitors are welcomed into the haymow, where they can make themselves comfortable on a bale of hay beside a collection of antique farm implements that hangs on the walls and listen to Don introduce the state of the farm, ca. 1900. Visitors are then free to wander through the active henhouse, the pungent silo, and the livestock pens, while interpretive staff explain how domestication and agricultural practices have evolved over the years. Kids get a special thrill out of romping in the hayloft, where Don has left several heavy ropes hanging from the rafters for swinging. A modest fee is charged to visitors, and the place is open to the public by arrangement. Organized tours are welcome, too. For directions, call (320) 693-7750 or go to nelsonfarm.com.

In 1956 Minnesota's last surviving Civil War veteran died in Duluth at the venerable age of 106. Since his death, anyone wishing to visit the state's most enduring memorial to the War of the Rebellion has had to travel to **Litchfield**, where the **Grand Army of the Republic Hall and Museum** has proudly stood since its construction in 1885. Facing a large park in the center of town, the building's distinctive brick facade—replete with a large castlelike half-tower in the center and small turrets on the corners—creates an unmistakably military aura. It is the only building erected by the GAR veterans' organization that is still in use in Minnesota and just one of thirteen in the country.

When visitors pass through the small entrance beneath a recessed portrait of Abraham Lincoln, they enter the original library, which now also serves as an exhibit space for a small but very interesting collection of items left behind by local veterans of the American Civil War. Most of the men who built the Litchfield GAR hall first came to Minnesota after the fighting was over to take advantage of the land grants allotted to Union soldiers in lieu of pay. Thus the stories generated by the museum's artifacts reflect the experiences of such famous fighting units as the First Minnesota Volunteer Infantry, whose members led a decisive and near-suicidal charge at Gettysburg, as well as those of men from other parts of the country.

One exhibit case displays a leather belt whose buckle reads "CSA," that is, Confederate States of America. According to museum staff the belt was exchanged for one bearing the Union army's insignia when a pair of soldiers who had been friends in Ohio before the war confronted each other as "enemies" during a battle. On another shelf rests a photograph of a Minnesota volunteer who died of starvation in Georgia's infamous Andersonville prison camp. Elsewhere in the building a framed drawing of the camp depicts the desolate site at which eleven thousand Yanks died of starvation and disease in the one-year period that the facility was in operation. Also on display are rifles and muskets, a pair of prized boots (many soldiers were reduced to wrapping their feet in rags), articles of clothing, and various personal effects.

The walls of the interior meeting room are hung with portraits of many GAR members, paintings of battle scenes, and original furnishings. In large letters just below the ceiling are rendered two proclamations: IN MEMORY OF OUR LOYAL DEAD and WE ARE THE BOYS OF '61.

Adjacent to the rear of the hall is the *Meeker County Historical Society Museum*, which features items of local history. Both buildings, located at 308 North Marshall Ave., Litchfield, are open Tues through Sun for a small fee throughout summer. Call (320) 693-8911 or visit meekercomuseum.org for more information.

Though you might not guess it today, in the early years of Meeker County's history, the little town of *Forest City*, six miles northeast of Litchfield on MN 24, was a community of some consequence. By the early 1860s enough bustling activity had been generated by a sawmill and flour mill located on the banks of the north fork of the Crow River that for a time the town was designated the Meeker County seat (an honor later permanently bestowed upon Litchfield). This explains why so many of the area's settlers simultaneously sought protection at Forest City during the panic that swept the countryside immediately following the outbreak of the Dakota conflict in late August of 1862.

On September 3, the settlers, using logs and lumber from the sawmill, hastily erected a 120-square-foot stockade around a two-story log cabin and barn, which now houses antique farm tools, ca. 1860–80. Today a reconstructed *Forest City Stockade* stands near the site of the original, looking much the same as the first one did more than a century ago.

Strolling about inside the enclosure's ten-foot-high walls, one feels a little claustrophobic, considering that this cozy space was shared for ten days by 240 men, women, and children. It was largely the women and children, however, who bore the brunt of this confinement, as many of the men ventured out to work their fields during the daylight hours despite the fact that the stockade was attacked the first night. Throughout the event there were no casualties— even a thirteen-year-old girl whose frightened family left her behind in the fields to find her own way to Forest City arrived safely at the stockade by nightfall.

The stockade, located just east of MN 24 on the south edge of town, is open daily from mid-June through Aug. An annual Furtrade Rendezvous is held at the site the third weekend in Aug, featuring black-powder shooting, craft demonstrations, and plenty of characters camped out in 1860s regalia. For more information go to forestcitystockade.org.

Kandiyohi County

Prairiewoods Environmental Learning Center sits on five hundred acres of woodlands and prairie among a scattering of lakes northwest of Willmar. And though they do mainly group programs and classes, the center has six miles of hiking trails and four miles of mountain bike trails open to anyone. They groom trails in the winter for cross country skiing and fat tire biking, and they rent ski gear, fat tire bikes, snowshoes, and kicksleds. Besides these activities the center also offers various educational programs and public events. Contact them at (320) 354-5894 or visit prairiewoodselc.org.

Larry and Barb Levins are natural history buffs and collectors with an interest in sharing their collection of butterflies, seashells, rocks, minerals, artifacts, dinosaur bones, and books with others. With this in mind, they started *Raptor Ridge Museum*, located about eighteen miles northeast of Willmar. Among their collection you'll find a massive egg from the extinct elephant bird, a flightless bird that stood around ten feet tall and lived on the island of Madagascar. They also have a thirty-two-pound piece of amber that Larry believes is the second largest in the world, and some items from a headhunting tribe in the Philippines from when Barb lived there. Raptor Ridge Museum is open by appointment only. To schedule a visit contact Larry or Barb at (320) 295-3838 or email them at kabsat.bl@gmail.com.

Chippewa County

A walk down the main street of the little Minnesota River town of *Milan*, population 429, is enough to convince a visitor that this Norwegian American community maintains an exceptionally strong tie with the old country and its traditions. Several wall murals depict Norwegian themes and locales, and the

Just Go Get It!

One of the more interesting, and some would say humorous, events in state history occurred in *Lac Qui Parle County*. As settlers moved into this western Minnesota county in the 1860s, small towns started popping up throughout the rolling landscape. As the population increased, residents elected a slate of county officials before officially being designated a county.

The battle over which town would get the county seat erupted between the residents of Madison and Lac Qui Parle. The competition finally culminated on the evening of November 12, 1886, when 150 men and forty teams of horses met on the Leather Breeches farm near Madison. The group went to Lac Qui Parle, put the courthouse on wagons, and moved it fifteen miles across the prairie to Madison.

Now Madison had the building and records, while the officials stayed in Lac Qui Parle, stopping any county business for a month. After much political maneuvering—this time in the courts and legislature instead of on the prairie—the county seat finally ended up in Madison.

trim on many storefronts displays the work of Milan's two gold medal–winning rosemalers (only four artists in the state have achieved this national recognition for their delicate and highly stylized painting on backgrounds of painted wood).

Drop in to the ***Arv Hus Museum and Gift Shop*** on Second Street to get a feel for the range of talents the citizens of Milan have to offer. A gift shop of Norwegian craft items features samples of *hardanger* (embroidery), wheat weavings, pottery, and rosemaling.

In the back of the store there's a museum dedicated to the life's work of a local inventor, William Thompson, who in 1925 created a toaster-size device called the radio booster that enabled rural listeners to pick up a dozen stations instead of only two or three. Thompson was also a pioneer in portable-radio technology. Wrapping one hundred feet of wire back and forth over the roof of his Model T enabled him to boast of owning the region's first car radio. In the 1930s he built the country's first portable broadcast truck.

A block away from the Arv Hus Museum, at ***Karen Jenson's studio*** (104 Lincoln), visitors are welcome to stop by and see works in progress by one of Milan's top rosemalers. More locally generated artistry is also on display one block behind Jenson's home, at the ***Kviteseid Lutheran Church***. A beautiful baptismal font with a rich green-and-red floral design was produced by Karen's brush, as were four playful murals in the church's downstairs bathrooms. The altar and pulpit parapets are handmade *hardanger* designs by another of Milan's artists.

I can't confirm this, but Milan must have one of the only authentic, built in Norway *stabburs*. What's a *stabbur*? It's a small Norwegian building, comparable in size to a garden shed but much more ornate, that serves as an outdoor pantry to store food, clothing, and for extra sleeping quarters. The ***stabbur*** ended up in Milan through a relationship established between local resident Don Peterson and Halvard Pettersen from Vinstra, Norway. Pettersen wanted to thank the American people for gifts and food sent to Norway during and after World War II and decided to build a *stabbur*, disassemble it, and reassemble it in Milan. The completed *stabbur* has a bell tower, sod roof, and ornately carved designs and names of communities near Pettersen's home in Norway. For the full story and location of the *stabbur* visit milanmn.com. This website is also an excellent source of information and links with information on the area.

Milan's folk traditions have developed such a following that a folk school, ***Milan Village Arts School***, offers weekend workshops and classes for those interested in developing the old-world skills of weaving, silversmithing, painting, carving, and, of course, rosemaling. For information on classes, call (320) 734-4807 or visit milanvillageartsschool.org.

For American Indians and European explorers alike, the earliest highway through this part of the state was the Minnesota River. Enough water flowed down the river to make for an easy passage throughout the summer, and the heavily forested banks offered shelter from the surrounding open prairie. Thus, when the area's first missionaries set out to begin their work, they had good reason to choose a place like the *Lac Qui Parle Mission*, found today in a wooded grove south of Milan.

Lac Qui Parle was a thriving mission outpost from 1835 to 1854, focusing on a nearby Dakota village of four hundred. Of the half-dozen buildings that were once clustered at this site, only a rebuilt church stands today. The towering cottonwoods surrounding the church and the exhibits inside make this prairie oasis well worth a visit.

It was here that the Bible was first translated into the Dakota language in a written alphabet developed by the missionaries. Lac Qui Parle was also the location of the valley's first school and the first place in the state where thread was woven into cloth. During the mission's active years, it included a school, a corn mill, cabins for the missionaries, and a spring. Exhibits in the church, which was constructed in 1841, show the work of the mission; the life of Joseph Renville, an early fur trader in the area; the archaeological excavation of the site; and the history and culture of the Dakota. The site is open daily, free of charge, during the summer. For more information contact the Chippewa County Historical Society at (320) 269-7636 or chippewacohistory.org

Lutefisk Capital of the United States

Today Madison claims another important title besides county seat of Lac Qui Parle County. It's also known as the *Lutefisk Capital* of the United States. As a dish only a Scandinavian could love, lutefisk is cod cured in lye and boiled, before being served with potatoes and lefse, a traditional Norwegian flatbread similar to a tortilla. In June 1993 the town dedicated a twenty-five-foot fiberglass model of a cod, named Mr. Lou T. Fisk.

The smell before cooking and texture after are the most distinguishing features of lutefisk. Uncooked lutefisk smells like something someone forgot about for months in a refrigerator, while mushy comes closest to describing the texture. Despite these less-than-appetizing traits, die-hard Scandinavians love it and feast on it during the holiday season.

Each year during Norsefest at Madison, lutefisk lovers gather to celebrate Scandinavian heritage. Activities include a lutefisk-eating contest and the Norsky Outhouse Race. Though it's hard to say if future generations will still eat lutefisk, this delicacy should stay popular in Madison.

Yellow Medicine County

The name of this western Minnesota county comes from the river that flows through it before merging with the Minnesota River near Granite Falls. The Sioux named the river Yellow Medicine for the bitter yellow roots of the moonseed plant that grows as lush vines in thickets along the riverbanks. This long, narrow county borders two distinct areas: the prairie of South Dakota and the rugged Minnesota River Valley.

Granite Falls is a pleasant little city. It has an impressive park system, densely wooded residential avenues, and an attractive business district near the banks of the Minnesota River. The community's traditional small-town values are reflected in one of its historic sites: the *Volstead House*, at 163 Ninth Ave., which was the residence of congressional representative Andrew Volstead, author of the bill that instituted Prohibition in 1919.

Four miles south of town on MN 23 you will find an attraction you wouldn't really expect to find in western Minnesota. At 2450 540th St. the *Fagen Fighters WWII Museum* has an extensive collection of aircraft,

Salt on the Prairie

If you're the type of person who likes to dazzle or confuse your friends with your knowledge of the obscure and unique, here's one for you. Among Minnesota's more than ten thousand lakes, do any of them contain salt water?

One does, and it's appropriately named *Salt Lake*. This briny body of water, which is one-third as salty as an ocean, sits on the border of Minnesota and South Dakota, west of the small town of Madison and just north of Yellow Medicine County. An anomaly in a state known for freshwater but not salt water, Salt Lake attracts many species of birds and has a variety of unusual plants that have adapted to the saline environment.

Brinewater lakes are more common in the western US, including North and South Dakota, and it's rare to find a saline lake as far east as Minnesota. Salt Lake is popular with bird-watchers who come to see the prairie and saltwater birds not found elsewhere in the state.

To reach the lake, follow MN 40 west from Madison for 11.5 miles, turn south at the Salt Lake sign, go three miles south and finally west for one mile. And while you're in the area, take some time to visit some of the native virgin prairie sites in Lac Qui Parle County. Although you won't find heavy surf at Salt Lake, you will have the satisfaction of visiting a unique attraction in Minnesota and one that is most definitely off the beaten path. For more information on Salt Lake and native prairie reserves in western Minnesota, go to prairiewaters.com.

vehicles, and assorted memorabilia from World War II. With the exception of their gliders, all aircraft in the museum can fly and occasionally do on sunny days. The museum also has a collection of military vehicles, a library, and art exhibits. The museum is open Thurs through Sat. Admission is a suggested donation of $10 per person. For more information on the museum call (320) 564-6644 or visit fagenfighterswwiimuseum.org.

But that's not all, for beneath the surface of Granite Falls's all-American facade, two of Minnesota's most exotic environmental features have been cleverly hidden. If you're a nature-minded sleuth, head to the **Yellow Medicine County Historical Museum**, at the junction of MN 67 and MN 23 just south of downtown, where a sign in the parking lot gives one of the secrets away.

World's Oldest Rock, the placard states boldly. You peer behind it to see a lichen-covered clump of Morton gneiss (pronounced "nice")—a protrusion of gray, red, and black bedrock that probably looks no older than any other rock you've seen. But to be fair, when you're face-to-face with an object that's well over three billion years old, it may take a moment for its significance to sink in. Climb on top, make yourself comfortable, and give yourself a few minutes to think. Consider the sweep of monumental events that have occurred in the world since the time of Christ. Then imagine that if the entire existence of the rock beneath you were reduced to the scale of an average human lifetime, all that has passed in the last two thousand years would have been experienced by the rock in slightly more than one second.

When you've had enough of such mind-bending contemplation, stretch your legs by walking west across the highway and into the woods that crown

Prairie and Valley

Two geographic features best define Prairieland. The first is the omnipresent prairie, which stretches for miles and offers the big-sky views normally associated with the Dakotas and Montana. The Minnesota River Valley is the other dominant feature of this region, carved by a torrent of glacial meltwater and flowing for more than three hundred miles through the rolling prairie and patches of hardwood forest.

The Minnesota River meanders through the wide and often steep-walled valley, a remnant of the waterway that carved this great gash in the landscape. When the glacial flood subsided, it left behind a valley that is up to five miles wide and 250 feet deep. The terraced valley walls, irregular channels, and rock ridges form a rare landscape found in few areas. The Columbia River of eastern Washington and parts of Oregon and Idaho shows the same characteristics that formed from a short but catastrophic flood. The area around Granite Falls in eastern Yellow Medicine County is a good place to see the unique features left behind by an ancient river.

another outcrop of ancient gneiss. You have now entered the **Blue Devil Scientific and Natural Area**, a thirty-five-acre tract of land set aside by the Minnesota Department of Natural Resources as one of the state's five natural habitats for an endangered lizard called—that's right—the blue devil. Also known as the five-lined skink, the blue devil is one of Minnesota's two indigenous lizards. In fall and winter the quick little metallic-blue creatures burrow into the crevices in the rock for protection. In spring and summer they tend to prefer cool, damp shelter, such as that offered by rotten logs and humus. Note that Minnesota Scientific and Natural Areas do not have maintained hiking trails. Brochures on the blue devil can be found inside the Yellow Medicine County Historical Museum, which has exhibits on local history and is open free of charge Tues through Sun in the afternoons.

Lincoln County

Besides being the wind-power capital of the Midwest, this county that borders South Dakota is easy to overlook. And though most travelers won't plan a special trip to this lightly populated area of farms and prairie, two attractions make it worth visiting if passing close by.

Hole-in-the-Mountain Prairie runs south from Lake Benton and offers visitors a look at both virgin and restored prairie. Consisting of what was once 4,300 acres of prairie, Hole-in-the-Mountain runs partially through a valley the American Indians called "Mountain Pass" or "Hole-in-the-Mountain." Though not a mountain pass in the true sense, the valley does cut through the often steep hills of Buffalo Ridge, which is part of the Coteau des Prairies.

Besides having more than sixty species of grasses, sedges, and rushes; ten species of trees and shrubs; and two hundred species of wildflowers, the 1,364-acre preserve also provides good habitat for rare prairie-dependent insects. One, the Dakota skipper butterfly, survives on only a few scattered sections of virgin prairie in the Dakotas, Minnesota, and Iowa. For more information call (612) 331-0750.

Tyler, Home of the Nissemaend, is a fun place to stop. According to Danish lore, *nissemaend* are tiny elves who occupy each Danish home. Cousins to Irish leprechauns, they are never seen, and they are helpful or mischievous depending on how much food their hosts set out. Other attractions in Tyler include the Danebod Complex, one of the few buildings that survived a 1918 tornado that destroyed the town; Aebleskiver (ball pancakes) Days; and three special guided tours through the area. For more information call (507) 247-5556.

Lyon County

Most people who visit this county come to Marshall, one of the largest towns in southwestern Minnesota and home to Southwest State University. Most don't know that the Redwood River, which runs through the county and through a beautiful valley that many years ago was an oasis in the harsh prairie for animals and humans, received its name from American Indians.

The name came from the reddish bark of the dogwood that grows along the river. American Indians called it *kinniqkinnic,* and they used the white inner bark as smoking "tobacco." This farming county also has a couple of attractions that are definitely off the beaten path.

Most people think of an oasis as a stand of palm trees surrounding a small pond in the middle of a desert. Ten miles south of Marshall near the town of Lynd lies a different type of oasis—one that sheltered human and animal inhabitants of the plains.

Today this oasis is named **Camden State Park**, and it's a true anomaly in a region of gentle rolling hills and thousands of acres of corn, soybeans, and pasture. Located in an area called the Coteau des Prairies, the park is a shaded valley with thick stands of deciduous trees. The Redwood River carved this valley eons ago, and animals and humans have long found shelter here from the blazing summer sun and the cold winter winds that whip across the landscape of southwestern Minnesota. Camden State Park still shelters wildlife from the changeable weather of this area. If you find yourself driving through this part of Minnesota, take the time to stop at this oasis of the plains.

In the small town of **Minneota**, north of Marshall, visitors will find the Big Store Opera House, which in the 1800s was the only store between Mankato and Watertown, South Dakota. Each Sept this small town also hosts Box Elder Bug Days, a celebration that revolves around this orange and black insect. Festivities include bug races, a parade, and a concert. For more information go to boxelderbugdays.com.

Redwood County

If you are visiting or passing through Redwood Falls, which is the county seat and largest town, it's well worth your time to stop at the **Redwood County Museum**, located on MN 19 just west of downtown. The museum is open afternoons Wed through Sun, May through Sept, or by special appointment. For information call (507) 641-3329 or (507) 430-5781.

The historical museum occupies an imposing building constructed in 1908 as the county poor farm. Among a variety of local history exhibits is a room

Coteau des Prairies

One of the most surprising geographic features in Minnesota cuts across the southwestern part of the state from northwestern Iowa to northern South Dakota. The *Coteau des Prairies* ("highland of the prairie") is a plateau made of glacial till piled high on a base of quartzite rock, the remains of an ancient mountain range. Only the hills along Lake Superior are higher than this plateau. While the glacial moraines left some rugged terrain along the edges, the top is mostly smooth and gently rolling.

Many streams flow from the top of the coteau, dropping through steep gorges on both sides of the plateau. To both animals and humans, these wooded valleys provided free-flowing spring water and shelter from the summer heat and winter storms of the prairie. While many species of wildlife still live on the coteau, unfortunately the populations of bison, elk, wolf, prairie chicken, and golden eagle have disappeared within the last one hundred years. In one quirk of geography, trout survive in the Redwood River, an extremely unlikely occurrence in southwestern Minnesota.

The four major rivers that flow from the plateau and into the Minnesota have three distinct stretches. Each has a swift and rocky section as it drops from the coteau, followed by a slow meandering course across the plains, before ending with a fast two-hundred-foot plunge into the Minnesota River. In fact, these rivers resemble streams in northern Minnesota as they tumble down the final stretch. Some of the best places to see the impact of the coteau on the southwestern Minnesota landscape and rivers include Camden State Park near Marshall (507-865-4530), Upper Sioux Agency State Park near Granite Falls (320-564-4777), and Alexander Ramsey Park in Redwood Falls (507-616-7444).

dedicated to the career of Richard W. Sears, founder and first president of Sears, Roebuck and Company. In the early 1880s sixteen-year-old Sears was employed as a station agent with the Minneapolis and St. Louis Railroad in the little community of North Redwood. One day a shipment of watches mistakenly arrived at his depot. Rather than return them to the manufacturer, Sears arranged to sell them himself to other agents up and down the line. The resulting profit spurred the growth of his famous mail-order business, which, by the time he retired in 1908, had achieved an annual sales volume of $50 million.

When Colonel Samuel McPhail and some companions set about founding the town of **Redwood Falls** in 1864, they had the good taste to establish the community around a beautiful wooded glen formed by the junction of Ramsey Creek and the Redwood River. The creek, named after Minnesota's first territorial governor, tumbles over a steep, narrow waterfall surrounded by pines. The waterfall soon became the focal point of this little oasis of forestland in the heart of the prairie. Today the 217-acre **Alexander Ramsey Park** is the largest municipal park in Minnesota.

A network of trails and roads winds through the rugged terrain, attracting hikers, joggers, cross-country skiers, and those who simply enjoy a drive through inspiring scenery. Visitors will also find a zoo, an exercise course, a public golf course, two playgrounds, and plenty of space for camping and picnicking.

Although the history of the Dakota people is integral to that of the Minnesota River Valley, there are few sites in the area that provide opportunities for visitors to learn about the traditional lifestyle of these American Indians. An exception is the **Lower Sioux Interpretive Center** within the boundaries of the Lower Sioux Indian Reservation on CR 2, nine miles southeast of Redwood Falls. Exhibits and films at the center provide an appreciation of the Dakota perspective of the events surrounding the tragic conflict of 1862. Visitors are also given an overview of the past two hundred years of Dakota culture, from the time the Dakota were pushed westward out of the woodlands of eastern and central Minnesota by the Ojibway up to the present.

When the **Lower Sioux Agency** was built in the 1850s, it was one of two US government administrative centers along the Minnesota River charged with the task of transforming the nomadic Dakota into Christian farmers. At the height of its operation the agency's population approached one hundred whites and thirty-two hundred Dakota. There were stables, storehouses, a blacksmith shop, a school, a boardinghouse, and staff quarters. But by the summer of 1862, following a crop failure the previous year, the Dakota were faced with starvation. The gross insensitivity of the head agent—who refused to allocate food supplies held in storage and, through a representative, admonished the Dakota to "eat grass" instead—was more than the Dakota could take. Tribal elders, moved to act against their better judgment by a group of enraged younger braves who had murdered a settler family, declared war. When the fighting ended six weeks later, three hundred settlers and soldiers had died, whereas the surviving Dakota (no one knows how many were killed in battle) had been either arrested or driven from their lands.

Today a stone warehouse that predates the conflict still stands behind the interpretive center, which is open free of charge daily, year-round. Call (507) 697-8674 for hours and information on special events or go to mnhs.org.

Once you've had a chance to look into Dakota history, you may want to visit several other sites on the reservation that will give you a flavor of life there today. The sporting crowd can check out the **Jackpot Junction** high-stakes bingo and casino facility, replete with Las Vegas–style entertainment. Jackpot Junction is a couple of miles west of the Lower Sioux Interpretive Center on CR 2. At the **Lower Sioux Trading Post**, near Jackpot Junction, Dakota-made pottery and beadwork are sold and craft demonstrations are given. And across the street in an outdoor staging area next to the community center, a large **powwow** is held in mid-June each year. For information about trading post hours and powwow dates, call (507) 697-8000 or visit jackpotjunction.com.

The lack of trees on the prairies of southwestern Minnesota posed an interesting problem for the area's first settlers: how to build a house. The solution most commonly reached was to slice up bricks of topsoil sprouting the ubiquitous prairie grasses and build dwellings made of sod. As strange as the idea may seem today, Stan McCone of Sanborn, in southeastern Redwood County, has proved that, properly made, a sod house is a downright comfortable place to call home.

Stan first tried constructing the **Sod House on the Prairie** of second-growth prairie grass, but he found that without the extensive root system characteristic of virgin prairie, the sod just didn't hold together. Then he spotted an area of virgin prairie grass on an accommodating neighbor's farm and proceeded to plow up strips of the stuff with a special plow. After carefully stacking an estimated three hundred thousand pounds of sod in a cross-linked pattern and installing a wooden floor, rafters, six windows, and a sod roof (which he says weighs in at about twenty-four thousand pounds), in August of 1987 Stan and his family proudly beheld their creation.

The thirty-six-by-twenty-one-foot, one-room "soddie"—furnished with two high-backed antique double beds, a wood-burning cookstove, tables, chairs, and even a leather fainting couch—is as cozy as can be. Two-foot-thick walls

Traverse Gap

Way up in the northwestern corner of Prairieland, visitors will find a geological site that is both subtle and significant. It's easily missed when passing through this remote area of Minnesota, yet it marks the thin line between the headwaters of the Red River and the Minnesota River and the drainage between Hudson Bay and the Gulf of Mexico.

The **Traverse Gap** marks the point where around twelve thousand years ago Glacial Lake Agassiz broke through the ridge of the Continental Divide and began flowing southeast through central Minnesota. Known as Glacial River Warren, this immense river flowed through this breach for almost three thousand years and carved out what we now call the Minnesota River Valley.

The gap separates Lake Traverse and Big Stone Lake, bodies of water that form the respective headwaters of the Red and Minnesota Rivers. The channel carved by the ancient river measures one mile wide by 130 feet deep. Though not nearly as spectacular as the canyons of the West, it must have been an awesome sight as this torrent of water rushed through the cut in the divide.

keep the place cool in summer, warm in winter, and insulated from the sound of the persistent prairie winds. The house is no longer open for lodging, but those wishing to tour the structure may do so for a token fee. To find the house, look for the first dirt road on the south side of US 14, one mile east of US 71. Stan can be reached at (507) 723-5138; you may also check out sod house.org for more information.

A pioneer alternative to the sod house was the "dugout"—a less labor-intensive dwelling built into an embankment or hillside that required fewer sod bricks. One famous resident of Redwood County whose family constructed a prairie dugout in 1874 was Laura Ingalls Wilder, the author of the popular children's book series on pioneer life that gave birth to the *Little House on the Prairie* television series. The site of the **Laura Ingalls Wilder Dugout** on the banks of clear-flowing Plum Creek is open to visitors for a small fee; it is located on the Harold Gordon Farm, a couple of miles north of Walnut Grove on CR 5. *Little House* fans may want to peruse the Wilder memorabilia at the free **Laura Ingalls Wilder Museum** and gift shop on CR 5, just south of US 14. Also, **Fragments of a Dream**, an effectively staged pageant based on anecdotes drawn from the *Little House* books, is presented the first three weekends of July each year at sunset in a park at CR 18 and CR 20 in Walnut Grove. For more information go to walnutgrove.org.

Brown County

The settler community most heavily damaged by fighting in the Dakota conflict of 1862 was the eight-year-old German enclave of **New Ulm**. The fledgling city was attacked twice—on August 19 and August 23—and citizens defended themselves behind barricades erected in the streets. By the end of the two battles, thirty-four settlers had been killed and 190 structures destroyed by fire. Dakota losses were unrecorded.

Today, more than 160 years later, New Ulm's strong German tradition is thriving. To find out just how much of a grip it still has on the town's fourteen thousand residents, drop in to see the **Brown County Historical Museum**—no doubt the only county museum in the state where exhibit labels are written in German as well as English. An interesting pattern of white-and-red brick-work graces the building's striking German Renaissance exterior, whereas the renovated interior of this former post office (ca. 1910) has three floors of exhibits dedicated to local art and history. The quality of the displays and their contents is several cuts above that of most county historical societies. One whole floor is dedicated to the interpretation of Dakota culture, and the museum often displays paintings from a large permanent collection of works by nationally

The Missouri River Connection

It's unfortunate that most people think of southwestern Minnesota as the epitome of flyover country. Although the scenery doesn't have the breathtaking qualities of the north shore of Lake Superior or the bluff country of southeastern Minnesota or the endless vistas of green common to the thick forests of northern Minnesota, this part of Minnesota has a subtle geographic feature some travelers may find surprising.

While the vast majority of streams and rivers in Minnesota drain into the Mississippi River, Hudson Bay, or Lake Superior, a handful of waterways in the southwestern corner of the state flow into the Missouri River. The largest of these is the Rock River, which originates on the Coteau des Prairies and is the only major stream in Minnesota that drains into the Missouri. So the next time you happen to drive through southwestern Minnesota on your way to somewhere else, enjoy the scenery and take an hour or so to stop, look at, and contemplate some of the unique characteristics of Minnesota's portion of the Great Plains.

renowned artist Wanda Gag. The museum, located at the corner of Center Street and Broadway, is open for a small fee on afternoons Tues through Sun. For more information call (507) 233-2616 or visit browncountyhistorymn.org.

The Victorian era was a time when the construction of large public monuments was very much in vogue, and according to Minnesota architectural historians, in no place was that trend given such grand expression as in New Ulm. *Hermann the Cheruscan*, a sword-wielding, winged-helmeted Teutonic warrior whose stern visage has been looming above the city since 1897, stands in ***Hermann Heights Park*** (along Center Street on top of the bluff) as further tribute to the city's proud German heritage. The thirty-two-foot copper statue of the Cheruscan tribesman who freed his people from Roman domination in AD 9 rests on top of a massive pedestal replete with ten stout Greek columns and a large dome. A circular staircase winds nearly to the top to afford sweeping views of the city.

The ***Glockenspiel***, a large carillon clock tower on Fourth and Minnesota Streets, is a more recent and decidedly less Wagnerian public monument in town. At noon, 3 p.m., and 5 p.m. daily, the Glockenspiel rings out a ten-minute concert, accompanied by the appearance of seven animated figures depicting aspects of the city's history. The figures slowly rotate on a circular stage midway up the forty-five-foot structure. On special occasions the thirty-seven-bell carillon is played manually as well.

What German American town worth its salt would be without a brewery, you ask? The answer, of course, is none. And New Ulm amply fulfills this expectation in a beautiful wooded glen along the banks of the Cottonwood River at the south end of town with the **Schell Brewery**. August Schell arrived in New Ulm in 1858 and quickly set up shop, rolling his first barrel of beer onto the delivery wagon within two years' time. His brewery survived the Dakota conflict unscathed (except for the unaccounted-for disappearance of two and a half barrels), and by 1880 Schell had outpaced New Ulm's five other breweries, establishing August as the dominant brewer in the vicinity.

Visitors to the Schell facility today discover that the *gemütlichkeit*, or congenial charm, of the place is arresting. From Memorial Day through Labor Day, visitors are free to wander through the lovely hillside gardens and beside the deer and peacock pens that surround a large European-style mansion built in 1885. The daily guided tours of the small processing plant, which produces only twenty-five thousand barrels annually, are instructive for those curious about the brewing process. And each tour ends in the tasting room, where visitors can sample the eleven beers and sparkling beverages the company produces. The brewery is located near the southeastern end of Franklin Street. For more information on tours, which cost a token fee, call (507) 354-5528 or visit schellsbrewery.com.

Although it borders on sacrilege to visit New Ulm and not enjoy beer, wine lovers now have a place of their own. **Morgan Creek Vineyards** (507-947-3547 or morgancreekvineyards.com) sits in the scenic Minnesota River Valley that cuts through the rolling prairies of this region. While it seems unlikely that a vineyard would operate in southern Minnesota, the hills along the river provide a hospitable location for grape production.

Established in 1993, the vineyard rolled out its first commercial vintage in 1998 and opened the first underground winery in Minnesota. Morgan Creek hosts private wine tasting for groups of five to twenty from May to Oct and conducts public tours on Sat and Sun from May to Dec. Who knows, a serious beer drinker might even enjoy a tour of the winery.

Festivalgoers with a taste for German culture may want to visit New Ulm during **Bavarian Blast** in mid-July or for **Oktoberfest**, which takes place over two weekends in mid-Oct. Both festivals feature German food and music, including performances by New Ulm's acclaimed Concord Singers. At **Heritagefest** there are also a parade, running races, and traditional arts-and-crafts exhibits. For further information call the New Ulm Convention and Visitors Bureau at (888) 463-9856.

Nicollet County

In the early 1870s the steamboat was the primary means of transportation for river towns such as New Ulm. As the settlement of the prairies gradually resumed in the wake of the 1862 Dakota conflict, little communities up and down the river looked forward to years of growth and prosperity. Such was the case in the village of **West Newton**, nine miles upstream of New Ulm on Nicollet CR 21, where Alexander Harkin opened a general store in 1869.

Today visitors who drop in at the **Harkin Store**, where tours are offered Tues through Sun from Memorial Day through Labor Day, step back to that era of hope and budding economic development—expectations that were dashed for West Newton in 1873, when the railroad was routed through New Ulm, effectively ending the steamboat era, and when a devastating grasshopper plague wiped out crops. The Harkin Store hung on until 1901, when it was closed with most of its merchandise left intact.

Today 40 percent of the items stocking the shelves at the Harkin Store date back to the turn of the twentieth century, though visitors would be hard-pressed to identify anything inauthentic. In keeping with its former function, the Harkin Store is a sociable gathering spot where news of the outside world, ca. 1873, can be obtained from costumed guides and from notices posted on the walls. Evidence of the store's role as a post office, apothecary, and dry

Sleepy Eye

The town of **Sleepy Eye** got its name from the lake it sits beside. The lake is named after a peaceful and friendly Dakota chief named Ish Tak Ha Ba, which translated in English to Sleepy Eyes. Historians believe his name came from his slightly droopy eyelids.

Born around 1780 at Swan Lake in what became Nicollet County, Ish Tak Ha Ba became chief of the Sissetons by order of the Bureau of Indian Affairs. Significantly, he was not a hereditary chief since neither his father nor his grandfather held such a position, but he did sign several treaties.

While reluctantly signing the Traverse des Sioux Treaty, he said he wanted to live the rest of his days in the "Lake of Many Swans." Granted this wish, he lived along the lake until 1857. Ish Tak Ha Ba moved to a lake west of his village, which eventually became the town of Sleepy Eye.

Ish Tak Ha Ba died around 1860 in South Dakota, and in 1902 Sleepy Eye residents disinterred his remains and buried them with proper ceremony in the Minnesota town. Today the park sits in the middle of Sleepy Eye, with a tall obelisk marking the final resting place of the peaceful chief.

goods, food, and implement dealer abounds. Coffee is advertised at thirty-five cents per pound, and bottles of Ayers Tonic promise relief from just about any conceivable ailment. Even the well-used checkerboard, whose hand-carved wooden pieces sit on top of the cracker barrel next to the woodstove, is genuine. For information on tour times (a token fee is charged), call the Nicollet County Historical Society in St. Peter at (507) 934-2160 or the store at (507) 628-5591.

Fort Ridgely State Park, nine miles farther upstream at the junction of CR 21 and MN 4, combines fascinating history with a variety of recreational opportunities. The only Minnesota state park with a golf course, Fort Ridgely also has eleven miles of hiking trails, four miles of groomed cross-country skiing trails, and seven miles of trails for horseback riders and snowmobilers, in addition to camping, picnicking, and playground facilities.

The partially reconstructed fort occupies a prominent site on a bluff-top field surrounded by steep ravines. These natural wooded depressions sheltered hundreds of Dakota warriors during the two battles that took place at the fort on August 20 and 22, 1862. The restored commissary building, which now houses excellent exhibits on the history of the fort, military life in the 1860s, and the role Ridgely played in the Dakota conflict, is the only historic structure that today appears much as it did originally.

Chances are that nothing at all would have remained of the small garrison had the Dakota decided to attack one day earlier, on August 19, instead of assaulting New Ulm, for on that day only twenty-nine soldiers were stationed at the fort, the rest either having been killed in earlier fighting elsewhere or being out on maneuvers to the north. The recruits who were on duty were almost all fresh volunteers with no fighting experience. But the extra day given the soldiers at Ridgely enabled them to boost their ranks and set up defenses for the attack they knew was coming. In the end—thanks to the effective use of the fort's cannons, which primarily fired canister shot (collections of small lead balls that disperse when fired, like shot from a shotgun)—180 greenhorn soldiers repelled 800 Dakota while losing only 3 of their number. For more information about Fort Ridgely, call (507) 426-7840.

Each year in late June at Ridgely, the mid-1800s are brought back to life through the *Fort Ridgely Historical Festival.* Surrounded by more than a hundred tepees and period tents, the old fort grounds come to life with military and cannon drills by the historic New Ulm Battery, a fur traders' rendezvous encampment, folk arts exhibits, bluegrass and folk music, and traditional foods and beverages. For more information on the festival, for which there is a small daily charge, call (507) 426-7840.

St. Peter, a Minnesota River community in eastern Nicollet County, is a town that has had to settle for second best. Following a well-planned, marginally ethical, and ultimately unsuccessful attempt to wrest the state capital from St. Paul in 1857, St. Peter was instead designated the site of Minnesota's first public hospital for the insane. Today at the **St. Peter Regional Treatment Center** (as the hospital is now called), which is south of downtown on US 169, an interesting museum chronicles the history of the institution and the sort of care it has provided to its wards since the hospital's construction in 1866.

In contrast to many visitors' notions of the stereotypically primitive "insane asylum," when the state hospital first opened its doors it offered a variety of relatively humane therapeutic services in an effort to rehabilitate its patients. It was only sixty years later, during the Great Depression, that funding for rehabilitative treatment dried up and the hospital essentially became a warehouse for people who couldn't live elsewhere in society. Photographs on display from this period, which lasted until the 1950s, show huge dorm-like rooms filled with beds no more than a foot apart. In another section of the museum, mannequins depict a variety of early twentieth-century treatment methods, including early electric shock technology, insulin shock (whereby patients were sent into temporary comas with large and sometimes fatal doses of insulin), and hydrotherapy (whereby agitated patients were wrapped in wet sheets to dissipate their hysterical energies). Tours of the museum are by appointment only and can be arranged by calling (507) 985-2249.

Though never out of line enough to warrant a visit to the state hospital, the eccentricities of one of St. Peter's more colorful nineteenth-century community leaders, Judge E. St. Julien Cox, did get him into the kind of trouble that made headlines throughout the region. You can learn about the good judge's exploits by visiting the magnificent **E. St. Julien Cox House**, located at 500 Washington St., a completely restored structure that one historian describes as the "most impressive example of a Gothic Revival dwelling still standing in Minnesota." The house and carriage house, with their high-pitched roofs, board-and-batten walls, tower, and round-hooded windows, were considered flamboyant by community standards when they were built in 1871, though they apparently were well enough suited to the tastes of their builder.

In the midst of an impressive career in public life that included leading a regiment from St. Peter to assist the beleaguered citizens of New Ulm in August of 1862 and serving as St. Peter's first mayor, a Democratic member of the state legislature and senate, and a district magistrate, Judge Cox ran afoul of his Republican enemies in 1878. It seems they took exception to the usual etiquette in the Cox courtroom, which reputedly entailed sending defendants out for a bucket of beer before they were sentenced and the staging of mini concerts—on a melodeon—by the judge himself, who was not above stealing an occasional catnap during moments of uninspired testimony. Cox was ousted from the bench following a sensational six-month trial that resulted in a whopping seven thousand pages of proceedings, only to be exonerated and reinstated a few years later by a Democratic-controlled legislature. Costumed guides relate the history of the Cox House and family on Wed through Sun afternoons during summer and on weekends in Sept. For information call (507) 934-2160 or go to nchsmn.org.

Le Sueur County

After visiting the **W. W. Mayo House** in Le Sueur (north of St. Peter), it's easy to see why rural Minnesotans in the 1850s consulted doctors only with trepidation and as a last resort. There were no licensing procedures for those who wanted to practice medicine, no required course of study beyond several months of internship with another doctor, no minimum required skills. But as costumed guides at the 1859-vintage dwelling explain, in that era's hack-filled medical profession, William Worrall Mayo, founder of Rochester's famed Mayo Clinic, was an exception.

Mayo's upstairs examining room provides some insights into the forty-year-old doctor's far-reaching vision even at that relatively early stage of his stellar career. The primitive microscope on his desk, for example, is similar to his own, which was the first microscope to be used in the state. Meanwhile, the fully functional 1850s kitchen downstairs, which on any given day may well be exuding aromas of fresh-baked bread or muffins, re-creates the home life of the Mayo family. There is a gift shop, and a token fee is charged to visitors for tours, offered Thurs through Sun in summer; call (507) 357-8580 or (507) 665-3250 for times.

A statue of two mothers and three small children engaged in a delightful dance stands in a little park adjacent to the Mayo House. The statue is known as the **Mothers Louise** sculpture, and it is Louise Mayo, William's wife, and Louise Cosgrove, a later resident of the Mayo House, who, along with three of their children, have been immortalized in bronze. The Cosgrove family gained prominence in Le Sueur by founding the Minnesota Valley Canning Company—which eventually became Green Giant Company—in 1903.

If the romance and imagery of the steam age—the ponderous metal engines, the billowing smoke and steam, the wide leather belts stretched great distances between wooden pulleys, the sweat and heat of the boiler—catch your imagination, you must pay a visit to the **Geldner Sawmill**. Rounding the eastern shore of Jefferson Lake on CR 13 a few miles northeast of Mankato, you'll find the weathered shed-like building with a very tall smokestack on the west side of the road. Inside is a fully operable machine that played an essential role in the rural Minnesota landscape of the late nineteenth century.

The second Sun afternoon of each month, May through Sept, engineer John Zimmerman fires up the boiler to raise the pressure in the system. Sawyer John Ballman and an assistant secure a hardwood log on the carriage, and the sawdust begins to fly. (The mill is also open for tours on the remaining Sun afternoons throughout the summer). This bustling activity is as interesting to watch as these men are enlightening to listen to.

As they describe the technical evolution of the machinery, the conditions under which employees worked, and the lifestyles of the farmers who slowly cleared the big maple, basswood, oak, and elm off their land, a picture of Le Sueur County ca. 1870 begins to form in your mind's eye. It was a place where the official dirt roads were often so impassable that most hauling of heavy loads took place on an informal network of "winter roads"—primarily the surfaces of frozen lakes. Thanks to places such as the Geldner Mill, the log homes first constructed by the early pioneer farmers were gradually replaced by wood-frame dwellings. It was also a time when Minnesota's Big Woods were slowly giving way to the neat rows of crops that are found today. For information on special sawing demonstrations, call (507) 357-8201.

In **Elysian**, the **Le Sueur County Museum**, housed in an 1895 brick school building on top of the largest hill in the middle of town, is of special interest for art-history buffs as well as those curious to learn more about local history. Dorothy I. Hruska, the museum's director and curator, says that more than a quarter of a million dollars' worth of paintings, drawings, and prints are part of the museum's permanent collection. Among these are works on display by several world-renowned artists, including Adolf Dehn and Roger Preuss, who hail from nearby Waterville. These exhibits are complemented by a wide-ranging assortment of historic items: a ten-thousand-year-old skull of a now-extinct species of bison, four hundred glass slippers, a large church vestments collection, and an exhibit dedicated to the work of a NASA scientist from Elysian who developed a meteorite detector for Explorer 1, America's first satellite to orbit in space. The museum is open Wed through Sun afternoons in summer, weekend afternoons in May and Sept, and by special appointment; call (507) 267-4091.

Blue Earth County

The city of **Mankato** grew up around the confluence of the Blue Earth and Minnesota Rivers, drawing its name from the Dakota word for "blue earth," *mahkato.* The community of forty-four thousand occupies the slopes and floodplain of a broad wooded valley at the southernmost point of the Minnesota's run to the Mississippi.

Blue Earth is a bluish-green clay layer that formed from the decomposition of prairie grasses over the past nine thousand years or so. American Indians used the clay for decorating their faces and bodies. It also attracted the attention of French explorer Pierre Charles Le Sueur, who believed the clay contained copper because its blue-green color resembled copper salts. Le Sueur and some fellow miners dug thirty thousand pounds of the clay out of the bluffs overlooking what became known as the Blue Earth River and took some of it back to France. It did not contain copper but ended up becoming known as fool's copper.

Each July the ten-day ***Bend of the River Festival***, featuring canoe races, a parade, and other family activities, reflects Mankato's prominent position at the elbow of the long arm of the Minnesota. Then on the third weekend in Sept, hundreds of American Indians and others return to ancient Dakota ceremonial grounds at Land of Memories Park for the ***Mahkato Mdewakaton Pow Wow***. For more information on these events and others, contact the Mankato Area Convention and Visitors Bureau by calling (507) 385-6640 or go to visitgreater mankato.com.

One of the first buildings encountered upon crossing the Minnesota River to enter the heart of Mankato's business district is an unremarkable structure with surprising historical significance. The simple, modern design of the ***Blue Earth County Library***, located at 100 East Main St., gives no hint that the site on which it stands is one of special importance to the history of the Minnesota Valley and the conclusion of the Dakota conflict of 1862. Yet it was here that thirty-eight defeated Dakota warriors were simultaneously hanged from a huge gallows in the largest mass execution in US history. A statue of a sorrowful Dakota chief and a plaque commemorating the event stand outside the northwest corner of the building.

In the children's wing of the library, past the lobby's impressive boulder-filled fountain, is a special collection of books and memorabilia concerning Mankato-born author Maud Hart Lovelace. The *Betsy-Tacy* book series that Lovelace wrote in the 1940s and 1950s centered on her Mankato childhood, and many houses, buildings, and geographical landmarks mentioned in the books are recognizable around town today. *Betsy-Tacy* enthusiasts can visit the library to look through the Lovelace scrapbooks, listen to a taped interview with the now-deceased author, view a video inspired by the books, and chat with Shirley Lieske, librarian of the children's section and Lovelace expert. A ***Betsy-Tacy walking tour*** guide is also available.

Not long after its incorporation in 1868, Mankato rose to prominence as an important center for flour milling and limestone quarrying. On MN 68, five miles west of town, is an interesting site that pays tribute to both aspects of Mankato's economic history. The *Seppmann Windmill* was built by Louis Seppmann in 1862 on top of a hill in what is now *Minneopa State Park*. The European-inspired conical shape of the mill's limestone base is pleasing to the eye, and its massive beams and burr stones only hint at the tremendous amount of labor that must have been required to build the now-inoperable structure. Thirty-five-square-foot canvas sails were supported by four huge wooden arms until the mill was afflicted by a series of natural disasters late in the nineteenth century: In 1873 Mr. Seppmann's mill was struck by lightning, losing two arms; then in 1880 a tornado took off two arms again; and finally in 1890 another storm wrecked the mill beyond repair.

Before leaving Minneopa State Park, you may want to visit a spectacular double waterfall along Minneopa Creek (*Minneopa* is translated from Dakota as "water falling twice"). The forty-five-foot falls, which are a short hike from a picnic area in the southern part of the park, spill into a steep wooded gorge over a protruding lip of Jordan sandstone. For more information on the park call (507) 386-3910 or visit dnr.state.mn.us.

Faribault County

The little town of *Winnebago* in northwestern Faribault County (south of Mankato) derives its name from the fact that from 1855 to 1863 a group of Wisconsin's Winnebago, driven from their traditional lands by settlers and by other hostile tribes, lived on a reservation nearby. American Indian history and prehistory are the main attraction at the *Winnebago Historical Society* as well. From postglacial times—when this continent's first human inhabitants migrated southward from the Bering land bridge about twenty thousand years ago—until the first contact between American Indians and Europeans in the 1700s, the museum chronicles very effectively the evolution of the area's American Indian cultures in a changing natural environment. A headdress that once belonged to Chief Red Cloud and some beautiful Ojibway ceremonial beaded clothing bring the prehistory exhibit into historic times. The free museum, located at 16 South Main St., is open Tues from 9 a.m. to noon and Wed through Sat from 1 p.m. to 4 p.m. or by appointment. For information call (507) 893-4660 or visit winnebagoareamuseum.org.

A statue of a different kind awaits those who approach the town of Blue Earth (not to be confused with the county of the same name) from the north on US 169 near I-90. Here, sporting a forty-eight-inch smile and wearing size seventy-eight green fiberglass slippers as he gazes contentedly down on a shopping center, is a sixty-foot rendering of the **_Jolly Green Giant_**. The Minnesota competition for most kitschy roadside attraction is a hot one—what with the many manifestations of Paul Bunyan and Babe the Blue Ox up north and the various civic animal totems elsewhere. But whatever you may say about all the rest, Blue Earth's entry is surely the greenest—though whether from envy or inexperience (he's only been here since 1979), it's hard to say.

Cottonwood County

This southwestern Minnesota county received its name because the Cottonwood River touches the northeast corner of the county. The Sioux called the river _Waraju_ for the dense stands of cottonwoods that grew on the banks. Sparsely populated, the county remained so until after the Civil War and the end of the bloody Dakota uprising of 1862. **Windom**, the largest town in the county, has two buildings of historical significance. The courthouse is on the National Register of Historic Places, and the power plant is the first municipal building in the US to be listed in the Art Deco Registry.

Heritage Village in Mountain Lake, northeast of Windom, is essentially a pioneer village—a museum built of a variety of transplanted historic buildings construed to represent a typical bygone town—but it's one with a couple of unusual twists. First, there are an extensive collection of historic telephone equipment and a general store stocked much as it was when it went out of business early in the twentieth century. Second, the area's Mennonite traditions are preserved in the **_Heritage Ayte Shtade_** (meaning "eating place") restaurant, located on the village grounds on CR 1, one mile south of MN 60.

The inexpensive meals served by costumed staff at the Ayte Shtade reflect the fact that the Mennonites traveled widely throughout Europe in their search for social environments tolerant of their religious beliefs. Such Mennonite dishes as _moos_, a delicious cold fruit soup; _klups_, a meat loaf patty with vegetables; and _perischki_, dumplings with fruit, reflect ethnic influences from much of northern Europe. The restaurant is open summer evenings (it's closed in winter) Thurs through Sat and at noon on Sun.

Each Sept Mountain Lake holds the annual **_Heritage Fair_**, or _Utschtallung,_ at Heritage Village. Festivities include music, Mennonite and other foods, and kids' activities. For more information, go to heritagevillage mountainlake.com.

The **_Jacob Harder House_** has been described by one architectural historian as looking like a "pregnant spaceship . . . sheathed in fish-scale shingles which really look more like chicken feathers." Looked at another way, this

TOP ANNUAL EVENTS IN PRAIRIELAND

FEBRUARY

Ole & Lena Days
Granite Falls, early Feb
(320) 321-3202
granitefallschamber.com

JUNE

Buffalo Days
Luverne, early June
(507) 283-4061
luvernechamber.com

Aebleskiver Days
Tyler, late June
(507) 247-5556

OCTOBER

Oktoberfest
New Ulm, first two weekends in Oct
(507) 233-4300

NOVEMBER

Norsefest
Madison, early Nov
(320) 598-7373
ci.madison.mn.us

circular dwelling, with its two bug-eyed bay windows separated by a proboscis-like bulge in the wall, just might be the visage of some extraterrestrial insect. Check it out for yourself by driving down Eighth Street between Second and Third Avenues.

Extraterrestrial influences may also come to mind upon visiting the *Jeffers Petroglyphs*. There are nearly two thousand rock carvings at this site, located several miles east of Jeffers and a couple of miles north of MN 30 on CR 2. Each figure was chiseled into an exposed ridge of red quartzite bedrock at some undetermined prehistoric date. Together they represent the state's largest group of petroglyphs.

The circular trail begins at a tepee-shaped interpretive center managed by Minnesota Historical Society staff. After picking up a guidebook, visitors are free to wander the quarter-mile walkway, which is surrounded by virgin prairie, at their own pace. Many of the figures encountered seem to have been suggested by aspects of the natural environment, including such animals as bison, bear, wolf, turtle, and elk. Human forms, sometimes wearing what look to be horned headdresses (perhaps similar to those used by Dakota medicine men in historic times), imply the possibility that at least some of the glyphs held spiritual significance. Others are simple geometric designs, hand- or footprints, or so abstract as to defy description. But whatever they may have meant to their creators, it's clear that making these figures required a lot of work. Each of them was pecked into the hard quartzite surface by a pointed rock that was held in the fist and struck with a hammerstone.

The site is open daily for a small fee during summer and on weekends through Sept. For more information call (507) 628-5591 or go to mnhs.org.

Watonwan County

Named after the Watonwan River, a word meaning "good fish bait" or "where fish abound," this county (east of Cottonwood) has a site related to one of the most infamous events in Minnesota history. On September 21, 1876, Jesse and Frank James, the three Younger brothers, and three other gang members robbed the single bank in Northfield, the only criminal act the gang pulled off in Minnesota. The robbery was also the only real mistake Jesse made as an outlaw.

A gunfight in Northfield killed two gang members, and the James brothers escaped to the Dakota border. Two weeks later the Younger brothers and Charlie Pitts stopped at a farm near St. James for food, but the son of the family recognized them and fled to get help. A posse formed and soon caught up with the gang in the Watonwan River bottoms. In the ensuing gunfight, Pitts died and the Youngers surrendered. The *Younger Brothers Monument* sits a half mile south of LaSalle on CR 3. For information call the St. James Chamber of Commerce at (507) 375-3333.

Nobles County

Ask serious windsurfers for their favorite place to ride the wind, and most will say the Columbia River Gorge between Washington and Oregon, Maui, or some big reservoir in the windy western US. Many Midwestern windsurfers probably don't realize that the best wind in the Midwest blows across *Lake Okabena* in Worthington.

Called "Gorge of the Midwest," this prairie lake has a reputation for strong and consistent winds that some say make it the best windsurfing lake in the Midwest. Entrepreneurs have built electricity-generating windmills throughout southwestern Minnesota, and now windsurfers have discovered this inexhaustible natural resource. For more information call Worthington Okabena Windsurfers (WOW) at (507) 372-2919 or visit Worthington Windsurfing Regatta (and Music Festival) on Facebook or its website at worthingtonwindsurfing.net.

Worthington's *Nobles County Pioneer Village*, more than most other collections of antique, historically furnished buildings in the state, has the feeling of a real town. Practically every institution that a thriving turn-of-the-twentieth-century prairie community would have had is represented among the forty-seven structures. There's a law office, a hospital with an iron lung

Mystery at Blue Mound

For avid viewers of the *X-Files* or anyone who has pondered the origin of Stonehenge and the statues on Easter Island, another such mystery awaits at *Blue Mounds State Park*. In this prairie park located in Rock County, a 1,250-foot-long line of rocks sits aligned from east to west.

While no one knows who built it or why, on the first day of spring and fall, sunrise and sunset line up on this stone arrangement. Did prehistoric humans align the stones to mark the changing of the seasons? Did visitors from light years away do it to let us know they were here? Or did some locals build it more recently as a hoax? While the first scenario seems the most likely, we'll probably never know definitively. And it's probably better the mystery remains.

and a primitive X-ray machine, a train depot, a church, a millinery shop, two life-size grain elevators, a well-equipped schoolhouse, and even a doghouse. Enter most of these establishments, and the furnishings and artifacts arranged casually about create the illusion that everyone has just stepped out to lunch. Walk out on the empty street and you *know* you're in a ghost town.

The village, located just west of the Nobles County Fairgrounds, south of I-90, is open daily in summer for a nominal fee. For further information call (507) 295-5397 or go to noblescountyhistory.org.

Rock County

As one might expect, Rock County received its name because of rock. In this case, the rock is a ledge of Sioux quartzite (also called red rock or jasper) that starts in Blue Mounds State Park and extends northwest to the town of Jasper. Rock County also has the distinction of being the only county in Minnesota where all its streams flow into the Missouri River, a unique feature in a state dominated by the Mississippi.

Driving north from Luverne on US 75, *Blue Mounds State Park* grabs your attention as soon as it comes into view. In a landscape of largely treeless, boulderless, and flat agricultural fields, suddenly you confront a ridge running at odd angles to the highway, as if a mountain were beginning to emerge from the well-groomed surface of the earth. Against a background of colorful prairie grasses, you can see boulders and protrusions of Sioux quartzite bedrock, which are covered with lovely constellations of lichens and surrounded by clumps of prickly pear cacti. And as you approach the entrance to the park, a small herd of bison is visible in the distance. The sensation is uncanny: You've returned to the prairie of a hundred years ago.

Approached from the east, as they were by the westward-migrating settlers, the mounds appear bluish against the predominant prairie sky, hence the origin of their name. The face the Blue Mounds presented to these travelers was a rugged one—a steep escarpment 2.5 miles long and up to 100 feet high, with a ragged line of oak trees at its base. Mound Creek, which flows along the northern edge of the ridge, has been dammed in two places to form small reservoirs; otherwise, little in the park has changed over the centuries.

Hiking trails follow the top and bottom of the cliff and meander across the top of the mounds, offering many vistas of the surrounding countryside and a chance to wallow in the rich prairie environment. Swimming is possible in Lower Mound Lake, and camping and picnic grounds are located nearby. The bison can be viewed from numerous locations. And at the southern edge of the park is an interpretive center containing exhibits on the natural history of the prairie environment. For more information call the park at (507) 283-6050 or visit dnr.state.mn.us.

If you've ever looked at a *National Geographic* magazine, you have likely seen amazing photos from noted photographer *Jim Brandenburg*. Few people probably know he is based in the northern Minnesota town of Ely, but fewer still know he is from Luverne in far southwestern Minnesota. In cooperation with the local chamber of commerce, he opened a gallery in downtown Luverne that displays over one hundred pieces of his work. The gallery is within the chamber of commerce building at 213 East Luverne St. The gallery is open Mon through Fri 8 a.m. to 5 p.m. and Sat 10 a.m. to 5 p.m. For more information call the chamber at (507) 283-4061.

Brandenburg was also involved in starting the Brandenburg Prairie Foundation, which in a partnership with the US Fish and Wildlife Service bought more than eight hundred acres of untilled prairie north of Luverne. Now known as *Touch the Sky Northern Tallgrass Prairie National Wildlife Refuge*, it is being restored to its natural state as a tallgrass prairie. There is a two-mile out-and-back hiking trail at the refuge that gives visitors the experience of being in the prairie landscape rather than only seeing it from afar. For more information and directions to the prairie, go to luvernechamber.com.

Pipestone County

The Sioux quartzite formation that gives rise to the geology of Blue Mounds State Park breaks through to the surface again just north of the city of *Pipestone*. But here a second kind of stone, softer than the quartzite and of a distinct reddish color, is visible, too. It is called pipestone, or, after nineteenth-century itinerant artist George Catlin, catlinite. And the site now known as **Pipestone National Monument** has for hundreds of years been a sacred quarry from which raw material was obtained to produce the stone pipes so widely associated with American Indians.

Despite whatever animosities existed between tribes, throughout most of its history the pipestone quarry was considered neutral territory to which American Indians from as far as a thousand miles away would travel on foot and remove the soft clay stone in peace. Pipe makers still quarry and work the stone today, though since 1928 the land has been under National Park Service jurisdiction.

A visit to the monument begins at the interpretive center, where a film on the history of the site is complemented by exhibits of pipestone artifacts, a gift shop, and craft demonstrations by native carvers. A three-quarter-mile footpath leads from this building through the quarry grounds. The trail winds through stands of trees (which have matured in the absence of the once-frequent prairie fires) along Pipestone Creek to beautiful Winnewissa Falls, which was formed where the creek pours over a quartzite ledge. Several quarry pits are passed along the way, appearing as gashes in the ground surrounded by discarded quartzite rubble. Notations chiseled into a trailside boulder are evidence of cartographer Joseph Nicollet's expedition in 1838. Even bird-watching is excellent in this special place.

Pipestone National Monument is found to the west of US 75, adjacent to the north side of the city of Pipestone. Open daily, it has a small admission charge. For more information call (507) 825-5464 or visit nps.gov.

Murray County

When the railroad finally reached the town of **Currie** in 1901, it was faced with a little problem. Like many small Minnesota towns that were off the main rail routes but still large enough (or politically savvy enough) to warrant being served by the iron horse, Currie was at the end of a spur line. And, having made the thirty-eight-mile jaunt from Bingham Lake to the southeast, the engines needed some way to get turned around for their return trip.

The solution was to build a turntable—a section of track resting on a pivot upon which the engine and coal car could be swung around 180 degrees by the efforts of a single worker. When it was built, the Currie turntable was an unremarkable bit of engineering similar to many others of the time. But today it is one of only two still in existence in the state, making the **End-o-Line Railroad Park and Museum** an unusual attraction.

Once you're through marveling at how one puny human could spin a locomotive as if it were a top, there's much more to see in the depot and engine shed. The shed, which originally housed locomotives that weren't in use, is full of antique railroad equipment and memorabilia, such as a full set of section foreman's tools and a couple of track-inspector vehicles—including the trusty velocipede.

Nearby, the depot has been restored in detail to its former glory, incorporating such touches as the strategic placement of a tobacco tin in the telegraph set to improve its reception. The building's two waiting rooms reflect a tradition of segregation by sex that was in effect until the 1920s. Under this Victorian arrangement, the men were able to spit tobacco and the women to nurse children without compunction or embarrassment. The depot's baggage room has been devoted to an outstanding HO-scale model train display that depicts the Currie railroad yards as they looked in the 1940s. Outside there's a restored caboose to be explored, the reconstructed Currie Store (the first general store in the area), and the region's first school.

The End-o-Line Museum is open free of charge daily during summer and by special arrangement at other times. For information call the End-o-Line Railroad Park and Museum at (507) 763-3708 or visit endoline.com.

WAY, WAY OFF THE BEATEN PATH

Box Elder Bug Days
mid-Sept, Minneota
While one is more likely to find turtle races and frog races as part of a town festival, it's rare to come across someplace that devotes an entire festival to a lowly bug. And given how common (i.e., annoying) box elder bugs are around here in September, this is the perfect way to "celebrate" their arrival. boxelderbugdays.com

Birthplace of Sears
north Redwood County, on MN 101
Although Sears has fallen on hard times in the past few years, it's still remarkable that a multibillion-dollar company had its beginning in a small farming community in southwestern Minnesota.

King Turkey Days
second Sat after Labor Day, Worthington
For many years, Worthington was one of the top turkey producers in the US. In 1939 the town started this festival as a way to celebrate and promote the role of turkeys in the local economy. Although Worthington is no longer the top turkey producer, this festival, which includes a turkey race between a local bird and one from Cuero, Texas, continues. kingturkeyday.org

Lake Shetek State Park, two miles north of Currie on CR 37, is in the center of what is commonly known as the Great Oasis—a lovely hardwood grove surrounded by a network of lakes amid the dominance of farm and prairie. Within the 1,175-acre park are no fewer than five small lakes and ponds, complemented by extensive footage on the shore of the much larger Lake Shetek. Thus there's lots to do for water-sports enthusiasts besides the usual state park fare of hiking, camping, and picnicking.

But Shetek is also the memorial site of one of the more gruesome encounters between the Dakota and settlers in the conflict of 1862. Since 1987— the war's 125th anniversary, which was commemorated as the Year of Reconciliation—staff at the park have held an annual *Shetek Revisited* program over a late-Aug weekend to illuminate the complex tragedy that led to the killing of eleven settlers and several Dakota at Slaughter Slough. The program includes a bus tour of sites related to this event. For more information call (507) 763-3256 or visit dnr.state.mn.us.

Places to Stay in Prairieland

BLUE EARTH

AmericInn
MN 169 and I-90
(507) 526-4215
wyndhamhotels.com

GRANITE FALLS

Super Motel
845 West Hwy. 212
(320) 564-4075

LITCHFIELD AND WILLMAR

Best Western Plus
1525 Hwy. 12 East
Litchfield
(320) 693-1600
bestwestern.com

Best Western Plus
2100 Hwy. 12 East
Willmar
(320) 235-6060
bestwestern.com

Country Inn & Suites
201 Twenty-Eighth Ave.
Southeast
Willmar
(320) 214-0300
choicehotels.com

Holiday Inn Express & Suites
250 Twenty-Third St.
Southeast
Willmar
(320) 231-2601
ihg.com

LUVERNE

Grandstay Hotel & Suites
908 South Kniss Ave.
(507) 449-4949
grandstayhospitality.com

Econolodge
801 South Kniss
(US 75 South)
(507) 283-7189
choicehotels.com

MANKATO

Courtyard by Marriott
901 Raintree Rd.
(507) 388-1234
marriott.com

Hilton Garden Inn
20 Civic Center Plaza
(507) 344-1111
hilton.com

Holiday Inn Express & Suites
2051 Adams St.
(507) 388-1880
ihg.com

River Hills Hotel
1000 Raintree Rd.
(507) 388-8688
riverhillshotel.com

MONTEVIDEO

Crossings by Grandstay
Inn and Suites
1805 East Hwy. 7
(320) 269-8000
grandstayhospitality.com

Viking Motel
1428 East Hwy. 7
(320) 269-6545
vikingmotelmontevideo
.com

NEW ULM/SLEEPY EYE

Bingham Hall Bed
& Breakfast
500 South German St.
New Ulm
(507) 276-5070
bingham-hall.com

Best Western Plus
2101 South Broadway
New Ulm
(507) 359-2941
bestwestern.com

Microtel Inn and Suites
424 Twentieth St. South
New Ulm
(507) 550-0922
wyndhamhotels.com

AmericInn
1100 Main St.
Sleepy Eye
(507) 312-6036
wyndhamhotels.com

PIPESTONE

Grandstay Hotel
and Suites
915 Seventh St. Southeast
(507) 562-1100
grandstayhospitality.com

REDWOOD FALLS

Redwood Valley Lodge
1382 East Bridge St.
(507) 644-5700
redwoodlodge.com

Travelodge
1305 East Bridge St.
(507) 637-0580
wyndhamhotels.com

The Vintage Inn
103 East Second St.
(507) 627-1875
vintageinnredwoodfalls.com

WINDOM

AmericInn Lodge
and Suites
2270 Hwy. 60 East
(507) 832-8300
wyndhamhotels.com

WORTHINGTON

AmericInn
1475 Darling Dr.
(507) 376-4500
wyndhamhotels.com

Comfort Suites
1447 Prairie Dr.
(507) 295-9185
choicehotels.com

The Historic Dayton
House Bed and Breakfast
1311 Fourth Ave.
(507) 727-1311
daytonhouse.org

Holiday Inn Express
1250 Ryan's Rd.
(507) 372-2333
ihg.com

Places to Eat
in Prairieland

BLUE EARTH

Farmer's Daughter
(American)
1430 Giant Dr.
(507) 526-2120

Average Jo's Bar
and Grill
(American)
115 East Sixth St.
(507) 526-3032

Cedar Inn
324 North Grove St.
(507) 526-5612
cedarinndrivein.square.site

GRANITE FALLS

Bluenose Gopher
Public House
(American)
681 Prentice St.
(320) 564-0034
bluenose.coop

Jimmy's Pizza
776 Prentice St.
(320) 564-3737
jimmyspizza.com

Tolley's Bar and Grill
(American)
1316 Hwy. 212 West
(320) 379-1325

Carl's Bakery
810 Prentice St.
(320) 564-2531
carlsbakery.net

Falls Café and Canoe
723 Prentice St.
(507) 401-5566

LITCHFIELD

King's Wok
(Chinese)
305 Sibley Ave. North
(320) 693-2259
kings-wok-litchfield.edan.io

Mimi's Bistro and Bakery
(American)
215 Sibley Ave. North
(320) 693-2150

Parkview Grille
(American)
311 North Sibley Ave.
(320) 593-2835
parkviewgrille.com

Jimmy's Pizza
637 Hwy. 12
(320) 348-7982
jimmyspizzalitchfield.com

Sonora's
(Mexican)
637 Hwy. 12
(320) 593-0022

LUVERNE

The Bean
(coffee)
309 West Edgehill
(507) 449-0294

Sterling's Café and Grille
(American)
105 East Main St.
(507) 449-0220
sterlingsluverne.com

Pizza Ranch
110 East Main St.
(507) 283-2379
pizzaranch.com

Take 16 Brewing
509 East Main St.
(507) 369-2801
take16beer.com

MANKATO

**El Mazatlan
Mexican Restaurant**
1525 Tullamore St.
(507) 625-2406
elmazatlanfood.com

Fillin Station
(coffee)
630 South Front St.
(507) 344-0345
fillinstationcoffeehouse.com

Wooden Spoon
515 North Riverfront Dr.
(507) 345-4114
woodenspoonmn.com

Great Wall Restaurant
(Chinese)
1814 Commerce Dr.
(507) 345-5758
newgreatwallnm.com

Jake's Stadium Pizza
330 Stadium Rd.
(507) 345-5420
jakesstadiumpizza.com

Olives
(American)
20 Civic Center Plaza
(507) 274-7010
olivesmn.com

Pagliai's Pizza
524 South Front St.
(507) 345-6080
pagliaismankato.com

Pub 500
(American)
500 South Front St.
(507) 625-6500
pub500.com

MONTEVIDEO

Art's Dairy Freeze
1307 Black Oak Ave.
(320) 269-6282

Table 212
(American)
4490 Hwy. 212
(320) 321-1281
table212.com

Jake's Pizza
207 South First St.
(320) 297-6091
jakespizzamontevideo.com

Java River
(coffee)
210 South First St.
(320) 321-1555
javarivercoffeeshop.square
.site

**The Rivers Family
Restaurant**
(American)
610 Hwy. 212 West
(320) 269-8662
riversfamilyrestaurant.com

Topper's Bar and Grill
311 State Rd.
(320) 269-9401
toppersbar.com

NEW ULM

The Backerei
(coffee)
27 South Minnesota St.
(507) 354-6011
thebackerei.com

Joni's Restaurant
(American)
24 North Minnesota St.
(507) 359-2018
jonisrestaurant.com

Kaiserhoff
(German)
221 North Minnesota St.
(507) 359-2071
kaiserhoff.org

Lola American Bistro
16 North Minnesota St.
(507) 359-2500
lolaamericanbistro.com

Main Jiang House
1702 Westridge Rd.
(507) 354-1228
mainjianghouse.com

Plaza Garibaldi
(Mexican)
1707 North Broadway St.
(507) 359-7073
plazagaribaldinewulm.com

Turner Hall & Rathskeller
102 South State St.
(507) 354-4916
newulmturnerhall.org

**George's Fine Steaks
and Spirits**
(American)
301 North Minnesota St.
(507) 354-7440
georgessteaks.biz

PIPESTONE

Dar's Pizza
MN 30 and Eighth Ave.
Southwest
(507) 825-4261

Eighth Avenue Diner
101 Eighth Ave. Northeast
(507) 562-2540

**Los Tulipanes
Mexican Restaurant**
607 Eighth Ave. Northeast
(507) 825-9959

Hatfield Roadhouse
(American)
340 Second St. Northwest
(507) 845-0069

REDWOOD FALLS

Roadhouse Bar and Grill
(American)
713 Main St.
Wabasso
(507) 342-2006

Duffy's Riverside Saloon
110 Front St. East
(507) 616-1002
duffysmn.com

Grandview Valley Winery
(American)
42703 Grandview Ave.
Belview
(507) 938-9463
gvwinery.com

Pizza Ranch
1360 East Bridge St.
(507) 644-5936
pizzaranch.com

Plaza Garibaldi
(Mexican)
1211 East Bridge St.
(507) 627-7073
plazagaribaldiredwood.com

WILLMAR

**The Goodness
Coffeehouse**
333 Litchfield Ave.
Southwest
(320) 403-5025
downtowngoodness.com

Frieda's Cafe
(American)
511 Benson Ave. West
(320) 235-2865
friedascafe.com

Giovanni's Pizza
1312 Southeast
Lakeland Dr.
(320) 235-5555
giovannisofwillmar.com

Middle Fork Café
309 Lakeland Dr.
Southeast
(320) 262-5171

Jake's Pizza
316 Litchfield Ave. West
(320) 235-1714
jakespizzaofwillmar.com

Lu Lu Beans
(coffee)
1020 First St. South
(320) 214-9633
lulubeans.net

Panda Garden Buffet
1305 First St. South
(320) 235-1288
pandagardenbuffetmn.com

WINDOM

Godfather's Pizza
112 Third Ave. South
(507) 831-4836
gogodfathers.com

Jack Slades Steakhouse
2390 Hwy. 60
(507) 831-2280

WORTHINGTON

Blue Line Cafe
(American)
Hwy. 60 Northeast
(507) 372-4038

El Taco Restaurant
418 Tenth St.
(507) 372-5039

Phileos Coffee
212 Tenth St.
(507) 727-1480
phileoscoffee.com

Forbidden Barrel Brewing
900 Third St.
(507) 343-3880
forbiddenbarrel.com

Panda House
(Chinese)
913 Fourth Ave.
(507) 372-5155

Godfather's Pizza
1097 West Gateway Dr.
(507) 727-1627
godfathers.com

SELECTED WEBSITES IN PRAIRIELAND

Blue Earth Area Chamber of Commerce
(507) 526-2916
blueearthchamber.com

Granite Falls Area Chamber of Commerce
(320) 321-3202
visitgranitefalls.com

Le Sueur Area Chamber of Commerce
(507) 665-2501
lesueurchamber.org

Lincoln County Promotion and Tourism
(507) 694-1429
co.lincoln.mn.us

Litchfield Chamber of Commerce
(320) 693-8184
litch.com

Luverne Area Chamber of Commerce
(507) 283-4061
luvernechamber.com

Mankato Area Chamber of Commerce
(507) 385-6640
visitgreatermankato.com

City of Milan
(320) 734-4411
milanmn.com

Montevideo Area Chamber of Commerce
(320) 269-5527
montechamber.com

New Ulm Convention and Visitors Bureau
(888) 463-9856
newulm.com

Pipestone Convention and Visitors Bureau
(507) 825-3316
pipestoneminnesota.com

Redwood Falls Area Chamber and Tourism
(507) 637-2828
redwoodfalls.org

Sleepy Eye Area Chamber of Commerce
(507) 794-4731
sleepyeyechamber.com

Willmar Lakes Area Convention and Visitors Bureau
(320) 235-3552
willmarlakesarea.com

Windom Area Chamber of Commerce
(507) 831-2752
windomchamber.com

Worthington Area Convention and Visitors Bureau
(507) 372-2919
worthingtonmnchamber.com

Red River Country

This region covers the northwestern corner of Minnesota and has a landscape of dramatic contrasts. The Red River Valley covers the western and northern parts of this region and features some of the flattest landscape found anywhere in the world. The valley is not a valley in the true sense of the word because the river meanders north in a channel that sits only a few feet below the surrounding rich farmland.

East of the flat valley floor, rolling hills left by glaciers form a dramatically different landscape. Tabletop flat becomes endless rolling hills of all shapes and sizes, mile after mile of unbroken cultivated land becomes forest, and a landscape of scattered rivers and lakes turns into one of countless lakes and marshes. The change is not sudden, but it leaves no doubt that you have visited two areas of distinctive geologic characteristics. The *lake country of Otter Tail and Becker Counties* will make travelers wonder where all the water comes from as they wind around countless lakes, ponds, swamps, and streams.

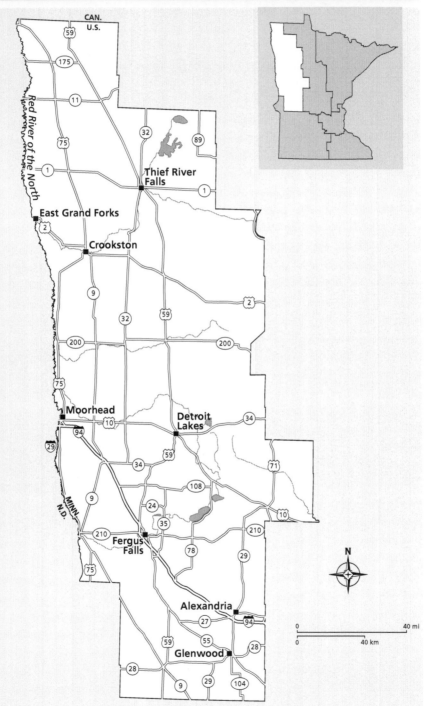

Douglas County

Due to its proximity to the Red River Valley, you would think this popular vacation destination's lakes and rivers would form part of the watershed of the Red River. But thanks to glaciations, the waters of Douglas County drain north and east to eventually join the Mississippi and south to join the Minnesota. Again the often subtle differences in what we see prove the role glaciers had in shaping the landscape of Minnesota.

Standing in the middle of downtown *Alexandria*—an attractive town of 11,580 surrounded by numerous lakes and resorts—is a brightly painted statue of a huge Viking whose shield is inscribed with a brazen claim: ALEXANDRIA/ BIRTHPLACE OF AMERICA. This dubious geographical declaration was inspired by an object housed across the street inside the *Runestone Museum*.

The story goes that in 1897 a large flat stone with a long inscription of unknown characters was discovered entwined in the roots of an old tree in the nearby community of Kensington. The man who claimed to have found the stone, a Swedish immigrant farmer named Olof Ohaman, forwarded a copy of the inscription to a Scandinavian languages professor at the University of Minnesota. The professor and his colleagues, unable to render a translation of the script, concluded that it was a fraud. But nine years later a historian of Norwegian immigration, Hjalmar Holand, succeeded in deciphering the runic script and became convinced that the Kensington runestone is proof the Vikings predated Columbus's journey to the New World by at least a hundred years.

Though the stone's authenticity has never enjoyed widespread scientific support, for some residents of Alexandria there exists not even a shadow of a doubt. A visit to the Runestone Museum—where the inscription is translated as describing the activities of a group of "8 Goths [Swedes] and 22 Norwegians" on an "exploration journey from Vinland [the East Coast] through the west" in 1362—will allow you to make up your own mind. The Discovery Room, where

AUTHOR'S FAVORITES

Glacial Lakes State Park
Glenwood/Starbuck
(320) 239-2860

**Lake Country of Otter Tail
and Becker Counties**

Lake Minnewaska at Glenwood

Maplewood State Park
Pelican Rapids
(218) 863-8383

Phelps Mill
Phelps (near Fergus Falls)
(218) 826-6159

the stone is on display, features a video about the runestone, as well as Viking artifacts. Other exhibits detail the more recent history of Douglas County, including a series of historic log and wood-frame buildings grouped together under the banner of Fort Alexandria. The museum, located at 206 North Broadway, is open daily and charges a small admission fee. Call (320) 763-3160 for more information or visit runestonemuseum.org.

Pope County

An imposing sight greets travelers arriving in the town of Glenwood from the north or east. The flat roads that pass through the Bonanza Valley, a sand plain formed by a melting glacier, suddenly drop down a steep ridge to *Lake Minnewaska*. As the thirteenth largest in Minnesota, the lake lies between the flat landscape of glacial outwash and the hilly land of countless glacial deposits of rock and gravel. Surrounded by a ridge that alternates between steep and gradual, the lake doesn't seem to belong in this area of farms. Obviously the glaciers thought otherwise.

Glacial Lakes State Park, located five miles south of Starbuck, provides visitors with an exceptional display of the effects glaciers had on this part of Minnesota. Besides the distinct geological formations, the park also sits in a transition zone between prairie and forest. Only one-tenth of 1 percent of the original Minnesota prairie remains, and this park has a section of it. For more information call the park at (320) 239-2860.

The *Glacial Ridge Trail* provides another way to see the glacier-scoured landscape of west-central Minnesota. This scenic route follows highways and county roads for 220 miles through five counties and traces a ridge left by the last glacier to cover this region. For more information on the trail, call the Glenwood Chamber of Commerce at (320) 334-3095.

When the flour mill was built along the banks of the Chippewa River in the little community of Terrace in 1903, there was trouble in the air. The railroad had passed Terrace by, and with it went the main source of hope and prosperity for Terrace's residents: a mill that had been built by the town fathers in 1870. The new mill was constructed in a doomed attempt to revive the community's economy.

After decades of observing a steady decline in population, the post office finally abandoned Terrace in the early 1970s and the little hamlet was threatened with complete oblivion. Then came a startlingly successful effort to restore the decrepit old mill.

Several times each summer, tens of thousands of people descend on *Terrace Mill* for some of the most innovative arts and music festivals to be found

Name that Glacier

Most of Minnesota bears the marks of glaciers, the last of which covered much of the state about ten thousand years ago. Although it's not easy for most of us to identify the landscape formations left behind, some are easier to see than others. Some of the more common glacial features in Minnesota include:

- *Drumlin*—a long hill made of glacial debris.

- *Erratic*—a rock carried and deposited by a glacier.

- *Esker*—a long wormlike ridge formed by debris-laden meltwater. Eskers probably mark the channels of subglacial streams.

- *Kame*—a conical hill of glacial debris deposited in contact with glacial ice. Imagine a snow cone tipped upside down.

- *Kettle*—a depression (which usually becomes a lake or marsh) that formed when a block of ice melted after separating from the glacier and being covered by glacial debris.

anywhere in the state. The internationally acclaimed Minnesota Orchestra has performed an outdoor concert beside the wooden structure that culminated in a stirring rendition of Tchaikovsky's "1812 Overture," replete with the firing of sixteen historic cannons. Minnesota's premier theatrical company, the Guthrie, has used the mill's portable stage and nineteenth-century atmosphere for such period productions as the Civil War–era *Red Badge of Courage*. Terrace Mill is also the site of an annual Heritage Festival Art Show in mid-June that showcases Norwegian-inspired rosemaling painting; classes and seminars are offered during the festival in this and other crafts. And each season ends with a concert in late Aug and an *Oktoberfest* celebration and Fiddle Contest the first Sun in Oct, which draws fiddlers from far and wide.

Tours of the now fully restored building are given daily during summer (a small donation is requested). Terrace's Historic General Store has been renovated, too, and is now stocked with dry goods and gifts. Restoration of the miller's home and the town's original log cabin qualified most of the community for inclusion on the National Register of Historic Places.

For more information about events at Terrace Mill, call (320) 278-3728.

Grant County

Herman is exactly the kind of quiet hamlet preferred by Minnesota's legendary stoic, hardworking bachelor Norwegian farmers. In fact, until recently the tradition had become so entrenched that seeing a woman about town was nearly as unlikely as spying a man without a seed cap. Then the national media decreed there was news in the fact that a town existed where bachelors outnumbered the womenfolk by evolutionarily suicidal odds, and eligible women began to show up in Herman's pool halls and taverns from as far away as Montana and California.

It's a safe bet that those stoic Norwegian farmers never envisioned groups of brightly clad, two-wheel-equipped humans invading the quiet farm and lake country of Grant County. But thanks to the *Central Lakes Trail*, that's just what happens when the weather warms as cyclists of all shapes, sizes, and ages take to this gorgeous paved trail. Running for fifty-five miles from Osakis to Fergus Falls, the fourteen-foot-wide, nearly level trail passes through the town of Ashby, which is located close to the halfway point of the trail.

The trail follows a former railroad line, and connects to the Lake Wobegon Trail near St. Cloud, which increases the total paved mileage to an incredible 103 miles. Recreational trails like this go through many small towns, so it's always easy to find food and water, and since they're separated from roads, they offer a safe and relaxing route for bicyclists. From Ashby to Fergus Falls the trail runs through the rural countryside, isolated from roads.

Besides great cycling, the trail is the site of *Quilts Along the Trail*, an exhibit every September that showcases quilts from local quilters. The event is set up alongside the trail in the town of Osakis and also includes arts and crafts and food and beverage booths.

For more information contact the Central Lakes Trail at (320) 763-0102 or visit centrallakestrail.com.

Otter Tail County

This popular vacation area sits in a scenic pocket on the edge of the Red River Valley. Many lakes dot the rolling landscape, as fields of corn, soybeans, and forage grasses form a patchwork with thick stands of stately hardwoods. Some archaeologists think humans may have lived here as long as ten thousand years ago along the shores of Glacial Lake Pelican. Today the glacier-scoured landscape attracts many visitors to this watery playground.

Though newspaper magnate William Randolph Hearst Jr. may not have been intending to start a trend when he imported the first South American llamas to the US in the early 1920s, these graceful, woolly domesticated pack animals have found a fast-growing niche in American society. A visit to *Horseshoe Valley Llamas*, three miles south of Fergus Falls on CR 25, gives travelers a sense of why.

A couple of dozen llamas serenely chew their cud while monitoring with an attentive gaze everything that transpires in the surrounding pasture. They have long necks, skinny legs, dignified faces, and slender, curved ears that resemble bananas. Like their distant cousin the camel, llamas walk with a peculiar lateral gait, swinging both legs on one side forward simultaneously. With one touch it's easy to see why their wonderfully soft wool, which makes the animals' bodies look much bigger than they actually are, is prized for making fine wool sweaters. Call (218) 736-4707 to arrange a visit.

When you find your way back to **Fergus Falls** from Horseshoe Valley Llamas, awaiting you is one of the best county history museums in the state. Exhibits at the **Otter Tail County Historical Society Museum**, located at 1110 West Lincoln, are laid out in a labyrinth of passageways that traverse the distance from early prehistory to the present—all within the confines of a single large building.

The well-interpreted exhibits begin with the glacial events that helped give Otter Tail County its lake-strewn character. This sequence is followed by interesting displays on the Dakota and Ojibway, activities related to the fur trade, a scaled-down logging operation, and an impressive section on agricultural history that includes a life-size harvest scene in a shimmering "field" of real wheat. Victorian lifestyles are displayed in a winding "street" of homes and diverse businesses, each appointed in detail with appropriate furnishings and artifacts. By offering such a fine representation of Otter Tail County's past, the museum, which is open daily year-round, also gives visitors a good overview of western Minnesota history. A small fee is charged to adults for admission. Call (218) 736-6038 for more information or go to otchs.org.

Minnesota's Kames

Red River Country lies in a geographical transition zone between Minnesota's western prairies and eastern forests. **Maplewood State Park** near Pelican Rapids provides an excellent example of a transition landscape. It sits in the Alexandria Moraine, a band of glacial drift two hundred miles long by ten to twenty miles wide. The park offers a startling change of scenery, as the terrain changes from flat to dramatically rolling.

Approaching the park, the observant visitor will notice many cone-shaped hills, known as *kames*. Maplewood has one of the best displays in Minnesota of this distinctive geologic formation. If you drive on Otter Tail CR 24 along the southern edge of the park, not only will you see an awesome collection of kames, but you will also find some unusual road signs marking places where the road curves around these huge mounds. In an age where technology seems to carve through any hill or under any mountain, it's refreshing to see that humans deferred to nature and rerouted a road.

Nature lovers visiting the Fergus Falls area have two attractions that should rank high on the must-visit list. *Prairie Wetlands Learning Center*, which is the first and only residential environmental education facility operated by the US Fish and Wildlife Service, covers 330 acres of native and restored prairie and twenty-eight wetlands on the southern edge of Fergus Falls. The center offers a wonderful example of prairie pothole topography, an important landscape for a wide variety of wildlife that is especially important for waterfowl. Over 180 species of birds have been identified at the center. Visitors will find nearly four miles of hiking trails, a visitor center with interpretive displays, and a gift shop. The center is located at 602 State Hwy. 210 East, Fergus Falls. For information call (218) 998-4488 or visit friendsofprairiewetlands.com.

Fergus Falls sits at the southern end of the *Pine to Prairie Birding Trail*, a two-hundred-mile route that follows highways through the transition zone geography of northwestern Minnesota. This part of Minnesota has a wide variety of habitats, including pine forests, deciduous woodlands, native tallgrass prairie, aspen parkland, sand dunes, fens, marshes, bogs, lakes of all sizes, and rivers. This incredible diversity of landscapes provides habitat for well over two hundred species of birds. For a map of the trail that lists forty-five sites for bird-watching, go to mnbirdtrail.com.

One of the pinnacles in Minnesota's less-than-alpine landscape is found about twenty-five miles southeast of Fergus Falls, near the tiny town of Urbank. *Inspiration Peak*, as the conical hilltop is known, is part of what geologists call a terminal moraine formed by ice age glaciers depositing quantities of sediment in a formation recognized today as the Leaf Hills. Along the wooded flanks of Inspiration Peak is a wayside rest and picnic area accessible from CR 38 about ten miles east of MN 78. Two asphalt footpaths ascend from the parking lot somewhat steeply to a clearing at the summit, 1,750 feet above sea level and 400 feet above Spitzer Lake immediately to the west.

The grand view from the top is well worth the half-mile round-trip hike. The Leaf Hills, covered with oak and other hardwoods, run in a rugged north–south line. To the east and west, rolling forest and farmland stretch to the horizons. More than a half-dozen lakes are visible, and numerous grain silos reflect the sunlight.

In mid-July each year, artists gather for the Phelps Mill Summer Festival in the tiny town of Phelps, twenty-five miles northeast of Fergus Falls on CR 45. At the center of this celebration sits *Phelps Mill* itself, which is open for self-guided tours throughout the summer season. From 1889 to 1931 turbines in this well-preserved wooden structure drew power from the clear-flowing Otter Tail River to grind wheat into flour. Farmers brought their wheat to Phelps from up to a hundred miles away, often seeking overnight accommodations at the mill's "Farmers Roost" while waiting to collect their flour. The mill remained popular during the heyday of the Non-Partisan League, when farmers didn't want to patronize the large mills owned by "capitalists" in Minneapolis. Finally the drought of the 1930s brought an end to milling activities at Phelps.

Now the mill, which is complemented by a historic country store and log cabin, is part of the Otter Tail County park system. Swimming, picnicking, and limited camping are possible just downstream of the dam. The Fergus Falls Convention and Visitors Bureau is located at 112 Washington Ave., Fergus Falls. For more information about the park and the arts festival, call (218) 446-0002 or go to visitfergusfalls.com.

One of the ethnic groups well represented in eastern Otter Tail County is the Finns, and a good place to explore their heritage is **Finn Creek Museum**, 55442 340th St., off MN 106 about six miles southeast of New York Mills (look for signs on MN 106). The museum consists of a complete farmstead that was built by Siffert and Wilhelmina Tapio in 1900.

The family's house—originally a one-room log building that was later expanded and covered with wood siding—is furnished much as it would have been at the turn of the twentieth century. A hand-pump supplies water in the kitchen, woodstoves heat each room, and straw mattresses cover the beds, including one on an adjacent porch that was slept in by a tuberculosis-afflicted daughter whose treatment called for lots of fresh air. Among the many smaller household items displayed is a sinister-looking collection of bloodletting equipment, including a razorlike instrument for making incisions and several hollowed-out animal horns that were sucked on to draw blood.

Outside there's a well with a large hand-hewn beam serving as a counter-balance to the bucket—an arrangement known in Finnish as a *vintti kaivo*. Other buildings include a blacksmith shop, two small barns full of historic farm implements, a summer kitchen, and two log saunas, one of which is roofed in birchbark and called a *savu*, or smoke, sauna. This building was heated by a chimneyless woodstove. Once the rocks surrounding the stove were hot, the building was aired out and used for its intended purposes—which included birthing babies.

An annual **Summer Folk Festival**, celebrating Finnish culture with traditional music, craft demonstrations, and food, is held at Finn Creek the fourth weekend in Aug. A slight fee is charged for this event; otherwise, the museum, which is open afternoons in summer, charges no admission. For more information call (218) 385-2233 or visit finncreek.org.

A small town in the middle of lake and farm country in northwestern Minnesota probably doesn't come to mind when you think of a hotbed of culture, but the **New York Mills Regional Cultural Center** (24 North Main Ave.) can

FEBRUARY

Polar Fest
Detroit Lakes, late Feb
(218) 234-2501
polarfestdl.com

MAY

Detroit Lakes Festival of Birds
Detroit Lakes, mid-May
(218) 847-9202
visitdetroitlakes.com

JUNE

Scandinavian Hjemkomst Festival
Moorhead, late June
(800) 235-7654

AUGUST

Ox Cart Days
Crookston, mid-Aug
(701) 215-1943
crookstonoxcartdays.com

change your mind. Located in this town of twelve hundred people, the center opened in 1992 with the goal of providing cultural and creative opportunities for those living in rural areas. The center offers programs that include gallery exhibits, a music series, literary and theater events, education programs, a sculpture park, and the *Great American Think-Off.*

The latter is called "America's premier amateur philosophy contest." Entrants write a 750-word essay about a new topic chosen each year, from which four finalists are chosen. The finalists meet in New York Mills to debate their essays, with the winner chosen by the audience attending the debate, and getting the title of "America's Greatest Thinker." For information on the cultural center and the Great American Think-Off, call (218) 385-3339 or visit kulcher.org.

Clay County

Not far over the Otter Tail County line on MN 32 is a tiny hamlet called Rollag, which consists primarily of three institutions. First is the *Rollag Store*, a wooden structure with peeling paint that is set back into the bushes next to an ancient kerosene pump. This quintessential general store provides its community with just about anything anyone could want that isn't found at Rollag's second institution: a large and thoroughly modern farm-implement dealership. Finally, just north of "downtown" on a dusty hilltop is a sprawling collection of mismatched buildings, unrecognizable pieces of heavy iron machinery, and a couple of steam railroad engines that seem, by the lay of the tracks, to go no place special.

On Labor Day weekend each year, this ghost town, known locally as Threshermen's Hill, comes roaring to life for the **Western Minnesota Steam Threshers Reunion**, an event that some claim is the largest gathering of steam-engine enthusiasts in the world (that's what they'll tell you at the Rollag Store, anyway). In truth, up to eighty thousand people converge on little Rollag for a celebration that includes just about every artifact ever made that ran on steam. There are steam threshers, of course, three steam-powered "Trains to Nowhere," merry-go-rounds that run on steam, steam-powered sawmills, and several monstrous steam engines with whirring flywheels up to seventeen feet in diameter. There are also more than a hundred antique tractors engaged in pulling matches, a pioneer farm, an antique flour mill, traditional craft demonstrations, shows of long-outdated fashions, threshermen's breakfasts, and a fiddlers' jamboree each evening. There is a modest fee for adults to participate in this gala festival; for children, it's free. Go to rollag.com for a complete listing of exhibits, schedules, and other information.

Driving from Rollag toward Moorhead, it is impossible to escape noticing how very flat the landscape becomes—a sign you've entered the valley of the Red River of the North. The river's floodplain has some of the most fertile agricultural land on Earth.

Despite the fact that almost anywhere you look in the Red River Valley you'll see row after row of crops running toward the horizon, not all the land around Moorhead is dedicated to farming. Here and there, patches of restored prairie have been maintained, partly in an effort to preserve environmental enclaves for the performance of one of the most unusual spectacles to be witnessed in Minnesota's animal kingdom.

The **Courtship of the Prairie Chicken** is a fascinating annual event in these parts that demands certain rigors of those who want to see it. Having made the necessary arrangements well beforehand, you must arise an hour or so before dawn and find your way to a "blind"—a cubelike canvas tent staked securely to the ground—somewhere in the middle of a field that seems as big as the endless prairie sky. Then you sit tight and wait. If all goes well (and it usually does if the blind is well placed), about a half hour before sunrise the chickens will begin stirring.

Probably before you can see anything at all, you'll hear a peculiar deep-throated whooping sound that hits three distinct notes. This is the "booming" that these birds are so well known for. When making this sound, the male chickens lift up special pinnae (feathers) on the backs of their necks into a vertical position while inflating the bright yellow air bags that the feathers normally hide; thus posed, in the dim light they could be mistaken for jowly rabbits. The booming, which is given off as the air bags deflate, is often followed by some frantic foot stomping, complete with appropriate sound effects and a sudden leap into the air, usually performed in tandem by two males against each other in a head-to-head duel.

These histrionics are accompanied by a wide range of other noises, resembling, among other things, tropical birdcalls, meows, the cooing of pigeons, an old woman's cackle, and an infant's forlorn crying. No one knows exactly what all this means, but the show you're watching has to do with each male defending his oval breeding territory against other males while trying to attract the amorous attention of any females in the vicinity.

Once they get started, the chickens usually occupy themselves in this way for two or three hours, providing plenty of opportunities for you to preserve it all on film if you like. Active season on the booming grounds begins in late Mar and runs through Apr. For more information contact Brian or Sonia Winter at (218) 498-2679.

Two historic sites in **Moorhead** offer visitors distinctly different views of the community's early history. The first is the **Bergquist Cabin**, Moorhead's oldest permanent dwelling, which is located in a wooded glade on the banks of the Red River of the North. A small log building with simple period furnishings, the cabin accurately conveys the humble beginnings of its remarkable builder.

John G. Bergquist decided to leave Smaland, Sweden, for the New World in 1868 after receiving a severe beating from his father for having been caught playing a forbidden musical instrument, an accordion, in the woods near his home. He traveled westward by rail to Brainerd and then set out alone on foot, first to a land office in Alexandria and then northwest along the Red River Trail to what was eventually to become Moorhead. He arrived in the Red River Valley in midwinter and took shelter in the only building within sight—an abandoned stagecoach stop, which he shared with a fellow traveler who spoke only English. John, whose sole tongue was Swedish, undertook all this at the tender age of eighteen.

The following summer, in 1870, he built his cabin and set up a modest farm. Within five years the town was beginning to take shape around him, and he eventually started a successful brick manufacturing business, using the clay he found in the riverbank near his home. Tours of the Bergquist Cabin, which is found on a dirt road near the west end of Eleventh Avenue, can be arranged by contacting the Clay County Historical Society at (218) 299-5511 or hcscconline.org.

The **Comstock House**, at 506 Eighth St. South, is a well-preserved example of the kind of society to which the likes of John Bergquist might have aspired. Solomon G. Comstock built this gracious eleven-room Queen Anne–style home—whose foundation was provided by the Bergquist brickworks—in

1883 after having established himself as one of the community's most prominent residents. During a sixty-year public career, Solomon served Moorhead as
the Clay County attorney, a state representative and senator, and a member of
the Fifty-seventh US Congress. His relationship with railroad baron James J. Hill
helped secure an extensive railroad system in the Red River Valley. And he was
pivotal in the establishment of a state normal school in Moorhead, which later
became Moorhead State College.

Owned and maintained by the Minnesota Historical Society, the Comstock
House still has most of the family's original furnishings, reflecting a well-to-
do lifestyle that nevertheless falls short of the opulence found in some grand
homes elsewhere in the state. The house is open to the public on weekends in
summer and by appointment at other times. A small admission fee is charged.
Call (218) 291-4211 for more information.

Not far from the Bergquist Cabin, in a wooded park on the banks of the
Red River, is a monument that stands quite literally in recognition of a dream
come true. With its high-peaked twin towers and white tentlike shape, it even
looks a little dreamy. But the **Heritage Hjemkomst Interpretive Center** is
real enough, as is the magnificent wooden vessel within it.

Hjemkomst (pronounced "yemkomst") means "homecoming" in Norwegian, and it was the vision of paying a dramatic tribute to the seafaring Vikings
of his homeland that inspired a local teacher, Robert Asp, to begin work in
1971 on a project that dominated the last years of his life. His plan was to build
an authentic Viking sailing ship, the *Hjemkomst*, and to sail it from Duluth to
Norway. It was nine years before Robert was able to stand at the ship's helm
on its maiden voyage in Duluth Harbor, and not long afterward he died of

Red River

Although most rivers flood at one time or another, few do it with the vengeance of
the **Red River**. In this land of incredibly fertile soil and agricultural bounty, two geographic features cause the meandering and mostly insignificant Red to change from
mild-mannered to malevolent.

First, because the river flows north, when the spring melt starts upstream (which in
this case is south), the lower reaches remain frozen, and the water has nowhere to
go but out of its banks. Second, the Red flows in a small channel through the cutting
board–flat lake bottom of Glacial Lake Agassiz, and when it floods, the water spreads
out over hundreds of square miles. In the devastating flood of 1997, the swollen river
reached a width of more than thirty miles. Someone once said that the Red is the
only river that runs amok while standing still.

leukemia. But several members of his family saw his dream through to fruition, landing the *Hjemkomst* in Bergen, Norway, on July 19, 1982.

The multimillion-dollar interpretive center built in the *Hjemkomst's* honor is an impressive site. Beneath the building's steeply pitched fiberglass roof, the ship is displayed fully rigged, along with many artifacts associated with its construction and sailing. The well-interpreted displays are complemented by a moving twenty-minute documentary, shown in an adjacent auditorium, on the construction and voyage of the *Hjemkomst*.

In addition to this exhibit is a large space for traveling exhibitions and a gallery for items from the Clay County Historical Museum's permanent collection. The Heritage Hjemkomst Interpretive Center is open daily year-round; a small fee is charged (for information on special exhibits, call 218-299-5511). It can be found at 202 First Ave. North.

A visit to the **Plains Art Museum** in nearby Fargo, North Dakota, quickly reveals the lie behind the common misconception that cultural life in rural Minnesota is as arid as the land is flat. Occupying a renovated turn-of-the-twentieth-century warehouse in downtown Fargo, the museum displays works by prominent contemporary artists who have been professionally or personally associated with the upper Midwest. The influence of the northern plains environment is evident in some paintings in the permanent collection, as are historical and cultural themes expressed by Dakota and Ojibway artists. A large gallery downstairs provides space for traveling exhibits. The Plains Art Museum (704 First Ave. North; 701-551-6100; plainsart.org) is open Tues through Sat year-round. Admission is free.

Becker County

Besides being a popular summer vacation spot, the Becker County seat of Detroit Lakes happens to be the annual site of the Midwest's largest country-and-western music festival. During the **WE Fest**, held the first weekend in Aug, the likes of Waylon Jennings and Willie Nelson get together with many of their famous buddies for three days of outdoor music and fun.

It all happens at the **Soo Pass Ranch**, three miles south of Detroit Lakes on US 59. Campgrounds at the ranch, including one just for families, provide space for five thousand campers. A rock 'n' roll Fourth of July celebration called **Celebrate America** is also held at the ranch each year. Tickets and camping reservations for the WE Fest and Celebrate America, which start at about $70 per person, can be ordered by calling (218) 847-1681 or by going to wefest.com.

A nearby alternative to the festivities at Soo Pass is a lovely forty-three-thousand-acre wilderness area eighteen miles northeast of Detroit Lakes that's teeming with wildlife. The rolling wooded terrain and numerous lakes and marshes of **Tamarac National Wildlife Refuge** are popular with anglers, hikers, birders, and those looking for a pleasant drive through a fine stretch of northern Minnesota landscape. The refuge headquarters, at the junction of County Hwys. 26 and 29 (35704 County Hwy. 26, Rochert), features a beautiful interpretive center with an excellent multimedia presentation on the history and wildlife of Tamarac. Wilderness-oriented films are shown on summer weekend afternoons; for titles and show times, call (218) 847-2641.

There's a self-guided auto tour of the refuge that starts and ends at the headquarters, too. The drive follows winding gravel roads past duck wetlands, stands of wild rice, and peat bogs that support clusters of tamarack—Minnesota's only "evergreen" that drops its needles each fall. You may even see trumpeter swans that claim the refuge as a summer home. In winter the swans will be gone, but the refuge's eight miles of cross-country ski trails offer their own special appeal.

Red Lake County

Red Lake County is not only the smallest county in Minnesota; it also happens to be one of the flattest. And despite its size, passing through on US 59 or some lesser road is a little like traversing the boundless waters of an ocean. There are few landmarks to gauge the passing of the miles besides an occasional stand of trees rising like an island above the distant horizon.

But when you've just about decided that this monotony will never quit, all of a sudden you stumble onto a pleasant surprise. The **Red Lake River** winds across the prairie like a beautiful wooded oasis—one that offers clear, cool flowing water and the kind of recreational opportunities you'd expect to find only in a more woodsy environment.

The twenty-mile stretch of river from St. Hilaire in Pennington County to Red Lake Falls, which flows through steep clay banks lined with hardwoods, is fine for easy canoeing and fishing, particularly for channel catfish. Then just above Red Lake Falls, the pace picks up. Three miles of nonstop rapids support Minnesota's largest commercially developed inner tube float trip industry.

The first outfitter to begin full-scale operations along the banks of the Red Lake, **Voyageur's View**, claims to have hosted the world's largest inner-tubing flotilla. Some 749 persons, clinging to one another's tubes on a sunny day in 1986, made newspaper headlines as far away as Korea. This feat, however, belies the fact that most of the time tubing on the Red Lake is relatively uncrowded. Also, due to a stiff deposit required on all beverage cans, the tubing experience has managed to preserve the quality of this fine natural resource. Voyageur's View also offers camping facilities. For more information call (218) 253-4329 or visit voyageursview.com.

Pennington County

If official recognition were given to the most populous creature found roaming the countryside during even the coldest or roughest of Minnesota winters, the snowmobile might well be the uncontested recipient. In many rural communities there are sometimes more "sleds" parked on the streets and in front of taverns than cars and trucks, and Minnesota's backcountry is crisscrossed with snowmobile trails.

For those intrigued by the legacy of the snow machine, the Pennington County seat of Thief River Falls, where *Artco Corporation* turns out the Arctic Cat snowmobile line, is likely to be an interesting summer destination, for it's during the snowless months that the following season's machines are being assembled. Visitors are welcome to stop in at the plant, located on MN 32 just south of town, for scheduled tours given every workday (call 218-681-8558 or visit arcticcat.com for times).

Hundreds of employees on the assembly line turn out an average of 130 snowmobiles per eight-hour shift. Nearby dozens of welders are at work in a row of cubicles that collectively emit more dazzling explosions of light than a fireworks show. In another room men and women are dressed in what appear to be inflated space suits to protect themselves from a cloud of dust generated as they take the rough edges off various fiberglass parts. Also, a couple of delightfully primitive-looking Arctic Cats that hearken back to the snowmobile's infancy in the early 1960s are on display in the lobby.

Marshall County

If you're staying the night in Thief River Falls and don't mind rising at the crack of dawn, a drive to the *Agassiz National Wildlife Refuge*—located on CR 7, twelve miles northeast of town—may well result in a chance to see one of Minnesota's grandest mammals: the moose. The extensive upland and wetland areas of the one-hundred-square-mile refuge are maintained to provide an optimal habitat for this largest member of the deer family, as well as for 280 bird species and 49 other mammals. Opportunities for observing these creatures are provided by a network of roads that wind along dikes through the extensive marshes; a booklet outlining a self-guided auto tour is available at the headquarters. There is also a one-hundred-foot observation tower that commands a magnificent view of the flat countryside in all directions. For more information call (218) 449-4115.

Thirty miles west of Agassiz, along the banks of the lazy Middle River, is one of Minnesota's most obscure state parks. **Old Mill State Park** provides an attractive setting in which to hike among the trees (a rare commodity in these parts), swim in a clear swimming hole, picnic, and camp. But perhaps its greatest attraction is the historic steam-powered gristmill that still works.

The simple, small wooden structure near the banks of the river next to a settler's log cabin is actually the last of nearly a half-dozen mills built near this site by the Larson family. The first of these was a water-powered mill constructed in 1886. This building was destroyed in a flood a couple of years later and replaced by a wind-powered mill. When that didn't prove very effective, the Larsons went back to water power, moving the mill a couple of times to new locations, and then finally they converted to steam about 1896.

The steam engine is fired up several times each summer on special occasions to demonstrate the milling process. The large machine, which looks a little like a railroad engine, is surprisingly quiet as it turns the 2,700-pound French burr stones, which were hauled to the site by oxcart. For more information about grinding demonstrations, call (218) 754-2200 or visit dnr.state.mn.us.

Too Wet, Too Dry

To the casual observer or traveler, the Red River Valley is a boring place to pass through and should be done as fast as possible on the way to some other place. And though this flat, lakeless area doesn't inspire comments about its beauty, it occupies one of the most remarkable places in North America, if not the world.

This incredibly flat valley was formed courtesy of Glacial Lake Agassiz, a lake that at one time or another covered more than two hundred thousand square miles. Formed by the last glacier that covered northwestern Minnesota, the lake covered parts of Minnesota, South Dakota, North Dakota, Saskatchewan, Manitoba, and Ontario. It extended more than seven hundred miles from its southern tip in western Minnesota to near Hudson Bay.

While eastern parts of the ancient lake bottom became impassable wetlands, the western section drained better, becoming fertile farmland. Today residents curse and praise the landscape left behind. They curse the region when the Red River floods because the extremely flat landscape causes the floodwaters to spread incredible distances. And they undoubtedly praise the area when farmers harvest bountiful crops of sugar beets. Because it was a lake bottom, the thick clay soil that formed from decayed vegetation is difficult to farm. Soil scientist Jim Richardson summed it up best when he said, "We believe there is about one day a year when it isn't too wet or too dry, so you better be out there working on that day."

Minnesota Woman

In 1931 a road repair crew found a skeleton along US 59 north of Pelican Rapids. Originally called Minnesota Man, researchers finally determined that he was a she, and changed the name to Minnesota Woman. Although not all experts agree on her age, no one disputes that her remains date back thousands of years.

Archaeologists estimated the age of the skeleton to be ten thousand years old, which makes it the oldest human remains ever found in North America. Experts surmise that Minnesota Woman was fifteen years old when she drowned in Glacial Lake Pelican, a massive body of water that adjoined the even larger Glacial Lake Agassiz. Two artifacts found with the skeleton—a dagger made of elk horn and a conch shell—led archaeologists to believe that she fell in the lake while gathering food.

Places to Stay in Red River Country

ALEXANDRIA

AmericInn
4520 Hwy. 29 South
(320) 421-8926
wyndhamhotels.com

Cedar Rose Inn
422 Seventh Ave. West
(651) 303-4466
cedarroseinn.com

Hampton Inn & Suites
2705 South Broadway St.
(320) 763-3360
hilton.com

Holiday Inn
5637 Hwy. 29 South
(320) 763-6577
ihg.com

Spirit Cove Lodge Bed and Breakfast
7458 Thirty-Ninth Ave. Southwest
Garfield
(320) 834-7250
spiritcovelodge.elementor.cloud

CROOKSTON

AmericInn
1821 University Ave.
(218) 864-6021
wyndhamhotels.com

Cobblestone Hotel & Suites
2304 Sahlstrom Dr.
(218) 470-1111
staycobblestone.com

DETROIT LAKES

AmericInn
777 Hwy. 10 East
(218) 325-1024
wyndhamhotels.com

Quality Inn and Suites
615 Hwy. 10 East
(218) 847-4483
choicehotels.com

Best Western Premier Lodge on Lake Detroit
1200 East Shore Dr.
(218) 847-8439
thelodgeonlakedetroit.com

Holiday Inn on the Lake
1155 Hwy. 10 East
(218) 847-2121
ihg.com

FERGUS FALLS

AmericInn
526 Western Ave. North
(218) 739-3900
wyndhamhotels.com

Comfort Inn
425 Western Ave.
(218) 736-5787
choicehotels.com

Country Inn and Suites
925 Western Ave.
(218) 531-9992
choicehotels.com

GLENWOOD

Grandstay Hotel & Suites
114 West Minnesota Ave.
(320) 334-3700
grandstayhospitality.com

MOORHEAD/FARGO, ND

AmericInn
1423 Thirty-Fifth St.
Southwest
Fargo, ND
(701) 237-1634
wyndhamhotels.com

Bison Plains Lodge
3621 Eighth St. South
(218) 233-8880
bisonplainslodge.com

Courtyard by Marriott
1080 Twenty-Eighth Ave.
South
(218) 284-1000
marriott.com

Hilton Garden Inn
4351 Seventeenth Ave.
South
Fargo, ND
(701) 499-6000
hilton.com

Homewood Suites
2021 Sixteenth St. North
Fargo, ND
(701) 235-3150
hilton.com

Wingate by Wyndham
4429 Nineteenth Ave.
South
Fargo, ND
(701) 281-9133
wyndhamhotels.com

THIEF RIVER FALLS

AmericInn
1920 Hwy. 59 Southeast
(218) 681-4411
wyndhamhotels.com

Grandstay Hotel & Suites
1031 Wendt Dr.
(218) 681-9988
grandstayhospitality.com

Quality Inn
1060 Hwy. 32 South
(218) 681-7555
choicehotels.com

Places to Eat in Red River Country

ALEXANDRIA

Angelina's Restaurant
(American)
1215 Hwy. 29 North
(320) 762-1324
angelinasmn.com

Casa Jalisco
(Mexican)
523 Broadway St.
(320) 219-6055

Coffee Pot
(breakfast, lunch)
1518 Broadway
(320) 762-0855

Dunn Brothers
(coffee)
405 Fiftieth Ave. West
(320) 759-2287
dunnbrothers.com

**Great Hunan
Chinese Restaurant**
2919 Hwy. 29 South
(320) 763-6288
greathunanonline.com

La Ferme
(American)
613 Broadway St.
(320) 846-0777
lafermemn.com

Pike and Pint Grill
(American)
110 Thirtieth Ave. West
(320) 763-7468
pikeandpint.com

Pizza Ranch
1522 Broadway St.
(320) 763-4010
pizzaranch.com

Traveler's Inn Café
(American, Italian)
511 Broadway
(320) 763-4000
travelersinncafe.com

CROOKSTON

China Moon Restaurant
114 South Broadway
(218) 281-3136
thechinamoon.com

Caribou Coffee
1310 University Ave.
(218) 281-3174
cariboucoffee.com

**Happy Joe's Pizza
& Ice Cream Parlor**
705 East Robert St.
(218) 281-5141
online.happyjoes.com

IC Muggs
1500 University Ave.
(218) 281-7643
icmuggs.com

DETROIT LAKES

Brygge Taps and Tastes
(American)
111 Veteran Memorial
Pkwy.
(218) 844-5932
bryggetapsandtastes.com

Chinese Dragon
Washington Square Mall
(218) 847-2177

El Loro
(Mexican)
720 West Lake Dr.
(218) 844-5333
elloromn.com

La Barista
(coffee)
Washington Square Mall
(218) 847-8870
labaristadl.com

Main Street Restaurant
(American)
900 Washington Ave.
(218) 847-3344

Zorbaz at the Beach
(Mexican)
402 West Lake Dr.
(218) 847-5305
zorbaz.com

FERGUS FALLS

**Higher Grounds Café
and Coffee**
401 South Cascade St.
(218) 998-3102
highergrounds-coffeeshop
.business.site

Fiesta Brava
(Mexican)
218 West Cavour Ave.
(218) 531-1315

Mabel Murphy's
(American)
Hwy. 210 West
(218) 739-4406
mabelmurphysmn.com

**Union Avenue Bar
and Eatery**
114 South Union Ave.
(218) 998-8888

Viking Cafe
(American)
203 West Lincoln Ave.
(218) 736-6660

GLENWOOD

China Panda
8 East Minnesota Ave.
(320) 634-0688
chinapandaglenwood.com

**Minnewaska House
Brewing Company
and Grill**
(American)
24895 Hwy. 28
(320) 634-4566
minnewaskahouse.com

**Lakeside Steak
& Chop House**
180 Lakeshore Dr. North
(320) 634-0307
glenwoodlakeside.com

Pizza Ranch
14 East Minnesota Ave.
(320) 634-4261
pizzaranch.com

SELECTED WEBSITES IN RED RIVER COUNTRY

**Alexandria Lakes Area
Chamber of Commerce**
(320) 763-3161
alexandriamn.org

Crookston Chamber of Commerce
(218) 281-4320

Detroit Lakes Tourism Bureau
(218) 847-9202
visitdetroitlakes.com

**Fargo-Moorhead Convention
& Visitors Bureau**
(800) 235-7654
fargomoorhead.org

Fergus Falls Chamber of Commerce
(218) 446-0002
visitfergusfalls.com

**Glenwood Area Chamber
of Commerce**
(320) 334-3095
glenwoodlakesarea.org

**Thief River Falls Convention
and Visitors Bureau**
(218) 686-9785
visittrf.com

MOORHEAD/FARGO, ND

Acapulco
(Mexican)
1150 Thirty-Sixth St. South
Fargo, ND
(701) 297-0355
acapulcomexicanfargo.com

Giant Panda
(Chinese)
1331 Gateway Dr.
Fargo, ND
(701) 298-8558
giantpandafargo.com

Luna Fargo
(coffee, sandwiches)
1545 University Dr. South
Fargo, ND
(701) 293-8818
lunafargo.com

Passage to India
855 Forty-Fifth St.
Southwest
Fargo, ND
(701) 281-0277
passagetoindiafargo.com

Randy's University Diner
(American)
2130 University Dr. South
Fargo, ND
(701) 280-0414
randysuniversitydinerfargo
.com

**Rustica Eatery
and Tavern**
(American)
315 Main Ave.
(218) 227-5388
dinerustica.com

Blackbird Woodfire Pizza
206 Broadway Dr. North
Fargo, ND
(701) 478-1968
blackbirdwoodfire.com

*Note: The Fargo-
Moorhead area publishes
a Gourmet Guide that lists
all restaurants in the two
cities. Call the Convention
& Visitors Bureau at (800)
235-7654 or check their
website at fargomoorhead
.org.*

THIEF RIVER FALLS

Schooner Bar and Grill
212 Second St. East
(218) 681-4500

The Rusty Nail
307 North Main Ave.
(218) 681-6245

The Hive Bar & Grill
1582 Hwy. 59
(218) 683-5389
thehivetrf.com

Johnnie's Café
304 Main Ave. North
(218) 681-0436

**Las Ranitas
Mexican Restaurant**
1845 Hwy. 59
(218) 681-0644
lasranitasmexican
restaurant.com

Headwaters

In this region of north-central Minnesota, the Mississippi River begins its 2,350-mile journey to the Gulf of Mexico. From a humble start in Lake Itasca, the Mississippi grows to become North America's largest and longest river, draining all or part of thirty-one states and two Canadian provinces. In addition to the mighty river, the Headwaters region contains a good portion of Minnesota's ten thousand lakes.

The landscape ranges from fields of corn and soybeans in the southern part of this region to thick pine and deciduous forests dotted with lakes, rivers, and wetlands in the north. It's a land of amazing quantities of water. Rivers rise out of the massive network of bogs that covers a large part of northern Minnesota and gradually make their way out of state. It's an impressive landscape, subtler than the mountains and canyons of the West, yet spectacular in a quiet way because of the volume of water.

Sherburne County

From any major highway through this county southeast of St. Cloud, the area doesn't look like anything special. It's mostly

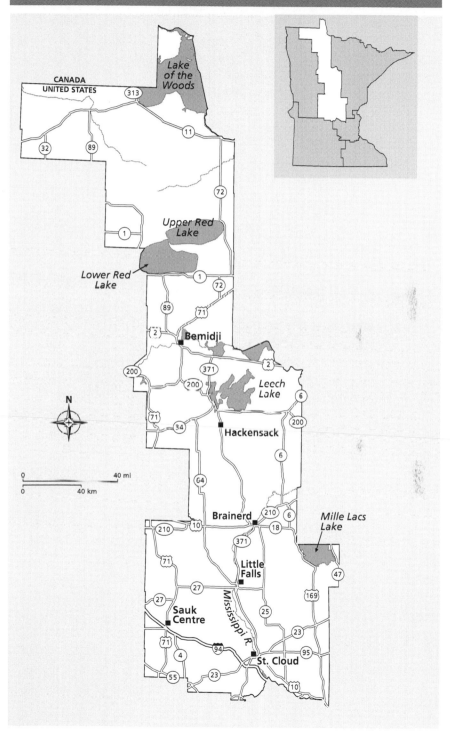

flat to slightly rolling, with a patchwork of farm fields, small sections of forest, and towns that have grown as more urbanites move from the Twin Cities. Most people don't realize that this county in central Minnesota sits in a unique geologic area called the Anoka Sandplain. As the last glaciers melted, outwash from the massive glacial rivers deposited fine material that eventually formed the largest area of sand dunes in Minnesota. Although it's not the best farmland, irrigation has helped it become reasonably productive.

When Minnesota was organized into a territory in 1849, most of the six thousand settlers who lived within it practiced a kind of subsistence farming. Following an agricultural tradition nearly as old as civilization, they grew a variety of crops to feed themselves, and whatever surplus there was supported a few nonfarming villagers.

Upon this scene came a young, educated son of a Boston tailor named Oliver Hudson Kelley, who staked a claim—the **Oliver Kelley Farm**—along the banks of the Mississippi River (three miles southeast of Elk River along US 10). What he lacked in experience as a farmer Kelley made up for by reading everything he could find about the new technology and crops just becoming available. He was a natural organizer and began to propagate information on "modern" farming through numerous newspaper articles and letters. His organizational efforts culminated in the founding of the Order of the Patrons of Husbandry—or, more commonly, the Grange—a national fraternal organization of farmers whose purpose was to advance the practice of agriculture and to promote the interests of farmers.

A visit to the Kelley Farm, which is now managed by the Minnesota Historical Society, is a step back in time to this turbulent period in American agriculture when subsistence farming began to give way to the raising of large single crops for shipment to fast-growing urban centers. Kelley's organization had a spectacular, if brief, popularity. The intentions of the Grange struck a chord with farmers across the land—more than a million of them quickly became members—but when their most pressing economic concerns weren't effectively addressed, membership dropped off sharply.

Exhibits and multimedia presentations at a modern interpretive center chronicle this populist agriculture movement, while costumed interpretive staff at Kelley's historic farm and farmhouse bring to life the farming practices of the time. Visitors can help feed animals and sample foods prepared on the cookstove in the kitchen. Outside, men wearing wool pants even on the hottest summer days demonstrate horse-powered plowing, planting, and harvesting. Special events, such as a Victorian wedding day and period games at the annual **Independence Day celebration**, make for great educational family fun. For more information call (763) 441-6896.

Stearns County

For a city with such an ethereal name, it's ironic that the Stearns County seat of **St. Cloud** has such a down-to-earth nickname: The Granite City. But make no mistake, this growing urban center of sixty-six thousand has its feet firmly on the ground, where the quarrying and processing of the area's distinctive red, pink, and gray granite have been a primary economic activity since the late nineteenth century and has continued into the twenty-first century.

The story of St. Cloud's contribution to the granite industry is told through several creative displays at the ***Stearns History Museum***, one of the best county history museums in the state. Inside the spacious, modern building is a convincing two-story replica of a 1930s quarry site that illustrates how the rock was drilled and blasted free in huge chunks weighing many tons. There are also exhibits on the area's natural history, early farming, immigration, and settlement, as well as revolving displays on other aspects of local culture. Thorough research in the museum's extensive archives combines with professional design and display techniques to result in the outstanding quality of the center's exhibits. There is also a nature center, with trails for skiing and hiking that shares the 106-acre wooded grounds with the museum. For more information on programs and hours (the museum is open most days of the week, year-round, and charges a small fee), call (320) 253-8424 or visit stearnshistorymuseum.org.

One of the most devastating natural disasters that confronted the early settlers of the Minnesota prairie was the periodic invasion of huge clouds of crop-destroying locusts. In response to a second consecutive year of this "grasshopper plague," in 1877 German Catholic farmers near the town of Cold Spring sought respite from their troubles by pledging to construct a chapel in honor of

AUTHOR'S FAVORITES

Brainerd Lakes Area
(218) 829-2838
brainerdlakeschamber.com

Heartland Bicycle Trail
Park Rapids
(218) 732-4111
parkrapids.com
Walker
(218) 547-1313
leech-lake.com

Itasca State Park
Lake Itasca
(218) 699-7251

Leech Lake
Walker
(218) 547-1313
leech-lake.com

Paul Bunyan Bicycle Trail
Brainerd
(218) 829-2838
paulbunyantrail.com

the Assumption of the Blessed Virgin. They made the vow and, as history has it, the grasshoppers disappeared the next day.

The wood-frame, Gothic Revival–style Locust Chapel built that very year survived until 1894, when it was destroyed by another violent prairie phenomenon: a tornado. In 1951 the Assumption Chapel—or, as it's commonly known, the **Grasshopper Chapel**—was reconstructed on the original site at the top of a lovely secluded knoll surrounded by oaks on Pilgrimage Road, just south of MN 23 in Cold Spring, about twenty miles southwest of St. Cloud. The new chapel is built of locally quarried granite left rough on the buttressed exterior and polished to a glistening sheen inside, where a statue of the Virgin and Christ child is the only remaining article from the original building. Over the entrance is a plaque depicting the Virgin Mary ascending into heaven on a cloud, with two grasshoppers below. The chapel is open for visitation spring through fall.

There is another sacred site in the St. Cloud area that is as grand and imposing as the Grasshopper Chapel is intimate and secluded. The famous bell banner above the entrance of **St. John's Abbey and University Church** can be seen for miles protruding above the wooded slope upon which the church stands. This architectural marvel has attracted such acclaim that, for the first ten years following its completion in 1961, it received more visitors than the state capitol did.

Among proposals from fifteen of the world's greatest architects, including Frank Lloyd Wright, the monks of the Benedictine Abbey selected a design for their church by Marcel Breuer, an Orthodox Jew. Breuer's concept of an unadorned, pillar-free sanctuary with walls of exposed poured concrete reflects the simplicity with which the monks carry on their lives. The prominence of the altar, near the center of the sanctuary beneath a cloudlike canopy, is a natural focal point. Illumination comes primarily from the north wall, where, behind a fantastic cantilevered, self-supported balcony, the largest stained-glass window in the world radiates magnificently. This abstract honeycombed design was created by a member of the St. John's University art faculty, Bronislaw Bak. His intent was to represent the seasons of the liturgical year—Advent, Christmas, Lent, Easter, and the Ordinary Time—through different vertical bands of color and subtly varied patterns of glass. Unifying this panorama is a series of roughly concentric circles, representing God, which draws the eye to the top and center of the window.

Outside, the bell banner stands as a monumental piece of modern poured-cement sculpture, 112 feet above ground and 100 feet across at the top, that is supported by four gracefully sweeping legs. High up in the center of this twenty-five-hundred-ton creation are a large white oak cross and five bells that ring on the quarter-hour.

River Pigs and Long Drives

While immigrant settlers plowed the rich soil of the prairie to form the farms that now cover most of the state, a different natural resource drew people to this area. Much of the Headwaters region lies in a part of Minnesota blanketed by thick forest. Huge old-growth white pines covered much of this area and lured the lumberjacks and future lumber barons who thought they had found an inexhaustible supply of trees.

From around 1855 until the last major log drive down the Mississippi in 1919, loggers hauled incredible amounts of timber from the forests. As in much of Minnesota, water also played an important role in the lumber industry. Teams of horses would drag out huge loads of logs on frozen roads, workers would pile them along riverbanks, and once the ice melted, huge log drives to sawmills downriver would begin.

Working a river drive was a dangerous job, and the crews even had to bear the indignity of being tagged with the less than complimentary title of "river pig." Hopping from rolling log to rolling log, the river crews occupied one of three positions. The driving crew worked at the front of the huge log rafts to keep the logs moving and out of side channels. The jam crew had the most dangerous duty, and the others considered them the elite of the three crews as they worked to prevent and remove jams. Finally, the rear crew brought up the back and gathered stray logs caught on snags or in backwater swamps.

Eventually the virgin timber ran out and the logging industry modernized, which changed the products and methods of this major Minnesota business.

You're welcome to drop in and visit the church anytime and to worship with the monks if you so desire. Inside the front entrance by the beautiful granite baptismal font, you can pick up a brochure for a self-guided tour. After touring the church, you may also walk the pathways of the surrounding twenty-four-hundred-acre wooded grounds, which have been designated as a wildlife sanctuary. Finding St. John's church is easy: Just take the Collegeville exit off I-94 and look for the bell banner to the south.

Sauk Centre has had a love-hate relationship with its most famous citizen ever since 1920, when Sinclair Lewis put the town on the world map with the publication of his American masterpiece, *Main Street*. The first reaction to the book's less-than-flattering portrayal of life in "Gopher Prairie" was outrage—apparently many citizens thought they could see themselves in Lewis's scathing critique of small-town middle-class life. But *Main Street* and its author, who in 1930 received America's first Nobel Prize in literature, gave Sauk Centre a certain notoriety, the value of which has not escaped the notice of at least some in this otherwise undistinguished dairy town of forty-six hundred. Today signs on I-94 point the way to the Sinclair Lewis Interpretive Center, and what was once the intersection of Third Avenue and Main Street—a crossing governed by Sauk Centre's only stoplight—is now the junction of The Original Main Street and Sinclair Lewis Avenue. Even the athletes at Sauk Centre Senior High, who compete as the Mainstreeters, honor the town's literary heritage.

Three sites in Sauk Centre relate to the life and work of its best-known native son. At a rest area near the freeway you can find the **Sinclair Lewis Interpretive Center**, which also serves as a local history museum and the chamber of commerce. The small exhibit area features samples of Lewis's writing in various stages of the publishing process, as well as first editions of his published works and historic photographs of the town and its founders. There is also a short videotape on Lewis's life.

Sauk Centre's celebrated main intersection is dominated by the **Palmer House Hotel** (500 Sinclair Lewis Ave.), which has been restored to surpass its former state of modest elegance with the addition of private baths in each of the twenty-two rooms, including several Jacuzzi-equipped suites. The appeal of the place is enhanced by the fact that Sinclair Lewis worked here as a night clerk while he was in high school, though the malcontent lad was fired for daydreaming and reading on the job. Nonetheless, the hotel found its way into literary history as the "Minniemashie House" in *Main Street* and as the "American House" in *Work of Art*.

Local legend has it that when it was built in 1901, the Palmer House was the first Minnesota hotel outside the Twin Cities to offer its guests hot and cold running water and electricity in every room. The traveling salesmen who frequented the hotel during its early years were reportedly so impressed with these novelties that they wore out the light switches in six months by playing with them so incessantly. The tin ceiling and chairs in the lobby, the furniture in many of the guest rooms, the wainscoting, and the stained glass in the arched first-floor windows fared better and have survived to the present day. The Palmer House charges modest to expensive rates. For reservations call (320) 351-9100 or visit thepalmerhousehotel.com.

A pilgrimage to Sauk Centre would be incomplete without a visit to the **Sinclair Lewis Boyhood Home**, located three blocks west of the Palmer House on Sinclair Lewis Avenue. This simple Eastlake cottage has been restored and appointed with period furnishings, earning a spot on the National Register of Historic Places. Some of the household items on display actually belonged to the Lewis family, including a junior-size bed that was occupied by Sinclair, who was often sick during his youth. The house is open for tours daily Memorial Day through Labor Day and by arrangement the rest of the year; call the Sinclair Lewis Foundation at (320) 429-5216 or visit sinclairlewisfoundation.org.

Morrison County

In central Minnesota the Mississippi River pauses. The Ojibway called this spot *KaKaBikans,* the "little squarely cut-off rock," which was a place where the river dropped over an outcrop of granite to form a waterfall. The Ojibway, Sioux, and Winnebago at times fought near the falls, and many fur traders, missionaries, and explorers wrote of it in their journals. Today Little Falls, the boyhood home of Charles A. Lindbergh, sits at this special place along the great river.

In one of Lindbergh's fond memories from his boyhood summers on a farm near Little Falls, he talks about lying on his back in tall grass, gazing for hours up at the sky. Oblivious to everything happening around him on Earth, he marvels at the passing cumulus clouds, imagining what it would be like to soar among them, birdlike, in an airplane. His early dreaming about flight was nourished in a family whose members had for generations excelled at everything they undertook. Lindbergh's father was a successful lawyer and congressional representative, and his grandfather had been a prominent member of the Swedish Parliament before immigrating to the Minnesota frontier in 1860. Lindbergh, following his own path to greatness, at age twenty-five climbed aboard the single-engine *Spirit of St. Louis* on an overcast day in May 1927 and in thirty-three and a half hours completed the first nonstop solo flight from New York to Paris. To his own surprise, Lindy became an international hero overnight.

Still, as you'll learn for yourself upon visiting the **Charles A. Lindbergh Historic Site**, the crossing of the Atlantic was only one of many accomplishments in the lifetime of this remarkable person. Exhibits at the modern interpretive center, which is also situated on the wooded banks of the Mississippi River, embrace the full range of Lindbergh's various achievements and interests. Parts of his first airplane, a World War I–vintage Jenny, are on display, as is a device Lindbergh helped design that is used to keep animal organs alive outside the body for the purposes of medical research. Lindy's political activities—initially he was a vocal opponent to the US entering World War II, just as his father had argued against America's involvement in the Great War—and his later concern with ecology are also well documented. The center houses a library of films on Lindbergh, his family, and the history of human flight and offers an attractive theater for viewing them. Admission is charged to the center, located on MN 238 just south of town. It is open daily from May through Labor Day and on weekends the rest of the year. Tours of the nearby **Lindbergh Boyhood Home** are also offered. For more information call (320) 616-5421 or visit mnhs.org.

You'll find the entrance to **Charles A. Lindbergh State Park**, named for the aviation hero's father, immediately across the street from the history center. Charles Jr., before he died in 1974, praised the establishment of this park as

Little Elk Heritage Preserve

When I first glanced at the brochure for the **Little Elk Heritage Preserve**, I dismissed it as either a petting zoo filled with semi-tame animals in pens or a large farm field with elk sauntering around. Closer inspection revealed this site near Little Falls to be the largest privately owned archaeological preserve of its kind in the Midwest. Stretching along one mile of undeveloped Mississippi River frontage, the Little Elk Heritage Preserve contains archaeological sites dating from at least 3,000 BC.

Visitors to this fascinating place—situated in an area where the prairie-forest transition zone meets the Mississippi River Valley—can take a self-guided hike through the preserve. Stops at seventeen points provide many details on important events and milestones of this patch of land. For more information contact the Institute for Minnesota Archaeology at fromsitetostory.org.

symbolic of civilization's greatest advancement: the valuing of life itself over the achievements of science and technology, such as the satellites now visible in the nighttime sky overhead.

Not far upstream from the Lindbergh home is an excellent museum dedicated to the Minnesota military experience. Located on the historic grounds of fifty-three-thousand-acre **Camp Ripley**—the largest National Guard training site in the country—the **Minnesota Military Museum** features professionally developed exhibits, including a series of displays illustrating the role Minnesota soldiers have played in every war since statehood in 1858. Another display area concerns Minnesota frontier forts, of which the original Old Fort Ripley was one. Elsewhere in the building is an exhibit on the development of small arms and a collection of war souvenirs brought home by Minnesotans from overseas. Among the latter are a handkerchief and napkin monogrammed AH—authenticated, says the label, as having once belonged to Adolf Hitler. The museum, located seven miles north of Little Falls on MN 115, is open free of charge Wed through Sun from Memorial Day through Labor Day. Call (320) 616-6050 or go to mnmilitarymuseum.org for more information.

Crow Wing County

If any area of Minnesota defines lake country, this north-central county does. As the home of many extremely popular lakes and countless resorts of all sizes, this region ranks as a favorite vacation spot for several generations of Minnesotans. The Crow Wing River enters the Mississippi barely after crossing the county line and splits into two parts. An island sits between the channels, and

American Indians thought it resembled the wing of a raven. Eventually their name for the river, Raven's Wing, through multiple translations became Crow Wing, which also became the name of the county.

Besides the Mississippi River, Crow Wing County is also home to the Brainerd lakes, a collection of lakes ranging from large to small and from crowded to quiet. The past decade or so has seen the area transformed from one of small family-owned, nothing-fancy resorts and cabins into one of expensive resorts with highly rated golf courses and lake homes the size and price of upper-end suburban houses.

Although the **Brainerd Lakes Area** is popular, it's still possible to get away from the crowds. Taking a bike ride on the **Paul Bunyan Bicycle Trail** is one of the best ways to find peace and quiet in this increasingly busy area. The trail currently runs 120 miles from Brainerd to the town of Bemidji and is paved for almost the entire distance. It passes twenty-one lakes, goes through sixteen small towns, and weaves through countless acres of forest and wetlands. Plans call for this recreational trail eventually to be paved all the way to Walker, where it will hook up with the Heartland Trail. For more information on this gorgeous trail, check out the website at paulbunyantrail.com.

The Cuyuna Iron Range is sometimes called Minnesota's forgotten iron range. Smaller than the larger ranges to the north, late to be discovered and early to be abandoned, the Cuyuna for seventy years was nevertheless a significant producer of iron ore and, during World War II, manganese. To commemorate the history of mining on the Cuyuna, two sites in Crosby are open to the public, both of them found by following signs along MN 6 in the heart of town.

At the **Cuyuna Range Historical Museum**, housed in Crosby's Soo Line Depot Museum, a collection of mining artifacts and photographs is augmented by other local history displays. The museum has photographs and memorabilia related to Cuyler Adams, who discovered iron on the range and named the area by combining his own name with that of his dog, Una. Also of interest are newspaper accounts and photographs of the famous 1924 Crosby mine disaster, in which forty-one miners died when their underground mine suddenly became inundated with water through an underground passage from a nearby lake. The museum is open Mon through Sat in summer. For more information call (218) 545-1166 or go to cuyunahistory.org.

If visiting museums and parks leaves you wanting some physical activity, you'll want to stop at the **Cuyuna State Recreation Area** just outside of town. This rugged area of former open-pit iron ore mines covers five thousand acres and has several crystal clear lakes, eight miles of paved bicycle trails, and over fifty miles of some of the best mountain bike trails in the state. The mountain bike trails wind up and down the piles of mining debris and, unless you're

Brainerd Pitted Outwash Plain

In a state covered with thousands of lakes, the area around Brainerd in north-central Minnesota has become a favorite among many people. The lakes in this area are shallow, warm, and clear, with gentle and sandy shores. Although thousands of tourists visit this area every summer, few probably give a thought about how the lakes in this region were formed.

Geologists call this area the **Brainerd Pitted Outwash Plain**, a mouthful for sure, but a simple idea to understand. As the glaciers receded, ice blocks of various sizes fell off, made depressions in the landscape, got buried by sand and gravel, and eventually melted. These dents became lakes and marshes, and the hundreds of such pits in the soil surrounding Brainerd represent a unique find. The ice blocks varied in size and formed depressions ranging from a few feet to several miles across. Geologists also estimate that 80 to 85 percent of Minnesota's lakes formed in ice-block depressions, providing further evidence of the role glaciers had in shaping our landscape.

really ripping around, will take the better part of a day to explore. A master plan calls for at least twenty-five miles of additional trails for an eventual total of seventy-five, and a redesign and some rerouting to make the riding even better. You'll come away with red tires from the iron in the soil, and if you wear a white bike jersey, that may come away stained red. For more information go to dnr.state.mn.us or call (218) 772-3690.

If you're hungry after spending a day or part of one at the recreation area, you'll find two great refueling stops in Crosby and a couple in Ironton, which is the smaller of the two towns. In *Ironton*, *The Hudson* (208 Curtis St.; 218-772-0096; hudson218.com) is located a short bike ride from the main mountain bike trailhead, or if you're heading home after riding all day, the first restaurant you come to after driving out of the park. Owned by the Lundquist family, this casual restaurant serves a variety of breakfast sandwiches and other handhelds, as well as coffee, beer, and mixed drinks. The restaurant has a large garage door they open as much as possible, and plenty of bicycle parking. If you need some sugar to fuel your biking, hiking, or kayaking trip to Cuyuna, you may want to stop at *MacDaddy's Donut Garage* (221 Fourth St.; 218-772-0222) in Ironton. They have a large selection of fresh-baked pastries, but close at noon.

In *Crosby* you'll find two excellent places to stop that have been around awhile and are go-to places for many riders. *Mixed Company* (128 West Main St.; 218-545-1010; enjoymixedcompany.com) is a great little coffee, ice-cream, and sandwich shop in downtown. The espresso is excellent, and the sandwiches will fill you up for the drive home. *Red Raven Bike Café* (2 Third St.

Pequot Lakes Legends

As you drive into the small resort town of **Pequot Lakes** in Crow Wing County, you may notice that the town's water tower resembles a large fishing bobber. Local tradition says it belonged to **Paul Bunyan**, the mythical lumberjack whose footprints formed many of the lakes in this region. Legend claims that Paul lost the bobber during a fight with a forty-foot northern pike and that he flipped it and the fish seven miles from Whitefish Lake to downtown Pequot Lakes.

One story also says that Paul's longtime companion, Babe the Blue Ox, helped form the Mississippi. According to the tale, a huge tank wagon being towed by Babe sprang a leak. The rushing water formed Lakes Bemidji and Itasca, while the overflow trickled down to New Orleans to form the great river. It's only fitting that Minnesota legend revolves around fishing and water. Of course, now that Minnesotans have added golf to their list of summer obsessions, some residents of Pequot Lakes want to build a new water tower modeled after a golf ball.

Southwest; 218-833-2788; redraven.bike) is a combination coffee, sandwich, and bike shop that also has a selection of microbrews.

Cass County

If you're heading north through Brainerd and need a break from the sometimes heavy traffic, or if you're searching for something a bit more restful and refined than the sort of action found at Brainerd's International Raceway and the Paul Bunyan Amusement Center, you may want to stop by **Maddens Resort** on Gull Lake for a game of croquet. Now this is not exactly the kind of backyard

TOP ANNUAL EVENTS IN THE HEADWATERS

MARCH

Perch Jerk
Walker, late Mar
(218) 547-1313

JULY

Sinclair Lewis Days
Sauk Centre, mid-July
(320) 352-5201
saukcentrechamber.com

AUGUST

Taste of Dorset
Dorset, early Aug
(218) 732-4111
parkrapids.com

**Lindbergh Symposium
and Celebration**
Little Falls, mid-Aug
(320) 632-5155

"guerrilla croquet" you may have played as a kid. Many players on the close-cropped bent-grass courts at Maddens will be dressed all in white. The hefty wooden mallets they swing with strategic precision cost upward of $250. They may even be drinking champagne while engaging in convivial patter between shots. This is croquet in the grand tradition of the sport, and Maddens is one of two such places in the state where the public is welcome to join in the fun.

Guest lawn fees, including equipment rental, at Maddens are moderate, and free clinics are offered several times each week. Stop by in mid-June to see some of the nation's best players compete in the Maddens Invitational and Minnesota Championship tournaments. Maddens is located twelve miles northwest of Brainerd on CR 77. For further information call (218) 829-2811 or visit maddens.com.

The 6,100-acre **Deep Portage Conservation Reserve**, located about ten miles east of Hackensack on CR 46, is a beautiful natural haven offering recreational and educational activities for individuals, families, and groups. There are twenty-five miles of trails wandering over hilly, wooded terrain shaped by the action of two ice age glaciers. The trails are equally divided for use between skiers and snowmobilers in the winter and are available for hiking the rest of the year. Naturalists operating out of the attractive interpretive center offer weekday and weekend programs using the surrounding lakes and forests as a classroom.

Since 2009 Deep Portage has installed solar, wind, and biomass systems, which has saved them hundreds of thousands of dollars in energy costs and made the campus completely carbon neutral. Especially impressive is the biomass system, which uses several wood gasification units to burn sustainably harvested wood from the surrounding area. If you're planning on visiting Deep Portage, I highly recommend scheduling an informational tour of their renewable energy systems. It's impressive. For directions and information about special events, call (218) 682-2325 or visit deep-portage.org.

Hikers may also want to explore a section of the **North Country Trail**, which, when completed, will provide a continuous footpath from New Hampshire to North Dakota. A sixty-eight-mile stretch of the trail now runs east and west through **Chippewa National Forest** between Remer and Walker. It may be accessed from MN 371 about five miles north of Hackensack or from a Chippewa National Forest road near Longville. Contact the forest supervisor of the Chippewa National Forest at (218) 335-8600 for maps and further information.

Rough Fish are Fish Too

When the burbot received the new designation from rough fish to game fish, the whitefish and cisco also gained the new classification. A group of anglers has continued to advocate for more Minnesota native fish to get changed from the designation of rough fish to game fish. A "No Junk Fish" bill seeks to change the designation from rough to game fish for redhorse suckers, bigmouth buffalo, gar, bowfin, mooneye, and goldeneye. For years most anglers in Minnesota have thought of rough fish as nasty, almost dirty species that should be killed and discarded. Most didn't realize that these native fish contributed to the health of the ecosystem of lakes and rivers by being a food source for game fish or birds of prey, fertilizing streams where salmon and trout lay their eggs, and competing and even eating invasive species.

Besides the ecological benefits, rough fish have long been valued by indigenous tribes as food, and more nonnative anglers have come to appreciate them as fun to catch and as tasty as game fish. Advocates hope that rough fish will gain the protections that game fish now have and get more respect as more people become of aware of their value.

Hubbard County

Food lovers will find a special treat in this county in the heart of lake country. The town of **Dorset** boasts the most restaurants per capita in the US. Of course that's not too difficult with a population of twenty-two, but Dorset still has four restaurants in its short downtown. During their annual **Taste of Dorset festival** or any busy summer weekend, the town may seem anything but off the beaten path, but it still ranks as one of the most surprising finds in Minnesota.

After you've eaten your fill at the Taste of Dorset, you may want to work some of it off with a leisurely ride on the **Heartland Bicycle Trail**. This trail runs forty-nine miles from Park Rapids to Cass Lake, with the twenty-seven miles from Park Rapids to **Walker** paved. It goes through the scenic lake country of Hubbard and Cass Counties, cutting through miles of northern forest and several small towns before coming to Walker, which sits on the shore of Leech Lake, one of the largest lakes in Minnesota.

Leech Lake is a reservoir and attracts anglers in pursuit of walleye (the state fish) and the elusive and aggressive muskie. The lake is so huge that there are several places along the shore where you cannot see across it, not unusual for the Great Lakes but uncommon for an inland lake. The town of Walker has a city dock that gives it a coastal feel; people staying on the lake more often than not take their boat instead of their car to town.

Walleye Season

Mention walleye to any avid angler in Minnesota and they will likely regale you with passionate stories about pursuit of this tasty fish. When walleye season opens, more than one million residents drop most of what they're doing and go fishing.

Harvesting the walleye has caused conflicts in several parts of the state. At Mille Lacs Lake in central Minnesota, tense standoffs have developed between American Indians exercising their historic treaty rights to spear walleye and anglers and resort owners who oppose spearing. Talks by resource officials about closing part of the lake to sport fishing borders on sacrilege for anglers.

On Lake of the Woods, a huge lake that covers most of the northwest angle of Minnesota and ranks as the state's most productive walleye lake, conflicts have erupted between sport and commercial anglers, as both groups compete for this prized fish. In such a water-blessed (or obsessed) state, it comes as no surprise that vehement arguments develop over fish.

The headwaters of the Mississippi River are a destination of such international renown that the point could be made that they don't belong in a guidebook dedicated to undiscovered—or at least untrammeled—places. But **Itasca State Park**, in which the Father of Waters begins its epic journey south by flowing northward at a mere trickle, has within it a number of genuinely obscure attractions that most people discover only by stumbling upon them.

Perhaps more than any other of Minnesota's sixty-four state parks, Itasca, the oldest in the state, has the feeling of a national park. The massive hand-hewn log-and-stone construction of the Forest Inn Interpretive Center and the Douglas Lodge (Itasca is the only Minnesota state park to offer meals and accommodations) are reminiscent of Yosemite or Yellowstone. The scale of these buildings reflects the size of the trees to be found in the surrounding forests, too. In fact, Itasca boasts the largest white and red pines on record in the state.

Both of these trees are found at marked locations along Wilderness Drive, a one-way road that winds through the northwestern quarter of the park. Having survived the past three hundred years, including the onslaughts of loggers near the turn of the twentieth century, the giant white today looms 112 feet high, protruding above the surrounding forest canopy. Its trunk is massive—fifty-five inches in diameter—and its limbs somewhat diminished, suggesting that this tree has spent most of its energy growing up, not out. Nearby, the big red, or Norway, pine tops out at 120 feet above ground. The bark of its three-hundred-year-old trunk has a scaly, reptilelike appearance, and visible at its base are scars from six different fires. Far overhead, a tangle of branches twists out in all directions like a frozen burst from a fireworks display.

The short path leading to the big red pine also passes by one of the state's more interesting archaeological landmarks. A plaque along the banks of a small creek marks a **bison kill site** where eight thousand years ago a group of prehistoric hunters slaughtered sixteen giant bison en masse, perhaps by driving them off a now-nonexistent cliff.

For more information about lodging, meals, recreational opportunities, and the extensive naturalist programs offered at Itasca, call (218) 699-7251.

One tourist-oriented destination near Park Rapids provides visitors with insights into the era that saw the transformation of Minnesota's woodlands from magnificent pine climax forests into a mixed bag of second-growth species such as aspen, birch, spruce, and balsam fir. The **Rapid River Logging Camp**, located five miles north of town on CR 18, features several logging exhibits and an all-you-can-eat lumberjack cook shanty—the camp's main attraction—that provides three inexpensive meals daily, Memorial Day through Labor Day. For more information about the camp, call (218) 732-3444 or visit rapidriverloggingcamp.com.

Beltrami County

Around 1700, explorers started searching for the source of the Mississippi. Some of the explorers included Du Charleville, a relative of New Orleans founder Bienville; Zebulon Pike, for whom Pikes Peak is named; and Lewis Cass, governor of the Michigan Territory and namesake of both Cass Lake and Cass County. Perhaps the flashiest explorer to search for the source, Count Giacomo Beltrami, arrived at Fort Snelling in 1823.

His route took him up the Minnesota River and down the Red River of the North. He got as far as Pembina, North Dakota, before heading southeast on foot and canoe. He ultimately named Lake Julia near Bemidji as the source but didn't explore another lake a Chippewa guide had told him about. That lake, Lac la Biche, later became known as Lake Itasca, the source of the great river.

Though they're miles from the UN, one day each summer Bemidji's **Concordia Language Villages** explode in a polylingual, multicultural celebration of world unity that casts a shadow all the way to the UN Plaza in New York City. For one day in July or Aug, hundreds of young people participating in the nine Concordia Language Villages programs throughout Minnesota converge on **Bemidji** for an **international festival**.

Participants in the acclaimed Concordia College–sponsored program live in Russian, Finnish, Chinese, Norwegian, French, Swedish, Danish, German,

Red Lake Peatland

One of the most striking geologic features of the Headwaters region, and for that matter, of the US, is also one of the most difficult to see. Found in only a few places in the world, patterned peatlands cover a large chunk of northern Minnesota. The *Red Lake Peatland* covers about 450 square miles of Beltrami, Koochiching, Lake of the Woods, and Roseau Counties and ranks as one of the largest continuous mires in the lower forty-eight states.

This massive wetland occupies the eastern part of the Glacial Lake Agassiz plain, and travelers can see a good example of it in northern Beltrami County. Follow MN 72 north from Blackduck along the east side of Upper and Lower Red Lake. Go about ten miles north of unincorporated Waskish and you will see an obvious example of the peatland. Large open areas of low shrubs and coarse grasses give way to patches of tamarack, black spruce, and dwarf birch.

Although most people who drive the few roads that traverse these marshes think of them as boring swamp, observant travelers will appreciate nature's work. Peat up to ten feet thick covers much of this swamp, as water aimlessly and slowly moves through the thick vegetation, discouraging humans from entering, but making it a rich habitat for wildlife.

While not spectacular like mountains and deep canyons, patterned peatlands have a subtler way of displaying nature's power.

Japanese, or Spanish "villages," in which their American belongings have been surrendered upon arrival at "customs." Students exchange their familiar language, their currency, and even their own names for those derived from their new culture.

Guests of the festival (it is open to the public free of charge) can participate in this experience as the young people emerge from their adopted cultures to share ethnic foods, crafts, music, and gifts. Professional folk dancers and musicians add to the entertainment. Festival revelers also have an opportunity to see the traditional German and Norwegian architecture of the Concordia Language Villages sites. For more information call (800) 222-4750 or visit concordialanguagevillages.org.

As you're passing through downtown Bemidji, you're bound to catch sight of one of Minnesota's classic pieces of oversize civic roadside "art." ***Paul Bunyan and Babe the Blue Ox*** stand so stiffly at attention at the intersection of Third Street and Bemidji Avenue that your limbs ache just looking at them. This structure, built in 1937, is one of the most photographed statues in the US—or at least that's what they'll tell you at the chamber of commerce next door.

Northwest Angle

Look at a map of Minnesota and you'll see a small point sticking up from the top. Called the **Northwest Angle**, it doesn't seem to fit with the rest of the state. In the 1783 Treaty of Paris, the border between Canada and the US was traced along the old voyageurs route to the northwest corner of Lake of the Woods and then west to the Mississippi. There was only one problem. No one knew the exact source of the Mississippi.

After explorers found the source of the great river, the two countries modified the border. After the War of 1812, a boundary commission decided that the 49th parallel would be the new border from Lake of the Woods to the Pacific Ocean. This didn't intersect in the right place near the lake, so the plotters dropped a line straight south to close the gap. Thus the Northwest Angle, now separated from the rest of Minnesota, became the northernmost point of the lower forty-eight states.

Lake of the Woods County

As one of the most northern counties in Minnesota, this sparsely populated region borders Ontario and its namesake, Lake of the Woods. As part of the watery boundary between Canada and the US, much of this remote region remains as it was during the time of the voyageurs. It's a land of water dotted by land instead of land dotted by lakes.

When French explorer Pierre La Verendrye built **Fort St. Charles** in 1732 on an island in what is now called Lake of the Woods, it was the most northwesterly settlement of Europeans in North America. For ten years the fort was an important fur trading post for La Verendrye and his sons, who used it as a base of operations for their explorations of the Canadian Northwest. The fort also became the burial place of a French Jesuit priest, Father Jean Aulneau, and nineteen of his companions, who were killed on another island by a Dakota war party in 1736.

WAY, WAY OFF THE BEATEN PATH

Wood Tick Race
Cuyuna, middle of June, open to "family pets"
Wood ticks are one of the most unpleasant insects around, so having a race with them is really strange, or weird, or funny. It's definitely off the beaten path. They encourage novice entries; the champions never return.

Visitors can reach the fort by boat from Warroad or Baudette (about a fifty-mile ride) or by car from Warroad, sixty-three miles (the final twenty-three of which are gravel) through a section of Manitoba to Minnesota's Northwest Angle, where a number of resorts can provide easy boat access to the fort on Magnusson Island. A reconstructed palisade and log chapel stand today on the site of the original fort, and markers show where other buildings once stood. For more information on the fort, go to fortstcharles.com

Places to Stay in the Headwaters Region

BEMIDJI

AmericInn
1200 Paul Bunyan Dr. Northwest
(218) 751-3000
wyndhamhotels.com

Hampton Inn and Suites
1019 Paul Bunyan Dr. South
(218) 751-3600
hilton.com

Lake Bemidji Bed and Breakfast
915 Lake Blvd. Northeast
(218) 556-8815
lakebemidjibandb.com

BRAINERD AREA

Baymont Inn & Suites
7208 Fairview Rd.
Baxter
(218) 822-1133
wyndhamhotels.com

Comfort Suites/ Rapid River Lodge
7376 Woida Rd.
Baxter
(218) 825-7234
therapidriverlodge.com

Country Inn & Suites
15058 Dellwood Dr. North
Baxter
(218) 297-4816
choicehotels.com

Days Inn & Suites
14466 Dellwood Dr. North
Baxter
(218) 829-3080
wyndhamhotels.com

Grand View Lodge Bed and Breakfast
23521 Nokomis Ave.
Nisswa
(218) 963-2234
grandviewlodge.com

LITTLE FALLS

AmericInn
306 LeMieur St.
(320) 632-1964
wyndhamhotels.com

Country Inn & Suites
209 Northeast Sixteenth St.
(320) 632-1000
choicehotels

PARK RAPIDS

AmericInn Lodge & Suites
1501 First St. East
(218) 732-1234
wyndhamhotels.com

Heartland Inn and Suites
1009 First St. East
(218) 732-1471
bestwestern.com

Heartland Trail Bed & Breakfast
20220 Friar Rd.
(218) 732-3252
heartlandbb.com

Super 8 Motel
1020 First St. East
(218) 366-9071
wyndhamhotels.com

ST. CLOUD

Best Western Kelly Inn
100 Fourth Ave. South
(320) 253-0606
bestwestern.com

**The Estates Bed
and Breakfast**
29 East Minnesota St.
St. Joseph
(320) 557-0300
estatesbedandbreakfast
.com

Holiday Inn Express
4322 Clearwater Rd.
(320) 240-8000
lhg.com

**The Pillar Inn Bed
and Breakfast**
419 Main St.
Cold Spring
(320) 685-3828
thepillarinn.com

Quality Inn
4040 Second St. South
(320) 251-1500
choicehotels.com

WALKER

Horseshoe Bay Lodge
8098 Hawthorn Trail
Northwest
(218) 547-2283
horseshoebayresort.com

Chase on the Lake
502 Cleveland Blvd.
(218) 547-7777
chaseonthelake.com

Country Inn Walker
442 Walker Bay Blvd.
(218) 547-1400
walkercountryinn.com

**Leech Lake Bed
& Breakfast**
11058 Steamboat Loop
(218) 547-2231
leechlakeresort.com

**The Park Street Inn
Bed and Breakfast**
106 Park St.
Nevis
(218) 652-4500
parkstreetinn.com

Places to Eat in the
Headwaters Region

BEMIDJI

Brigid's Cross Irish Pub
(Irish/American)
317 Beltrami Ave.
Northwest
(218) 444-0567

**Keith's Pizza
& Restaurant**
(pizza, American)
110 Paul Bunyan Dr.
Southeast
(218) 444-7940
keithspizza.com

Minnesota Nice Café
(American)
315 Irvine Ave. Northwest
(218) 444-6656
minnesotanicecafe.com

Mi Rancho
(Mexican)
677 Anne St. Northwest
(218) 444-8212
miranchobemidji.co

Raphaels Bakery Cafe
(American)
319 Minnesota Ave.
(218) 444-2867
raphaelsbakery.com

**Tutto Bene
Italian Ristorante**
300 Beltrami Ave.
Northwest
(218) 751-1100
tuttobene.us

**Wild Hare Bistro
& Coffee Company**
523 Minnesota Ave.
Northwest
(218) 444-5282
wildharebistro.com

BRAINERD/NISSWA

The Barn
(American)
711 Washington St.
Brainerd
(218) 829-9297

El Tequila
(Mexican)
7399 Garrison Rd.
Baxter
(218) 454-0618

Ganley's Nisswa Inn
(American)
25396 Main Street
Nisswa
(218) 963-2993
ganleysrestaurant.com

Slice on Oak
(pizza)
625 Oak St.
Brainerd
(218) 454-0750
slice-on-oak.business.site

Sage on Laurel
606 Laurel St.
Brainerd
(218) 454-7243
sageonlaurel.com

Lost Lake Lodge
(American)
7965 Lost Lake Rd.
Nisswa
(218) 963-2681
lostlake.site

The Local 218
(American)
723 Mill St.
Brainerd
(218) 270-3195
local-218.com

**StoneHouse Coffee
and Roastery**
14540 Dellwood Dr.
Nisswa
(218) 961-2326
stonehousecoffee.com

**Coco Moon Café
and Coffee Shop**
601 Laurel St.
Brainerd
(218) 825-7955

DORSET

Compañeros
(Mexican)
20427 State Hwy. 226
(218) 732-7624
companerosmn.com

Dorset House
(American)
20427 State Hwy. 226
(218) 732-5556

La Pasta Italian Eatery
Dorset General Store
(218) 732-0275
dorset-general-store.
business.site

LITTLE FALLS

A.T. the Black & White
116 Southeast First St.
(320) 632-5374
attheblacknwhite.com

Charlie's Pizza
1006 Haven Rd.
(320) 632-6727
charlies-pizza-pizza
-restaurant.business.site

Great Wall
113 First St. Northeast
(320) 632-1095

Little Fiesta
(Mexican)
310 Twelfth St. Northeast
(320) 632-2445

**Little Falls Bakery
and Deli**
(coffee)
121 East Broadway
(320) 632-6388

Caffe Strolaga
(American)
500 Broadway East
(320) 414-0400

PARK RAPIDS

Bella Caffé
118 Third St. West
(218) 732-7625
bellacaffeon3rd.com

Espresso 34
1310 First St. East
(218) 237-8500
espresso34.com

SELECTED WEBSITES IN THE HEADWATERS

Bemidji Chamber of Commerce
(218) 444-6081
visitbemidji.com

**Brainerd Lakes Area Chamber
of Commerce**
(218) 829-2838
brainerdlakeschamber.com

**Leech Lake Area Chamber
of Commerce (Walker)**
(218) 547-1313
leech-lake.com

Little Falls Chamber of Commerce
(320) 632-5155
littlefallsmn.com

Park Rapids Chamber of Commerce
(218) 732-4111
parkrapids.com

**St. Cloud Convention
and Visitors Bureau**
(320) 251-4170
visitstcloud.com

Four Seas
(Asian)
322 Main Ave. South
(218) 237-8888
4seasparkrapids.com

The Good Life Café
220 Main Ave. South
(218) 237-4212
thegoodlifecafepr.com

Great Northern Cafe
(American)
218 First St. East
(218) 732-9565
greatnortherncafe.com

Necces Italiano Ristorante
311 Main Ave. South
(218) 237-4625

ST. CLOUD

Bravo Burritos
68 Thirty-Third Ave. South
(320) 252-5441
bravoburrito.com

Café Renaissance
2140 Frontage Rd. North
Waite Park
(320) 253-9300
thecaferenaissance.com

Korppi Coffee and Bakeshop
71 County Rd. 120
(320) 217-5252
korppicoffee.com

Bello Cucina
(Italian)
15 East Minnesota St.
St. Joseph
(320) 363-4534
bellocucina.com

House of Pizza
4040 Second Ave. South
(320) 252-9300
houseofpizzamn.com

Jules' Bistro
921 West St. Germain St.
(320) 252-7125
julesbistrostcloud.com

Kinder Coffee Lab
203 Cooper Ave. North
(320) 330-9807
kindercoffeelab.com

The Local Blend
(coffee)
19 West Minnesota St.
St. Joseph
(320) 363-1011
thelocalblend.net

Park Diner
(American)
1531 Division St.
Waite Park
(320) 252-0080
parkdinermn.com

WALKER

Benson's Emporium
(American)
400 Minnesota Ave.
(218) 547-1896
bensonsemporium.com

Dancing Fire Restaurant
(American)
6800 Y Frontage Rd.
(218) 335-3190
northernlightscasino.com

Jimmy's Restaurant
(American)
Hwy. 371 North
(218) 547-3334

Village Square Pizza and Ice Cream
411 Minnesota Ave. West
(218) 547-1456

Walker Bay Coffee Co.
509 Minnesota Ave. West
(218) 547-1183
walkerbaycoffee.com

Arrowhead

If any part of Minnesota occupies a special place in the hearts of many residents, this is it. The appropriately named Arrowhead region encompasses thousands of square miles of untouched forest and impenetrable bogs, thousands of lakes, and the big lake itself, Superior. Nowhere else in the state will a traveler see such spectacular scenery. And though you will see countless scenic vistas of forest and water throughout the region, the Lake Superior shoreline truly defines the Arrowhead: rugged, isolated, and inhabited by people of hardy stock.

Drive along the shore of *Lake Superior* (we natives call it the North Shore, no other description needed) and you'll see the vast body of icy freshwater bordered by thundering rivers toppling through narrow gorges, rocky outcrops that soar a thousand feet above the lake, and a vast forest of pine, birch, and maple. This region also has patches of the boreal forest, a special northern ecosystem that covers Canada up to the Arctic.

From I-35, the most direct route from the Twin Cities to Duluth, travelers will find a variety of roads from which to explore the Arrowhead. The best scenery in the region is along MN 61 as it hugs the shore of Lake Superior. MN 1 climbs north from MN 61 into the hills bordering the big lake and runs to

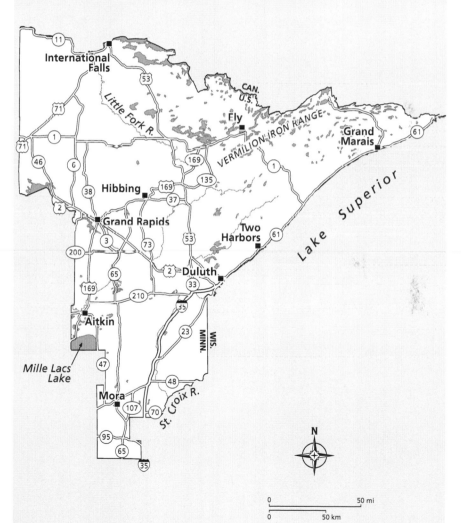

International
Falls

11

53

Little Fork R.

71

1

71

46

6

38

Hibbing

2

Grand Rapids

200

3

73

65

169

210

Aitkin

169

47

Mille Lacs
Lake

Mora

95

65

35

107

70

48

St. Croix R.

23

MINN.

WIS.

33

Duluth

2

53

Two
Harbors

61

Lake Superior

Fly

VERMILION IRON RANGE

CAN.
U.S.

169

135

1

Grand
Marais

61

37

N

0   50 mi

0   50 km

Ely through thousands of square miles of pine forest. Leaving Lake Superior behind, many other highways cut through the countless square miles of tamarack swamp, forest, and lakes.

Aitkin County

Aitkin, the largest town in the county, sits on the Mississippi River (at US 169 and MN 210) and owes its settlement in 1870 to a combination of the lumber industry, riverboats, and the railroad. It's also the site of the only diversion channel on the Mississippi. Although the town lacks a large tourist attraction, the residents have a sense of humor.

In 1991 Aitkin merchants, discouraged by the exodus of residents on shopping excursions to malls in bigger cities and tired of shoveling snow after a huge Thanksgiving Day storm, decided that a parade would draw people into town. And so began the ***Aitkin Fish House Parade***, held annually the Fri after Thanksgiving. Each year the parade grows as word spreads. Entrants show up with fish houses of all shapes and sizes to help celebrate the return of winter.

Besides the whimsical, Aitkin also has an important bird habitat at nearby ***Rice Lake National Wildlife Refuge*** and throughout the county. *Wildbird* magazine called this area the "best little unsung birding spot in America," and Aitkin County is becoming an important stop for serious bird-watchers. According to experts, the area has excellent bird-watching potential year-round. Harsh Canadian winters often force several species of owls south in search of food, and the low glacial hills of this region provide good habitat. Besides these winter visitors, many other species stop during their migration.

Although the Minnestalgia Winery and Gift Shop has closed, the family who ran it have formed a new business called ***Blaze Wild Rice***. They sell wild rice as long grain, soup grade, and flour, as well as berry jellies, jams,

AUTHOR'S FAVORITES

Cascade River State Park
west of Lutsen
(218) 387-600

Iron Range
(218) 749-8161
ironrange.org

Lake Superior

**Temperance River
State Park**
east of Schroeder
(218) 663-3100

Fun in Aitkin County

While most chamber of commerce and convention bureau representatives tend to be friendly, some take themselves much too seriously. You won't find that the case with the Aitkin Area Chamber of Commerce. Besides having a very friendly and helpful executive director, the chamber of commerce reflects the town's sense of humor in their area guide. The partial list that follows shows you what I mean:

Useful Facts for First-Time Visitors

Distance to Lake Wobegon: 1,200 miles and 16 toll booths

Electricity: Yes

Telephone: Yes

Highest Curb: Curb at Potter Bridge (Minnesota Avenue)

Cable TV: Yes

Parking meters: No

Most creative use of surveyor's transit: Minnesota Avenue

Indoor plumbing: Yes

Climate: Yes

Most famous landmark: Our stoplight (only one in Aitkin County)

Sense of humor: YoooBet!

and syrups, all made from either wild berries harvested in northern Minnesota or grown on small local berry farms. Wild rice is the only grain native to the US, and while some that is commercially sold still gets harvested the traditional way by canoe, much of it is now grown in paddies in northern Minnesota and machine harvested. This change in how it's grown has not diminished the nutritional benefits or taste of the grain. Blaze sells their products at a couple of local grocery stores in Aitkin and McGregor, and at The Roasting House, a great little restaurant/coffee shop located just north of McGregor at 47952 Hwy. 65, (218) 426-5466. Blaze Wild Rice can be reached at (218) 768-4917 or visit blazewildrice.com.

Kanabec County

This county received its name in 1858 after being part of three other Minnesota counties and one Wisconsin county. *Kanabec* (Kay-Nay-Bec) is the Ojibway word for "snake," which is also the name of the winding river that runs through

Dala Horses

In 1972 Mora erected a large *Dala Horse* to reflect its Swedish heritage and sister-city ties. Measuring twenty-two feet high and eighteen feet long, this landmark is a replica of the wooden Dala Horses carved by Swedish craftsmen.

The carving of Dala Horses began in the 1840s. Although two versions exist about who exactly started it, all seem to agree that the carvers chose the horse because they considered it the most valuable farm animal a family could own. The distinctive orange color and floral patterns painted on the Dala Horse came from the Dala paintings that decorated furniture and interior walls of Swedish homes. Carvers still do most of the work by hand, and because of this no two horses are exactly alike.

the county before emptying into the St. Croix. The unremarkable landscape in this part of Minnesota is a mostly flat mix of wetlands and varied forest. In fact, more than 80 percent of the original wetlands of Kanabec County remain untouched.

Mora, named after its sister city of Mora, Sweden, is the largest town in the county and home to several fun athletic events. Cross-country ski racers know it as the home of the Mora Vasaloppet, the second-largest ski race in the US and part of the three-race international Vasa series. This ski series has become more than a group of races. It has led to educational and cultural exchanges between the US and the other two countries that hold Vasa races, Sweden and Japan.

Besides the Vasaloppet, Mora also hosts a half marathon, a canoe race, and a bicycle tour for the athletically inclined. For those looking for less active endeavors, Kanabec and neighboring Isanti County host many other events, from the *Braham Pie Day* in Braham to the *Corn on the Curb* celebration in Ogilvie.

Mora is also home to the *Kanabec History Center* (805 West Forest). This local museum features rotating exhibits that tell the story of the Swedish settlers who arrived in the area with virtually nothing and began a new life. An authentic rural school also occupies the museum site. For more information, call (320) 679-1665 or visit kanabechistory.org.

People from other parts of the country often comment about our Minnesota (Meen-eh-sootah to us natives) accents, which apparently came from our Scandinavian ancestors. If you doubt the significance of Swedish heritage in this area, take a look at the festival brochure the county produces. It's printed in Swedish as well as in English.

Pine County

This north-central county defines the term "geographic transition zone." As you drive from south to north in Minnesota, you will notice that the farms get smaller, the patches of forest get bigger, and the mix of crops changes. Pine County provides a perfect micro view of this transition. Although it's not prime agricultural land, the southern part of the county has some decent-size dairy and livestock farms. In northern Pine County, the farms become fewer and smaller, while forests and bogs take over the landscape. Eastern Pine County borders the federally protected upper St. Croix River, one of the most scenic rivers in Minnesota.

While it's easy to see the influences of logging and agriculture in Pine County, it's much more difficult to see evidence of stone quarrying. The **Sandstone History and Art Center**, located at 402 Main St. in Sandstone, has interesting displays showing the quarrying of sandstone from the banks of the Kettle River, Minnesota's first Wild and Scenic River. For more information, call (312) 245-2138 or visit sandstonehistory.com.

As the first Europeans began making their way west to the land that was to become Minnesota, they arrived via a mode of travel that was true to the old adage "When in Rome, do as the Romans do." The birchbark canoes of American Indian design that these explorers used proved so well suited to the watery landscape that the canoe remained essential to the region's first commercial enterprise—the fur trade. Thus, the banks of a river like the Snake would have been the perfect place for an operation like the **Snake River Fur Post**, which today stands in all its early nineteenth-century splendor north of CR 7, about two miles west of Pine City.

This living-history site, managed by the Minnesota Historical Society, offers you an intriguing immersion into one of the state's most romantic eras. The French Canadian voyageurs, whom you will find "living" inside the exactingly re-created rough log palisade, were a notoriously colorful and lusty bunch. Paddling heavily laden canoes and portaging loads of 180 pounds and up from dawn to dusk throughout summer, the voyageurs were so high-spirited that they reputedly could not be kept from singing. In their boisterous way they will teach you how to throw a tomahawk and start a fire using flint and steel while spinning tales about how they spent their time at the post (which was occupied in the winter of 1804) trading guns, blankets, beads, and metal cookware with trappers from the local Ojibway bands.

The Snake River Fur Post—which is open free of charge Tues through Sat, May through early Sept—also gives you a glimpse into the incredibly vast scale of this Canadian-controlled fur trade empire. When the men at the post paddled to Grand Portage in early summer for their company's annual rendezvous, they were joined by compatriots from as far away as Montreal and the Arctic tundra of the Canadian Northwest. For more information call (320) 629-6356 or go to mnhs.org.

Perhaps the most tragic legacy of Minnesota's turn-of-the-twentieth-century logging boom was the devastating fire that completely consumed Hinckley and five other towns nearby in the hot, dry summer of 1894. The *Hinckley Fire Museum*—housed in the town's defunct train depot at 106 Old Hwy. 61 and open daily for a small fee May through Oct—has been dedicated to this singularly destructive event. Because of an accumulated effect of years of clear-cut logging, in which a thick mantle of limbs from the felled giant pines was left like tinder on the ground, there had been a number of small fires ignited through the summer, many by sparks from passing steam locomotives. Finally, on September 1 conditions were at their driest and a strong wind fanned one of these blazes into a firestorm that swept across 320,000 acres of land, destroying everything in its path. The museum's multimedia presentation, photographs, mural, and static displays of melted household artifacts recount the fate of the 418 persons killed in the conflagration, as well as those few who escaped by fleeing to nearby rivers and ponds. For more information call (320) 384-7338 or visit hinckleyfiremuseum.com.

Carlton County

By the time you reach Carlton County, which sits just south of Duluth, the transition from farm to forest is almost complete. While a few stubborn Scandinavians hang on to their small farms, logging and tourism begin to dominate the economy. Main attractions in the county include Jay Cooke State Park, which encompasses a wild section of the St. Louis River, and the Willard Munger State Trail, a beautiful bike trail that starts in Duluth.

Ask a knowledgeable Minnesotan to steer you toward the Grand Portage and you're likely to find yourself cruising along Lake Superior's spectacular north shore, headed for the Canadian border. The nine-mile climb from the shores of Gitche Gumee up and over the Sawtooth Mountains that was made famous by the voyageurs (see the section on Cook County later in this chapter) isn't the only grand portage in the state. The spectacular cataracts of the St. Louis River in its final descent before entering a placid estuary that leads to Duluth Harbor also precipitated a major carrying place for early explorers and fur traders seeking passage from the Great Lakes to the Mississippi watershed. This rugged valley, too, was known as the Grand Portage.

The Great Lake Superior

I don't remember my first visit to the north shore of Lake Superior. After my birth in November, my parents took me with them when they vacationed along the shore in June. Even though I don't remember that first trip, it must have ingrained in me a special affinity with that part of Minnesota. And while I still have not taken a canoe into the Boundary Waters Canoe Area (considered by some to be positively un-Minnesotan, especially for someone born and raised here), I have faithfully visited the big lake every year and in every season.

Besides good memories of the shore, I also have a poignant one. Because it had always been my mother's favorite place to vacation, we spread her ashes in the lake near the village of Grand Marais. From the beginning of life to the end, Lake Superior continues to draw my family to its rugged coast.

Today the area surrounding the St. Louis River Dalles is preserved as *Jay Cooke State Park*, which offers great hiking and skiing trails, camping, and picnicking along the banks of the river. But if you haven't the time or inclination to explore the area under your own locomotion, there's much to be gained by a drive along MN 210 between I-35 and MN 23, which parallels the river on the north side. The road winds up and over the rugged contours of the valley for nine miles and could almost fool you into thinking you've been detoured onto an Appalachian highway.

If hiking isn't adventuresome enough for your tastes, stop by *Superior Whitewater* (3212 River Gate Ave., Scanlon), just outside of Cloquet. Spring through fall, Superior Whitewater conducts professionally guided whitewater-rafting trips down an undeveloped stretch of the St. Louis just upstream of Jay Cooke State Park. The rafts accommodate six paddle-wielding passengers, each outfitted with a life jacket and instructed by experienced guides in the skills required to pilot the vessel; two-person inflatable kayaks are also available. The rapids on this section of the river begin gently enough and then grow in size and intensity as you progress downstream. By the time you reach Electric Ledge—a thrilling six-foot chute formed where the water tumbles over a river-wide bedrock dike—you're ready for the exhilarating splash in the face that you're likely to get.

The excitement of Minnesota's only whitewater-rafting experience lasts about two and a half hours and is expensively priced. You should make reservations in advance by calling Superior Whitewater at (218) 522-4446 or checking out minnesotawhitewater.com.

Before you disappear into the northern forests, a final stop in Carlton County should be made at the southeast corner of the junction of MN 45 and MN 33 in Cloquet. Here, amid gas fumes and the honking of cars, stands the world's only **Frank Lloyd Wright–designed service station**. Since 1957 this Phillips 66 franchise has been humbly serving the fossil-fuel needs of countless customers who have pulled up beneath the steep, angular cantilevered roof, perhaps unaware that they were in the presence of architectural greatness. Thus forewarned, you won't make the same mistake.

Itasca County

In the land of ten thousand lakes, this northern Minnesota county has its own monopoly on water. More than one thousand lakes surround Grand Rapids, which is the largest town in the county, and the Mississippi River flows through town as it begins its journey south. Although the two main highways that meet in Grand Rapids, US 2 and US 169, aren't especially scenic, a special treat awaits travelers. MN 38 running north from Grand Rapids to Effie is designated the Edge of the Wilderness Scenic Byway, one of the first of twenty National Scenic Byways.

Grand Rapids, the Itasca County seat, is an attractive old logging town that hasn't quit. The looming buildings of the **Blandin Paper Company**, which line the banks of a not-yet-so-mighty Mississippi River in the heart of the city, stand as living testament to the days when the decimated giant pine gave way to the cutting of pulpwood. Free tours of the facility are offered regularly and follow the high-tech step-by-step transformation of locally harvested balsam and poplar into fifteen-ton spools of glossy magazine stock that may eventually find its way into your home as *Time* or *Newsweek*. For more information on tours, call (218) 327-6200.

Back when pine was king, of course, life was a whole lot simpler, as you'll discover for yourself if you pay a visit to the Minnesota Historical Society's wonderful **Forest History Center**. You'll find this painstakingly resurrected turn-of-the-twentieth-century logging camp and interpretive center a few miles west of town at 2609 CR 76.

The modern interpretive center houses an excellent exhibit on the history of mankind's relationship with Minnesota's forests. From now-extinct American Indian cultural traditions to the most recent trends in conservation, this story is told through multimedia presentations, static displays, and photographs. A highlight is a short film of the last logging drive in Minnesota, which took place on the Little Fork River in 1937. Expert "whitewater men" can be seen hopping nimbly from log to log, while others guide huge "wanigans"—rafts supporting the crew's kitchen and bunkhouse—through the rapids.

Even though it may look like summer outside to you, it's December 15, 1900, in the **Northwoods Logging Company** camp, located a short hike through the woods from the interpretive center. In fact, as your guide explains before you enter the first of several hand-hewn-log buildings, the crew is still looking for some hardy men and women to fill a few jobs for the season. Highly entertaining and extremely knowledgeable costumed characters populating the camp provide opportunities for a little on-the-job training to help you decide if spending the winter as a "road monkey," assistant cook, or sawyer is for you. Unfortunately, as most folks quickly learn, their backwoods savvy qualifies them only for the bottom-rung position of road monkey, whose job it was to throw straw in front of log-burdened sleighs on the icy downhills and collect the "road apples" dropped in the wake of the powerful draft horses.

Besides visiting the bunkhouse, the notoriously ornery cook and her humble assistants, the earthy barn boss and blacksmith, and the solitary saw sharpener, you also get a chance to chat with a 1930s Forest Service ranger in his nearby cabin. Finally, you can visit a replica floating kitchen, or wanigan, of the type once used by logging crews as they drove their logs downstream. All facilities at the center are open daily mid-May through mid-Oct, and special events, such as a kids' weekend in mid-June and a woodcrafts festival in mid-July, are scheduled annually. The interpretive center and trails are open 10 a.m. to 2 p.m. Mon through Thurs in winter. There is a small admission fee. For more information call (218) 327-4482.

Since its construction in 1902, **Central School**—located at the intersection of US 2 and US 169 in Grand Rapids—has no doubt seen a lot of students gazing wistfully out of its Romanesque Revival arched windows. Today the attractive building has been preserved as a center for the area's historic heritage and the arts. Also, on the first floor, in what for many years was actually the first-grade room, is **Old School Café & Gift Shoppe**, an inexpensive restaurant serving very good homemade soups, sandwiches, and pies in an atmosphere likely to rekindle some long-forgotten grade-school memories.

Even more nostalgia is in store for visitors on the building's third floor, where the **Itasca County Historical Museum** has dedicated considerable space to Grand Rapids' most famous citizen. Judy Garland—born Francis Gumm in 1922 to Grand Rapids movie theater owner Frank Gumm—lived in town only until she was four. But by then she had already gotten a taste for the limelight, having delighted her father's customers by dancing on the movie house stage at age two-and-a-half. Commemorating her career are videos of *The Wizard of Oz* and other Garland films, a yellow brick road outside the building, and a collection of photographs, albums, and what is claimed to be the nation's largest display of Garland memorabilia. The *Gumm House*, not open to the public, can be seen a few blocks away at 727 Second Ave. Northeast. Also, an annual festival in honor of Judy Garland is held in Grand Rapids. Other exhibits in the museum—which charges a modest admission fee and is open year-round most days of the week—focus on aspects of Itasca County history. Elsewhere in the building a large art gallery features works of local artists.

In Ojibway mythology there is a sleeping giant called "Mesabi," and it was believed that the huge ridge of ancient granite stretching fifty miles north and east of Grand Rapids was its home. Though they may not have been able to conceive of just how their giant was to be awakened or what it would mean to America's burgeoning twentieth-century industries, the Mesabi and the adjacent Vermilion Range did indeed house a giant that for decades yielded vast quantities of the richest iron ore on Earth.

In Calumet—at the western end of the Mesabi, eighteen miles east of Grand Rapids on US 169—there is a must-visit site for anyone who wants to gain a firsthand perspective on just how Minnesota's iron ore giant was shaken to life. The *Hill Annex Mine* was in continuous operation from 1903 to 1978, when it was shut down practically overnight and sold to the state for a token fee. Run since 1988 by the Department of Natural Resources as Minnesota's sixty-fourth and newest state park, Hill Annex allows visitors to examine every aspect of the mining process—from the bottom of the pit to the top of the waste-rock piles looming more than five hundred feet overhead.

The tour begins at the old Hill Annex Clubhouse, which was built in the 1930s as a gathering place for managers who lived with their families in adjacent company houses at this "location" (a worker-habitation site) near the edge of the ever-growing pit; the miners, by contrast, kept to their own kind in bunkhouses on the other side of the tracks. Well-designed exhibits and excellent larger-than-life photographs in the clubhouse chronicle changing lifestyles and technologies at the mine. Upstairs are re-created living quarters, a chemistry lab, and a foreman's office. Another room has an oral history library and a computer-operated photograph file, all open to visitors.

This orientation complete, the visitor should get ready to board a colorful bus for a ninety-minute tour of the mine itself. Much of this time is spent exploring the processing plant, which separated ore from waste rock, and the complex network of conveyors that carried these materials to their respective destinations.

Though the Hill Annex was relatively small compared to other mines on the range, it is an awesome sight nonetheless. More than sixty-three million tons of ore were extracted from the 640-acre pit, whose bottom is now flooded with water. The decades of blasting and carving required to move all that rock have created a landscape that is simultaneously beautiful and discomforting to behold. Looking out from the rim, one sees the water glistening far below as if from the bottom of a spectacular desert canyon. But the place is also raw and desolate, occupied here and there by rusting hulks of machinery that look puny from afar and cumbersome and lifeless up close.

Bus tours at the Hill Annex are run on the hour, for a small fee, daily from Memorial Day through Sept. For information on special geology tours or for group reservations, call (218) 247-7215.

There are so few serious practitioners of the lost art of birchbark-canoe building in the US that they can practically be counted on one hand. But as is only appropriate to a state whose history is so deeply indebted to the canoe, one of the nation's greatest builders can be found in the heart of Minnesota's northwoods. As you're cruising north on MN 6 from Deer River, passing the settlements of Bowstring and Talmoon in a blur, the thick forests on either side of the road are suddenly interrupted by the Big Fork River and a large tar-paper shed on its banks, with a couple of graceful-looking bark vessels displayed out front. The sign above the door reads HAFEMAN BOAT WORKS.

Ray Boessel inherited this canoe-building business from his grandfather-in-law, Bill Hafeman, in 1981, and since then he has supported himself by producing up to seventeen canoes a year. The elder master learned the trade by necessity after moving to Big Fork in 1920, when the river route to town was a far better option than the area's rudimentary roads. Although Bill's maiden voyage in his first canoe carried him to town in four hours, it took him two days to get home. Over the years he greatly refined the canoe-building skills that Ray, in his gentle, friendly way, is glad to share with you. You'll learn all that's involved in his ancient trade—from cutting bark from live birches when the sap is flowing in early summer to collecting the long spruce roots for lashing the canoe together to completing the final stages of assembly. You can even test-paddle one of the finished products on the river to discover how strong, pliable, and lovely these canoes truly are.

In case you want to take one of these watercraft home with you to join the ranks of such proud owners as Charles Kuralt and Lady Bird Johnson, be prepared for a four-figure price tag. For more information you can call Ray at (218) 743-3709.

Koochiching County

Koochiching, the American Indian name for the Rainy River, referred to mist and spray from Koochiching Falls. As part of the great network of lakes and rivers that formed a portion of the Voyageur's Highway, the river played an important role in the settlement of this remote northern county, first as a watery highway and later as a source of power for industry. Made up of bogs, forest, and lakes, the county lies in a region blessed with a million acres of wilderness and cursed with long and often harsh winters.

In winter the Rainy River border town of **International Falls** often receives the dubious distinction of being identified as the nation's "cold spot." But when summer comes, the area around "Frostbite Falls" shows another face altogether. Eleven miles east of downtown, the magnificent 219,000-acre expanse of *Voyageurs National Park* (360 Hwy. 11 East), Minnesota's only national park, draws visitors seeking a full spectrum of waterborne recreational opportunities. So much of this relatively unknown park is covered with water—there are more than thirty lakes, five of which are large—that no roads lead into its interior. Thus the most common means of travel are by motorboat, houseboat, sailboat, canoe, kayak, and floatplane. Excellent hiking routes are found on the densely forested Kabetogama Peninsula in the interior, but the only access to the peninsula on the US side requires the services of an air- or waterborne ferry. During the chilly winter months, Voyageurs' thick lake ice and plentiful snow invite exploration by snowmobile and on skis.

The historical exhibits, orientation video, and bookstore at the Rainy Lake Visitor Center are well worth an hour of your time. Boat tours of Rainy Lake may be offered in summer; contact the park for current information. For more information about the park, call (218) 283-6600 or visit nps.gov/voya.

St. Louis County

As the largest county in Minnesota, St. Louis County stretches from Lake Superior to the Canadian border. Its hundreds of square miles of forest and bogs have made it an inhospitable place to try to carve out a living. But two features make it unique among northern counties. It has almost thirty miles of Lake Superior shoreline and can lay claim to two of the richest iron ore deposits in the world in the Mesabi and Vermilion Ranges. This combination of abundant natural resources and access to the big lake contributed to the growth of Duluth as the largest inland port in the world.

Much of Voyageurs National Park also is accessible from northwestern St. Louis County. The end of the Ash River Trail, CR 129, is a jumping-off place for the backcountry lakes of the Kabetogama Peninsula, which is also the site of the park's most unusual civilized attraction: Minnesota's remotest and perhaps most historically colorful hotel.

The **Kettle Falls Hotel** landing, located at 10502 Gamma Rd. (travel by boat is the only means of getting here), is close to the now-dammed Kettle Falls, which marks the international border and connects the Kabetogama Peninsula with Canadian soil. Following a comprehensive Park Service–funded restoration that was completed in 1988, the hotel sits proudly among the tall pines at the end of a long wooded walkway. The building gleams with fresh white paint, and cheerful red-and-white striped awnings adorn each window. A huge wraparound screened porch embraces the lower level and provides a pleasant site for dining, reading, or taking in the evening air. The rooms upstairs, which command a moderate price, are appointed with simple antiques and antique reproductions (all share common bathroom facilities).

According to its brochure, the Kettle Falls was built in 1910 to provide a "stopping place" for loggers who were endeavoring to rout the surrounding forests of the ubiquitous giant red and white pines. But corner the hotel manager, and you may learn just what induced those loggers to frequent the place. He can tell you about the extensive bootlegging and smuggling operations that were run out of the hotel during Prohibition (the woods on the Canadian side of the border provided an ideal site for a still). He may mention something of the pervasive gambling that took place, and he might just hint at another enterprise that was once central to the Kettle Falls's appeal.

But if the manager leaves some gaps in the story, just find your way to the hotel bar and, with luck, the bartender will fill in the rest. This room is adorned with signed photographs of leering sirens and framed calendar girls of a bygone era—perhaps the same faces that gazed down on the lumberjacks as they waited to take their turns upstairs with some of the hotel's female employees. In their exuberance these customers danced on top of the bar until it was reduced to splinters under their hobnailed boots.

If, after hearing about all this, you find you have a little trouble walking straight and the surroundings seem a bit out of kilter, console yourself with the knowledge that the barroom floor really does slope rather drastically toward the door. The reconstruction preserved in the warped foundation a two-foot drop in elevation when measured from the summit of a hump near the pool table (which appears to be desperately maintaining its equilibrium) to the distant corner.

The Kettle Falls has several housekeeping cabins available, as well as boat and canoe rentals. Home-cooked meals from a limited menu are served daily in the dining room. For more information call (218) 240-1724 or (218) 240-1726 or, from Nov 1 to May 1, (218) 875-2070; the website is kettlefallshotel.com.

Renting a houseboat from **Ebel's Voyageur Houseboats** (10326 Ash River Trail, Orr) is another way to gain access to the distant bays and numerous fishing holes of the park. Equipped with every convenience a landlubber could ask for, these floating mobile homes cruise at slow speed by day and are nosed up on protected beaches at night. Depending on size of party, length of trip, and degree of luxury sought, houseboat rentals are moderately to expensively priced. Contact Ebel's Voyageur Houseboats at (218) 374-3571; ebels.com.

The **Echo Trail** is a remote Minnesota back road that delivers all the pristine enchantment conjured up by its name. Flanked on both sides for most of its sixty winding, hilly miles by the famed million-acre Boundary Waters Canoe Area (BWCA) Wilderness, the Echo can afford drivers glimpses of deer, moose, bear, and possibly even the elusive eastern timber wolf. As it meanders between Echo Lake, about six miles south of the little town of Crane Lake on CR 24, and the north shore of Shagawa Lake near Ely, the Echo Trail skirts several lakeshores from which, on a calm summer evening, you may hear the resonant call of a loon across the water.

St. Paul YMCA Camp du Nord (3606 North Arm Rd., Ely) is one Echo Trail establishment that beckons families in search of an unusual summer vacation experience. Du Nord, located on CR 644 (also known as the North Arm Road) about 9 miles down the Echo from its eastern terminus, is a family camp—meaning it combines many of the features typically found at a resort with a creative variety of program activities for all ages. Upholding a strong wilderness ethic, du Nord staff leads families on canoe trips into the BWCA and offers naturalist-guided hikes and other environmentally oriented activities. Campwide cookouts and campfires develop a robust sense of community spirit, while daily activities for different age groups provide parents and kids with opportunities to mix with their peers. Families who attend the inexpensive weeklong summer sessions (advance reservations are required) can camp out or stay in rustic housekeeping cabins, many of which are perched along the rugged shore of the north arm of Burntside Lake. For more information, call (218) 248-2185 or visit dunord.org.

To get a sense of the breadth and depth of Ely's past, you may want to pay a visit to the **Vermilion Interpretive Center** at Vermilion Community College, located at 1900 East Camp St. Exhibits at the center capture the many ways the Ojibway, French Canadian voyageurs, Swedish loggers, and Finnish miners have interacted among themselves and left their mark on the woodlands that dominate the landscape. There is also an exhibit commemorating Ely resident Will Steger, leader of a spectacularly successful self-contained international dogsled expedition to the North Pole in 1986. The interpretive center is open Wed through Sat from Oct through Apr and daily in the summer. A modest admission fee is charged.

The howl of a lone wolf echoing across a lake conjures up images of the northern wilderness like nothing else. And the Minnesota legislature, which presides over a state graced with the largest population of wolves in the lower forty-eight states, decreed an interpretive center be built to honor the wolf and educate people about this much abused and misunderstood creature. The result is **Ely's International Wolf Center**, on MN 169 just east of town, which gives people the straight scoop about wolves through imaginative hands-on programs and an award-winning exhibit on the relationship of wolves to humans of all cultures.

Art, literature, interactive videos, a large diorama of a wolf pack bringing down a white-tailed deer, and other displays at the Wolf Center stimulate thinking about the many ways humans have mythologized and romanticized the wolf over the centuries and across the continents. Fables and images range from St. Francis of Assisi to Adolf Hitler, from Lon Chaney to Romulus and Remus.

Several times each day wolf handlers enter an enclosure and introduce visitors (who watch from behind glass windows) to the center's resident pack. A wolf ecology day camp for children, summer howling trips for families, and hands-on research expeditions for adults round out the offerings. The center charges a modest fee and is open daily, May through mid-Oct, and on Tues and weekends the rest of the year. For more information about programs, call (218) 365-4695 or visit wolf.org.

Fish Houses

In the north country, when the lakes develop a thick enough coating of ice, people tow little square shelters onto the lakes, drill holes through the ice, and fish. Obviously it's not a sight you'll see in warmer climates. Fish houses come in all different sizes and run the gamut from one-person canvas shelters to solidly built wood units that hold up to ten or more. The larger ones often have received substantial upgrades and may have a television, stereo, kitchen, bunk beds, and carpet. Whatever the size, all fish houses come with an important feature: a hole, or holes, in the floor.

Clusters of fish houses on lakes resemble an Arctic settlement, and on large lakes such as Mille Lacs, resort owners plow wide roads from shore to the temporary towns and put bridges over cracks in the ice. Although people fish everywhere, few go to such lengths to pursue their passion when the weather changes so drastically. Should you see a motley assortment of fish houses on some vast frozen wasteland, don't take pity on the inhabitants. They may be catching their limit of walleye.

Adjacent to the Wolf Center on MN 169 stand two log buildings that commemorate the life and times of a most unusual wilderness pioneer. Every log in the ***Dorothy Molter Museum*** was moved by volunteers, without mechanical assistance, from its original location on the Isle of Pines on Knife Lake in the heart of the Boundary Waters Canoe Area Wilderness. Here, from 1934 until her death in 1986, Dorothy lived a quiet life of service surrounded by nature's magnificence. As the Boundary Waters grew in popularity among canoeists, "The Root-beer Lady," as she became known, also sold homemade brew to many of the six thousand visitors who paddled to her door each year (her guest books, dutifully signed by all visitors, are available for your perusal).

Walk through the simple rooms of her two cabins and view portions of an excellent documentary about her life, and you may come to appreciate the many subtle things that make Dorothy's life remarkable. She evidently loved the long silences and solitary rigors of winter life at her island retreat, yet her summers were filled with enough uninvited visitors to make her one of the area's main tourist attractions. Without ever charging a fee, she used her training as a nurse to help wilderness travelers who were injured and sick. She even paid for an emergency floatplane evacuation for a man suffering from hypothermia whose party was unable to afford the flight. Perhaps that explains why an avalanche of signatures was easily gathered to petition the USDA Forest Service to allow her to remain on her island home in the late 1970s, when the Boundary Waters became closed to residents. Appropriately enough she was allowed the privilege of living out her days in the heart of canoe country.

The Dorothy Molter Museum is open weekends from her birthday, May 6, to Memorial Day each spring, then daily through Sept. Call (218) 365-4451 or go to rootbeerlady.com for more information and to make an appointment for visits outside normal hours.

Numerous resorts and outfitters in town can help even the most inexperienced adventurers gain access to the surrounding wilderness. Though the usual modes of travel in the BWCA are by canoe, skis, and snowshoes, explorers with more exotic tastes can arrange for kayak trips through ***Piragis North Woods Company*** (218-365-6745; piragis.com). In winter they can assume command at the helm of a sled-dog team under the guidance of polar explorer Paul Schurke at ***Wintergreen Lodge***; call (218) 349-6128 or visit dogsledding.com.

Scandinavians have made a fascinating ritual of the sauna—a ritual that has elements both sacred and profane—and there is no better place to partake of its traditions than at the ***Ely Steam Bath***. For more than fifty years, work-worn loggers and miners, grimy from a day's labor in the area's once-great open-pit mines, have made the trek into town to catch up on local gossip, cleanse their bodies, and replenish their spirits in the steam bath's penetrating vapors. A visit to this humble landmark institution, found on Harvey Street near First Avenue, will have the same effects on you, as well as providing a unique window to one of Minnesota's most engaging off-the-beaten-path communities.

The steam bath has separate public facilities for men and women, as well as smaller rooms available exclusively for couples. But for the full sociological experience, the public baths are the way to go. Typically the natives prolong their convivial ablutions by working up a sweat in the steam room, showering, and then sitting for a while in the antechamber to enjoy a cold drink before repeating the cycle a couple more times. By their last visit to the steam room, the men are so well softened that they often shave their bristly beards without need of shaving cream. Newcomers, however, may find themselves similarly poached after only one or two doses of Scandinavian heat.

Open for business Wed and Fri 4 to 8:30 p.m. and Sat 2 to 8:30 p.m. year-round, the Ely Steam Bath boasts extremely modest prices. Towels are provided. For information call (218) 365-2984 or visit elysteamsauna.net.

Minnesota's **Iron Range** is made up of the **Vermilion Range**, which runs south and west of Ely, and the larger and more famous Mesabi Range farther west. But what it lacked in size, the Vermilion made up for in the purity of its ore and in its stature as the place where Minnesota's iron ore rush began. The start of this world-class industrial bonanza was the **Soudan Underground Mine**—the oldest, richest, and deepest mine in the state and now one of Minnesota's most fascinating tourist attractions. As if sitting on an underlying bedrock formation that is 2.7 billion years old (try to wrap your brain around that number) wasn't enough of an attraction, in 2014 the state bought three thousand acres of land that includes shoreline on Lake Vermillion, and the new park is now **Vermillion-Soudan Underground Mine State Park**. Adding the land along Lake Vermillion made this a multi-faceted park.

Run by the Department of Natural Resources as a historic state park since mining operations ceased in 1962, the mine's several modest aboveground buildings and the 1924-vintage hoist (a huge cable, drum, and engine system that hauls loads up and down the Soudan's main shaft) are maintained in top working order. But instead of raising six-ton bins of dense reddish-brown hematite ore up to the surface every three to five minutes, as it has done for most of its working life, the hoist now transports rattling steel elevators, or "cages," full of visitors wearing hard hats.

After viewing a short film on the history of the Soudan, prepare yourself for a quick descent 2,341 feet below ground to level 27—the mine's deepest horizontal "drift," or passage, where the temperature year-round is a cool fifty degrees. The guide explains that the ride down will take three minutes traveling at about ten miles per hour, but the dizzying blur of rock and steel visible through the elevator's single window gives the impression of much greater speed. The elevator finally comes to a noisy halt, the door opens, and a small train awaits to take you a quarter of a mile down a dark tunnel to a reconstructed mining site.

The reality of what it was like to work in such a place dawns on you slowly. Solitary mannequins placed far apart in a large cavern stand poised to drill holes with deafening carbide-tipped, air-powered drills (the guide turns them on briefly). Under working conditions the headlamps the miners wore were the only sources of light (other lights illuminating the scene are momentarily turned off so you can appreciate the gloom), and a pervasive unhealthy dust frequently limited visibility even more. During lunch breaks and shift changes, the freshly drilled ten-foot-deep holes were filled with explosives, and the caverns were enlarged by blasting. Then, using heavy equipment, the laborers would load the ore into small railroad cars for the trip to the elevator. The best paid among the miners of this "Cadillac of underground mines" (conditions were considered excellent, and, with only thirteen deaths, the Soudan's safety record was very good) were the men who drilled and blasted the ceilings of vertical shafts that were up to two hundred feet high. In 1962 each eight-hour shift these men worked yielded a $24 wage.

If that doesn't sound like fun, consider the days before electricity and unionization brought their improvements. In the early 1890s, when the possibilities of open-pit mining at the Soudan site were exhausted and the enterprise went underground, miners wielded pickaxes for the duration of each twelve-hour shift. Illumination was cast by candles, one to a man. The mules that hauled the ore to the hoist stayed underground for six months at a time, and when they arrived at the surface for a well-earned six-month vacation, their eyes were wrapped in layers of gauze that were removed gradually over the course of a week to prevent blindness.

Underground tours of the Soudan mine are offered daily for a modest fee throughout the summer; they leave the surface each half hour and take about an hour. The interpretive film lasts ten minutes, there are aboveground exhibits in the information building, and the giant hoist can be seen in operation. Also, hiking trails lead to several of the Soudan's original open pits. For more information call (218) 300-7000 or visit dnr.state.mn.us.

Miners long ago discovered that nothing takes the chill off after a shift in the bowels of the earth better than an authentic home-cooked pasty—a delicious culinary tradition on the iron range that reflects the influence of immigrant Cornish miners. And the ***Sulu's Espresso Café***, just a mile west of the Soudan Underground Mine on MN 169 in the heart of Tower, has a variety of coffee drinks, from espresso to Lutheran-style coffee, fresh bakery items made in the kitchen, and soups and sandwiches. As their website says, "Skip the crowds in Ely and enjoy the quiet and laid-back vibe of Tower." Contact the shop at (218) 753-5610 or visit suluscafe.com.

Detour about a dozen miles south of Tower on MN 169 for an exploration of the Finnish heritage and architecture that characterizes much of the region's settlement history. **Finnish Heritage Homestead Tours**, in the little town of **Embarrass** (occasionally noted for having the coldest temperature in the lower forty-eight states), provides visitors with two-hour guided tours of several preserved pioneer homesteads. The informative guides strike a balance between explaining subtle differences in log-building techniques developed by Finnish master builders and providing insights into cultural traditions, such as the sauna, that were brought by the Finns to the northwoods. The tours are inexpensive and offered during summer Mon through Sat. For reservations call Finnish Heritage Homestead Tours at (218) 984-2084.

The **United States Hockey Hall of Fame**, on US 53 in downtown Eveleth, stands as a tribute both to the sport and to the prominence it has enjoyed on the iron range since 1903, when the first game was played in Eveleth. For current information call (218) 744-5167 or go to ushockeyhalloffame.com.

Traveling west from Eveleth on US 169 you'll encounter downtown **Chisholm's Minnesota Museum of Mining**, which provides a slightly different perspective on the area's industrial history. Surrounding a building of rambling indoor exhibits, where a detailed scale model of a taconite processing plant is displayed prominently, are several monstrous steam shovels, a railroad engine, and an evolutionary progression of trucks that culminates in one of today's 127-ton behemoths. Nearby, a twenty-ton drag bucket, once used to scrape up car-sized chunks of Mesabi ore, rusts in isolation on the grass, only hinting at the size of the crane that was its companion. The museum is open daily from mid-May through Sept and charges a small fee. Call (218) 254-5543 for more information or visit mnmuseumofmining.org.

Travel a few more miles west along the iron range's forested moonscape and you'll arrive at **Hibbing**. Follow the signs at the northeast edge of town for the Hull-Rust-Mahoning Mine overlook, where you can watch gigantic trucks and cranes removing what ore remains in the world's largest open-pit iron mine. The pit yawns two miles across, three miles long, and more than five hundred feet deep from the overlook interpretive center, where a short video and volunteer interpreters explain the operation. Blasting in the mine is frequently scheduled for Thurs at 11 a.m.

Retracing your steps toward downtown Hibbing, you'll pass through a skeleton of a ghost town. A grid of streets flanked by sidewalks with weeds growing in the cracks and an occasional lamppost is all that's left of what was once a thriving mining settlement called Hibbing. Like most communities on the iron range, Hibbing grew up on the edge of a mine. By 1918 industry managers determined that the town itself and all its inhabitants had to make way for the gaping pit that was to become the **Hull-Rust-Mahoning Mine**. The town site of Alice, two miles to the south, was selected as a suitable location for the transplanted population.

To make this move more palatable, the mining bosses built the town a high school that would match the immigrant miners' towering desire to better the lot of their children through education. Inexpensive tours of the fortresslike **Hibbing High School**, which was completed in 1923 at a cost of almost $4 million, are given Mon through Sat throughout summer (call 218-208-0841 for more information). Among Hibbing High's most noted alumni is Bobby Zimmerman, a musically talented student now known to the world as **Bob Dylan**; Dylan's boyhood home, not open to the public, can be seen at 2425 Seventh Ave. South.

The state-of-the-art **Paulucci Space Theatre** in Hibbing draws crowds year-round for mind-boggling multimedia programs on subjects that range from dinosaurs to outer space. Using a computer-driven arsenal of twenty-six slide projectors, a Spitz 512 Starball for stargazing, and a Cinema 360 fish-eye movie system that projects images all over the theater's domed ceiling, the Paulucci is among the top two-dozen planetariums in the nation. There is also an interesting gift shop. For information on the theater's inexpensive shows, call (218) 262-6720 or visit minnesotanorth.edu/campuses/hibbing /paulucci-space-theater.

Great Lakes shipping is the main economic force that put, and has kept, the city of **Duluth** on the map, and at this head-of-the-lakes international port, shipping primarily means iron ore. On any given day, spring through fall, there may be at anchor in the harbor several huge freighters from South America, Asia, or Europe. A good place to see them is from the breakwater that juts into the lake from **Canal Park**, found at the south end of Canal Park Drive and next to Duluth's most famous landmark, the aerial lift bridge. Ocean-size waves break against the shore, seagulls call stridently while winging overhead, and the exotic associations conjured up by the flags and foreign names on the ships can all conspire to transport your imagination far from the American heartland.

The **Lake Superior Marine Museum**, which faces the park and the breakwater, is an excellent first stop if you want to learn more about Lake Superior and the global shipping industry that it supports. Upon entering the building you'll pass down a sloping hallway lined above and on the walls with weathered signs bearing the names of ships that once traveled the lakes. The lower floor has an auditorium that shows films about shipping and the Lake

Superior environment several times daily. Large maps identify shipwreck sites and graphically depict the bottom contour of the world's largest freshwater lake. There are also exhibits on current underwater research projects and on the history of marine engine technology.

Upstairs three reconstructed staterooms, occupied by mannequins in period dress, convey a sense of what life belowdecks was like in the time of the Great Lakes steamer; also on display are numerous well-crafted models of historic ships. Another film-viewing area offers continually running shows on the US Army Corps of Engineers, which operates the museum, and on the modern bulk-loading process for freighters. The information desk on the second floor will alert you to the origin of any ships moored in the harbor, and against the plate-glass windows facing the lake you'll find telescopes available for studying these big vessels. The museum is open year-round free of charge. For information about the arrival of ships in Duluth Harbor, call (218) 727-2497 or visit lsmma.com.

Great Lakes Aquarium is a second Duluth waterfront destination that provides insights into Lake Superior's importance among the world's freshwater

TOP ANNUAL EVENTS IN THE ARROWHEAD

JANUARY

John Beargrease
Sled Dog Marathon
Duluth, Jan
(218) 461-1834
beargrease.com

FEBRUARY

Mora Vasaloppet Cross-Country
Ski Race
Mora, second Sun in Feb
(320) 679-2629
vasaloppet.us

JUNE

Summer Finnish Festival
Embarrass, early June
(218) 984-2084

JULY

Fisherman's Picnic
Grand Marais, late July/early Aug
(218) 387-2524
visitcookcounty.com

AUGUST

Braham Pie Day
Braham, first Fri in Aug
(320) 396-4956
pieday.com

Bayfront Blues Festival
Duluth, second weekend of Aug
(715) 817-6933
bayfrontblues.com

NOVEMBER

Aitkin Fish House Parade
Fri after Thanksgiving
(218) 927-2316
aitkin.com

resources. Since opening in July 2000, the aquarium has continued to add exhibits. Besides displays of assorted birds and one hundred thousand gallons of freshwater exhibits that contain many varieties of fish, the aquarium has several hands-on displays. A dune-making machine lets visitors turn a wheel and change the structure of dunes when the wind changes direction. Although most of us don't think of sand dunes around the Great Lakes, they are found along the eastern shore of Lake Michigan and on a smaller scale along Park Point near downtown Duluth. Another interactive exhibit, the *Great Lakes Water Table*, allows visitors to experience various hydrologic aspects of Lake Superior. For information call (218) 740-3474 or visit glaquarium.org.

The Great Lakes Aquarium has had some financial difficulties in the past, which resulted in the facility closing during the winter of 2002, but it has since started operating year-round again. With this in mind, make sure to call ahead or check its website before making a special trip to visit the aquarium.

Just west of Canal Park, in a slip beside Harbor Drive, sits the 610-foot freighter **SS William A. Irvin**. From 1938 to 1978 this steam-powered vessel served as the flagship of the US Steel Company fleet, the largest flotilla of ore carriers in the world. During summer, forty-five-minute guided tours that range from stem to stern are conducted, for a modest fee, many times daily.

The sheer mass of the *Irvin* can hardly escape your notice as you enter the gigantic middle hold through a door at the top of the gangplank. But somehow, it's through the smaller details of the ship's construction that the *Irvin*'s incredible size is driven home. After climbing and descending several of the sixteen steep staircases encountered during the tour, you find yourself outside the engine room on the stern deck. The links of a chain, supporting a three-ton emergency anchor nearby, weigh forty pounds each. A mooring rope coiled at your feet is almost as thick as your trunk.

To get this ship up to speed with its fourteen-thousand-ton load (eleven knots was tops, thirteen when running "light"), it took two one-thousand-horsepower engines burning a ton of coal per hour. It also took a lot of hard work and sweat. Even in Lake Superior's cool climate, temperatures in the engine room while the ship was under way ranged from 100 to 115 degrees, with 93 percent humidity. In balmy Detroit, temperatures were 115 to 130 degrees, and the poor guys stoking the boiler had to contend with a scalding 200 degrees. Above 115 degrees, the guide explains, everyone had to wear gloves to keep from getting burned when handling the brass equipment.

It was an entirely different kind of trip for the *Irvin*'s VIP passengers in their wood-paneled staterooms at the other end of the ship. Daily activities for these major stockbrokers and US Steel clients included trapshooting, driving golf balls into the lake, playing shuffleboard, and participating in an occasional game of baseball in an empty hold. Gourmet meals were prepared by a special chef and served in an elegant dining room following cocktails in the guests' private lounge. For a schedule of tours of the *Irvin*, call (218) 722-7876 in season, (218) 623-1236 off-season, or go to decc.org.

An enjoyable way to see Duluth's waterfront is aboard the **North Shore Scenic Railroad**. Day trips range in length from one and a half hours (Lester River) to six hours (Two Harbors) and are fully narrated, providing you with piles of information about the Duluth area. You'll learn about everything from how the port was built to how to keep the seagulls away from your window at the Edgewater Motel. For information on the North Shore Scenic Railroad, call (218) 722-1273 or visit duluthtrains.com.

In the evenings you can ride the **Dinner Train**, which features three different menus: Elegance and Romance, Buffet Dinner, and Pizza Train. The Scenic Railroad departs from the historic depot building that houses the Lake Superior Railroad Museum, 506 West Michigan St. Call (218) 727-8025 or visit lsrm.org for more information.

The tremendous wealth resulting from the burgeoning success of the iron ore industry at the turn of the twentieth century is evident in two Duluth estates along the Lake Superior shoreline on stately London Road, east of downtown. **Glensheen**, an elegant thirty-nine-room Jacobean-style manor house set in a seven-acre wooded glen, has become one of Duluth's most popular attractions. Since assuming ownership from the Congdon family in 1968, the University of Minnesota, Duluth, has been conducting tours that focus on Glensheen's outstanding architecture, extensive handcrafted woodwork, and furnishings that date from 1908, when the estate was completed. Glensheen, located at 3200 London Rd., is also available for rental. For information on rentals and for schedules of the inexpensive tours (reservations are recommended), call (218) 726-8910.

A slightly more intimate way to partake in Duluth's opulent past is to let a room for the night at **The Mansion**, a twenty-five-room bed-and-breakfast estate situated a half mile down the road from Glensheen at 3300 London Rd. Built between 1928 and 1932 for Marjorie Congdon Dudley (the daughter of Chester A. Congdon, master of Glensheen) and her husband, Harry C. Dudley, a mining engineer, The Mansion has seven acres of wooded grounds and more than five hundred feet of secluded Lake Superior shoreline. There are nine guest rooms in all, three in the former maids' quarters (which are moderately priced), five in the main part of the house, and an apartment that rents for a two-night minimum stay (moderately to expensively priced). All guests can enjoy the beautiful screened porch, the spacious living room, the upstairs den, and a library with a fireplace and lovely hand-carved-oak built-in bookcases lined with leather-bound volumes. A large country breakfast is served. For reservations call (218) 726-8932 or visit glensheen.org.

Visitors looking for a smaller bed-and-breakfast to stay at have a couple of options. *The Merryweather Inn*, located at 2316 East First St., sits in Duluth's old historic district. The ten-thousand-square-foot house was built for William Olcott, who earned a fortune through mining and railroads. Olcott worked directly for John D. Rockefeller, and the Rockefellers stayed at the house in 1928. After being saved from demolition by the Minnesota Teachers College, it was used as a music hall, Finnish seminary, radio station, and boardinghouse. It was turned into a bed-and-breakfast in 1997 and was known as the Olcott House Bed and Breakfast until the new owner took possession. For more information call the inn at (218) 728-1339 or visit merryweatherinn.com.

Solglimt Bed and Breakfast was built in 1910 as a two-room cabin on Lake Superior, and was renovated to match the exterior of a late 1800s seaside cottage. This unique bed-and-breakfast, located at 828 Lake Ave. South, sits right on the shore of the big lake just across the aerial lift bridge from Canal Park. Views of Lake Superior and St. Louis Bay cannot be beat, the gardens have received local and national recognition, and porches and decks surround the home. Solglimt has five guest rooms, each with a different feel. Canal Park, Lakewalk, the beach, and the Lake Superior Marine Museum are within easy walking distance. For more information call (218) 727-0596 or visit solglimt .com.

Duluth's historic train station, a striking 1892 châteauesque structure with steep-roofed towers and a great hall with a high cathedral ceiling, is several destinations in one. A permanent collection of paintings by Eastman Johnson is a cornerstone of the *Depot's* several art galleries. Johnson, who was America's most celebrated artist in the middle of the nineteenth century, lived and painted in the Duluth area for two years. As the displayed paintings and drawings indicate, he enjoyed producing portraits of presidents, as well as of the Ojibway he found on the Minnesota frontier. Also on display are exhibits on logging history and Norwegian wood carving.

A train museum in the boarding-platform area of the Depot features Minnesota's first steam engine, on display next to one of the largest locomotives in the world—the Mallet Number 227, which burned ten to twelve tons of coal per hour while hauling more than a hundred iron ore cars from Tower to the docks in Duluth Harbor. Surrounding the tracks is a boardwalk with reconstructed Duluth storefronts ca. 1910.

The historic Depot building is adjacent to Duluth's *Depot Theatre*, where ballet and theater performances and symphony orchestra concerts are held. The exhibit areas in the Depot, which is located at 506 West Michigan St., are open daily for a modest fee. For information on special programs, such as the annual *All American Railroad Days* celebration each July, call (218) 727-8025 or go to lsrm.org.

History buffs with a taste for documents have an interesting time at the *Karpeles Manuscript Library Museum*, 902 East First St. Founded by Dave Karpeles to "renew the sense of purpose our children are missing," this museum is a decidedly eclectic assemblage of historic documents and manuscripts. You'll find a page from Noah Webster's original dictionary and a stanza from Mozart's *Marriage of Figaro*. There's even a gas bill paid by Thomas Edison (suppose the rates hastened the invention of the lightbulb?). The list goes on and on, with each display seemingly as random as the next. Little historical background is given regarding any of the documents in the exhibit itself, but brochures with additional information about each piece are available near the entryway. The museum is open daily year-round and is free. Call (218) 728-0630 for more information or visit karpeles.com.

Lovers of old stadiums and baseball played on real grass should make it a point to see the *Duluth Huskies*. In days of old the Huskies (formerly the Dukes) were a Detroit Tigers farm team, and future stars such as Gates Brown and Denny McLain used the grounds of historic Wade Stadium, built in 1941, to learn their craft. Today the Huskies are one of six franchises in the independent Northwoods League. The baseball is not of Major League caliber, but neither are the prices—tickets, hot dogs for a family of four, and soft drinks cost less than $25. Best of all, the games are a lot of fun. Call Huskies Baseball at (218) 786-9909 for schedule and ticket information or go to northwoodsleague.com.

Though it's difficult to do, if you're passing through Duluth in autumn and can take your eyes off the oceanlike sweep of Lake Superior and the spectacular fall foliage along the shore, look skyward—you may well see something striking. Better yet, find your way to *Hawk Ridge* atop the string of hills behind the city, because, regardless of which direction you may be traveling, tens of thousands of hawks, eagles, and falcons will be winging their way overhead in their annual fall migration. And this small nature preserve, dedicated to observing and recording this singular event, offers what some say is the best viewing site in the country.

There are several observation posts at Hawk Ridge, each oriented to a different wind direction, as well as a network of hiking trails and a bird-banding station. Volunteer naturalists on duty daily from mid-Aug through Nov can assist you in the fine art of distinguishing between the various species. On a good day—one with clear skies and a wind from the west or northwest, creating updrafts upon which the grand birds can soar effortlessly about—you may see thousands of these beautiful winged predators. More than thirty thousand

ALSO WORTH SEEING

Artist's Point
Grand Marais
(218) 387-1400

**Koochiching County and
Bronco Nagurski Museums**
International Falls
(218) 283-4316
koochichingmuseums.org

Lutsen Mountains
Lutsen
(218) 663-7281
lutsen.com

Oberg Mountain
Lutsen
(218) 663-7804

sightings of individual birds of the same species have been recorded in a single twelve-hour period during the peak flyover time, which is usually mid-Sept.

Hawk Ridge is located along the Skyway Parkway, just north of the intersection of Glenwood Avenue and Forty-third Avenue East. Admission is free, though donations for the support of the reserve are encouraged. For more information call (218) 428-6209 or visit hawkridge.org.

Each summer Duluth hosts two cultural events that attract visitors from throughout the region. The *Bayfront Blues Festival*, held annually over a weekend in early Aug, attracts major entertainers from around the country. A week later the *Port of Duluth Festival* features (along with concerts, Jet Ski races, and other happenings) tours of selected US Coast Guard ships and giant wooden sailing ships, like the 179-foot *HMS* **Rose**, a replica of a British frigate that fought against the Bluecoats in New York Harbor during the Revolutionary War. For more information on these events, call the Duluth Convention and Visitors Bureau at (218) 722-4011 or visit visitduluth.com.

Duluth's annual *Winter Sports Festival* in Jan brings several other sorts of thrill seekers out of hiding. Competitors from all over North America come to Duluth for the grueling five-hundred-mile *John Beargrease Sled Dog Marathon*, which runs around the clock for four consecutive days. Large teams of powerful dogs driven by hardy mushers travel an old winter mail route from Duluth to Grand Portage and back. Not far behind them is a pack of snowmobile racers who buzz through town on their way from Thunder Bay, Ontario, to the outskirts of the Twin Cities. There are snowshoe races and, moving at a more soothing pace, a parade of antique horse-drawn cutters. For more information on these events, call the Duluth Convention and Visitors Bureau at (218) 722-4011.

Lake County

As you leave Duluth driving northeast on MN 61 you enter an enchanted realm. For 150 miles the North Shore Scenic Drive hugs the rocky, wooded, mountain-lined rim of the world's largest freshwater sea. Although there's no hint of salt in the offshore breezes and there are no tides, in almost all other respects the cold, clear water stretching blue and silver to the horizon may as well be an ocean. The moods of Superior—from its furious northeasters in late autumn to the infinite calm of August's doldrums—are just too grand to belong to a lake. The shoreline cliffs were built to the same larger-than-life scale. Even the mammoth ocean-bound freighters, which at night look like distant sparkling cities adrift beneath the stars, are dwarfed by the magnificence of this grand lake.

To help get yourself properly acclimated to the North Shore's maritime environment, a couple of shops in Knife River will fix you up with a supply of fish lured from Superior's depths. Depending on the month and the day's catch, **Russ Kendall's Smokehouse**—located along Scenic Drive—carries smoked or fresh lake trout, whitefish, herring, and salmon.

Next stop is Two Harbors, whose two natural bays became an early locale for iron ore shipping. As the staff and volunteers can tell you at the **Lake County Historical Society Museum**, which overlooks the huge ore docks from the corner of Waterfront Drive and South Avenue, Minnesota's first minuscule shipment of iron ore traveled from the Tower–Soudan mine in St. Louis County to Two Harbors in 1884. The amount of ore that passed through town that entire year—some sixty thousand tons—can today be carried by a single ship.

A short walk toward the lake from the museum leads to the permanent docking site of the *Edna G*, an extremely long-lived coal-fired tugboat that was in service at the docks from 1896 until the early 1980s, when freighters finally became capable of precise maneuvering in such small spaces as Agate Bay. The boat landing and breakwater at Lighthouse Point are good sites for watching these big ships dock and load. The museum staff can tell you which ships are coming and when.

Now then, let's say you have a question about sandpaper that's keeping you awake at night. Well, breathe a sigh of relief, because at Two Harbors' **Dwan Museum**, which contains the world's largest sandpaper exhibit, the answers to your most perplexing queries about abrasives are likely to be found. This one-of-a-kind museum occupies the former office of John Dwan, a Two Harbors lawyer who in 1902 became the first secretary of an obscure company called Minnesota Mining and Manufacturing—today known the world over as 3M.

The first of the museum's two rooms gives a brief history of 3M from its formation until 1919, when company headquarters moved from Two Harbors to St. Paul. An interesting display charts the company's growth and shows early models of some of its most famous products, including Scotch Tape and Post-it Notes. A portion of the second room documents changes in the company's logo through the years, and some of the museum has information on sandpaper, one of the most important products in the earlier days of 3M. For example, did you know that a very fine sandpaper is used to polish optical lenses? And that dentists use waterproof sandpaper to polish your teeth? And that 3M manufactures more than fifty *million* different sandpaper products for its customers around the world? For this and more impressive information, visit the Dwan Museum at 508 Second Ave. Admission is inexpensive, and the doors are open daily in summer and on weekends through the rest of the year.

A traumatic wait ended for pie lovers in early 1998 when two residents of the Twin Cities bought **Betty's Pies** and saved this venerable restaurant from extinction. Major reconstruction of MN 61 put part of the new road right through the existing building. The situation looked bleak for a while until the two new owners stepped forward and announced plans to rebuild farther back from Lake Superior. While the building and location have changed, the recipes won't, thanks to the two white knights in baker's aprons. The restaurant is located at 1633 Hwy. 61 East (two miles north of town), Two Harbors. Betty's serves breakfast, lunch, dinner, and, of course, awesome pies from 7 a.m. to 9 p.m. seven days a week. Call (218) 834-3367 or visit bettyspies.com.

You'll notice the landscape taking a turn for the dramatic just up the shore from Betty's as you approach the entrance to the Silver Creek Tunnel. Beside the entrance you can browse through the locally made crafts at **Pioneer Gallery & Gifts** (2821 Hwy. 61; 218-834-4175; pioneercrafts.com). From here to Thunder Bay, precipitous shoreline cliffs and awesome waterfalls are regular roadside attractions.

Because of the dangers posed by this inhospitable coast, the movers and shakers of the steel industry persuaded Congress to build the **Split Rock Lighthouse** in 1909. This plan was developed following a treacherous storm in November 1905, in which thirty ships were damaged or sunk, including two in the immediate vicinity of a prominent cliff located twenty miles northeast of Two Harbors. The Minnesota Historical Society now runs the site, and, as its guides will tell you, getting US taxpayers to fund the lighthouse was, in fact, a maneuver that enabled the steel barons to avoid having to institute costly safety procedures.

A beautiful interpretive center with an excellent film and exhibits complements the hour-long tour of the well-preserved lighthouse and the lightkeepers' residences (there were a head keeper and two assistants with families). The experience provides yet another perspective on the iron ore industry that has been so essential to Minnesota's livelihood. It also illuminates what life was like on Superior's shores in the early decades of the nineteenth century for local residents and for the employees of the strictly regimented and now-extinct US Lighthouse Service.

During the construction of the lighthouse, which required the assembly of a steam-powered derrick to hoist workers and materials up the one-hundred-foot cliff face, Split Rock was accessible only by lake. Soon after the North Shore Highway was completed in 1924, however, the facility became the most visited light station in the country. By 1969 the sophistication of navigational equipment had rendered obsolete the ten-second-interval beacon and foghorn (which were detectable more than twenty and five miles away, respectively), and Split Rock was deeded to the state.

The Split Rock Interpretive Center, MN 61, is open weekends in winter and daily through the summer months, whereas tours of the light station are offered only from mid-May through mid-Oct. A small fee is charged and an inexpensive state park sticker is required for admission. For more information call (218) 226-6372 or visit mnhs.org.

A view of the lake that surpasses even the one from the top of the Split Rock tower (itself 167 feet above the lake level) can be found about twelve miles farther up the shore. Just after passing the Palisade Baptist Church on the lake side of MN 61, you'll see an unmarked wayside parking area on the same side of the highway with a narrow, winding road leading out of sight up a steep embankment. This road leads to the top of **Palisade Head**, a spectacular two-hundred-foot promontory that presents a vertical face to the lake and that in summer is a popular playground for rock climbers. If you tire of watching men and women cheating death on the cliff, you can also look for a nesting pair of rare peregrines—falcons famous for attacking their prey in midflight—that have claimed this precipitous environment as a summer home. Also, the ground cover on top of Palisade Head offers outstanding blueberry picking in mid-to-late summer.

As grand as the views from Palisade Head may be, if you really want to take your measure against the North Shore's hills, you should spend some time on the **Superior Hiking Trail**. The rugged trail at present winds from Castle Danger to Grand Marais, connecting eight state parks in the process. Scenic overlooks punctuate the trail, as do occasional campsites (equipped with pit toilets and fire rings) and road crossings. The trail is designed so hikers can set out for just a few hours or hike for days. When the many, many hours of volunteer labor necessary to make the trail are complete, the Lake Superior Hiking

Trail will run the full distance from Duluth to the Canadian border. Trail maps are available free of charge at ranger stations and tourist information centers all along the shore. *Guide to the Superior Hiking Trail* is available from the trail association by calling (218) 834-2700 or visiting superiorhiking.org.

MN 1's winding sixty-mile journey from Illgen City on the Superior shore to Ely is one of those Arrowhead roads that continuously draws your attention out the window to witness tall stands of virgin timber, sparkling lakes and rivers, and moose and deer that momentarily break from their foraging to give you a mildly curious look. A little more than halfway along its length, this highway is intersected by Lake CR 2, very near the location of one of Minnesota's most unusual learning centers: the **Great Lakes School of Log Building** (1350 Snowshoe Trail, Isabella).

Since 1974, Ron Brodigan has been teaching experientially oriented courses in the basics of log construction for folks who've always dreamed of living in their own house made of trees. During the fourteen-day classes, students actually build a log structure such as the many that occupy the rustic school site (accommodations are in wood-heated bunkhouses, bathing is done in traditional Finnish saunas and solar showers, and participants provide their own food). At the end of each course, students with no previous construction experience or special strength return home with the necessary skills to under-take their own projects. Ron also offers rural skills short courses that concern various aspects of living in the backcountry. Per-day fees at the school are inexpensive. To register or to receive more information, call (218) 365-2126 or visit schooloflogbuilding.com.

Cook County

As the farthest northeastern point in Minnesota, Cook County is one of the most sparsely populated as well as one of the most scenic regions in the state. Although carpeted by hundreds of square miles of thick forest and home to a vast network of wilderness lakes, Lake Superior defines the character of this area. The big lake forms the southeastern border and exerts a powerful influence on the people and landscape of the county. Major tourist attraction, producer of heavy snowfall, summer air conditioner, moderator of winter tem-peratures, and at times inhospitable neighbor, Lake Superior affects all who choose to live by it or visit it.

If you're driving up the shore at a pace that's suitable for taking in all there is to see and do, by now you may well have happily consumed all the fish you purchased back in Knife River. No matter—in the tiny community of Schroeder, you can stop by the **Schroeder Baking Company** for a sandwich or fresh bakery treat. If you're not hungry yet, continue north about four miles to the town of Tofte and stop at *Coho Cafe, Bakery & Deli*.

Five miles north of Schroeder Baking Company, you'll cross the Temperance River, which at this elevation flows within the borders of *Temperance River State Park*. Some sources say this stream received its name in playful recognition of the fact that it was one of the few North Shore waterways without a sandbar at its mouth. Also, among the many rivers along the shore that have impressive waterfalls—such as the Gooseberry, Baptism, and Cascade—the Temperance is distinguished for having carved a fantastic series of cauldrons and spillways through the lava bedrock formation on the upstream side of the highway. A short trail winds along this section of the river, beginning from the parking area near the highway bridge.

The focal points for most of the state parks along MN 61 from Two Harbors to the Canadian border are the rivers that tumble down from the highlands to Lake Superior. The rivers all have waterfalls of various heights and intensities, and most have unique characteristics. Grand Portage State Park has the tallest waterfall in Minnesota at 120 feet, the high falls on the Pigeon River. The Temperance River has a series of falls where the water tumbles with such fury that it has carved smooth, round cauldrons from the billion-year-old volcanic rock of the canyon. *Cascade River State Park* has a spectacular series of several waterfalls that drop nine hundred feet from the top of the ridge bordering Lake Superior. All the parks have plenty of hiking trails that follow the rivers and the shoreline of the big lake.

Each park varies in size and amenities, from the 278-acre Grand Portage State Park, a day-use-only park with no camping, to 9,346-acre Tettegouche State Park with plenty of camping, hiking trails, and cross-country skiing and snowshoe trails. But even with all the camping and assorted activities available at each park, the most popular sights are always the rivers that cut through them.

Grand Marais is a focal point of North Shore recreational activity in both winter and summer. It is also a quaint coastal town in its own right, with a history steeped in fishing and logging traditions. When you are entering the community from the southwest, visible to your right is Grand Marais's harbor, where you'll find the North Shore's only sailboat instruction center outside of Duluth.

The *North House Folk School* offers several sailing programs, including the Lake Superior Adventure, a two-hour trip around the Grand Marais harbor and out into the big lake for an incomparable view of the Sawtooth Mountains and the North Shore. All trips leave from the Grand Marais harbor on the *Hjordis*, a fifty-foot gaff-rigged schooner. The school also offers a basic navigation and weather course, a Nuts about Knots class, and the Craft of Sail introduction to sailing.

North House provides instruction and programs to help participants learn and understand crafts of the past and present. Besides the sailing programs, courses include boat building, timber framing, shelter building, and woodworking, to name a few. For more information contact North House Folk School at (218) 387-9762 or northhouse.org.

Grand Marais's wilderness highway—the **Gunflint Trail**—is another Arrowhead road deserving of all the historic and romantic associations brought to mind by its name. Originally no more than a footpath, the road today meanders between lakeshores and climbs up and over steep rocky ridges for fifty-three miles before suddenly dispersing like a river delta into a network of boat landings along the shores of Lake Saganaga on the Canadian border. The Gunflint has numerous jumping-off points to the **Boundary Waters Canoe Area** (BWCA), which borders the trail for half its length. Boundary Waters travel information is available at the **Superior National Forest ranger stations** in Tofte and **Grand Marais**. Wilderness travel permits can be obtained by contacting the BWCA Reservation Office at (877) 444-6777 or by visiting recreation.gov.

There are plenty of resorts and outfitters along the Gunflint, too, the latter providing equipment, food, and route-planning services for those interested in canoeing the BWCA's pristine waters (call 218-388-2212 or go to gunflint -trail.com for a list of outfitters and resorts and for hiking, biking, and skiing information). Come winter, the Gunflint has several outstanding networks of snowmobile and cross-country skiing trails, including one that provides skiers with access to a most unusual type of accommodation: the yurt.

For centuries the people of the Mongolian plateaus have found cylindrical, peak-roofed tents, or yurts, to be practical places to live. Yurts are also much warmer than standard tents when outfitted with a woodstove, which they accommodate quite easily. Ted and Barbara Young of **Boundary Country Trekking** (Gunflint Trail 67-1) have established three of these dwellings an easy day's ski apart along the Banadad Trail. Each of the one-room canvas-covered yurts sleeps four to six, with accoutrements that include bunk beds, skylights, woodstoves, and an outhouse nearby.

You can either ski from yurt to yurt or to a recently built backwoods cabin reachable only on skis. The Youngs cheerfully shuttle your gear to the following day's destination and upon your arrival prepare outstanding meals, including such specialties as roast duck, grilled trout, and the almost-mystical Mongolian firepot dinner. Two lodges at either end of the Banadad Trail provide more civilized accommodations, or if yurts are too luxurious for your tastes, guided ski trips into the wilderness with dogsled support can be arranged. Prices for the yurt-to-yurt program are expensive, though they include the three meals per day, lodging, and shuttle. For more information contact Boundary Country Trekking at (218) 388-4487 or go to boundarycountry.com.

Another destination along the Gunflint Trail that's well worth the effort required to reach it is the 3.5-mile hike that will take you to the top of Minnesota's highest peak. You'll find the **Eagle Mountain** trailhead seventeen miles northwest of Grand Marais, at the junction of Superior National Forest Roads 153 and 158 (the Gunflint and Tofte ranger stations have maps). Throughout its length the trail winds through such dense forest that you really haven't a clue as to where you are. Then suddenly the sky opens up and you find yourself on the edge of a dramatic escarpment 2,301 feet above sea level that provides a sweeping view of the forested wilderness to the south, west, and north. It is a truly magical place to be during evening light, when the surfaces of a half-dozen lakes down below are set on fire—though make sure you bring a flashlight, as the hike back to the car is a nasty one in the dark.

The lure of the North Shore for those seeking a place to revel in nature's glories is not a new phenomenon. As soon as the highway was completed from Duluth to Fort William and Port Arthur (now Thunder Bay) in 1924, the Superior shoreline quickly became a popular destination for the touring crowd. It even attracted the mighty Babe Ruth, boxer Jack Dempsey, and writer Ring Lardner, who were part of a group that banded together to build an exclusive wilderness retreat near Hovland called **Naniboujou Lodge** (20 Naniboujou Trail). But perhaps the establishment's namesake—a mythological trickster of the North American woodland cultures—was a poor choice, for the project ground to a halt following the stock market crash of 1929, with only the main lodge and dining room completed.

Today Naniboujou's moderately priced rooms attract guests who come to collect agates on the beach or hike, ski, and fish beside the **Brule River** in the adjacent **Judge C. R. Magney State Park**. The dining room has an even larger clientele drawn by the very good fresh fish and poultry dishes (among others) and the fresh-baked breads and desserts served by owners Tim and Nancy Ramey. The setting for these moderately priced repasts is a large room whose lofty ceiling was painted in the 1920s with a bold, colorful motif inspired by Cree mythology. Ornate paper chandeliers hang above. The huge fireplace at one end consists of more than two hundred tons of native rock. Outside, the building's wood-shingled exterior blends nicely with the sprawling grounds that stretch down to the lakeshore. For more information call (218) 387-2688 or check naniboujou.com.

The last twenty miles of Minnesota's Lake Superior shoreline take you through the Ojibway-owned ***Grand Portage Indian Reservation***, one of the most historically significant and beautiful areas in all of Minnesota. After topping a steady incline that builds for several miles, MN 61 suddenly crests at

Worth the Hike

As with many places that are off the beaten path, sometimes even these areas get busier than one would expect. The hike to Eagle Mountain is a case in point. Most of the time you might encounter a few other hikers on this rugged trail, but on holiday weekends, and even some peak summer weekends, you might be surprised at the number of people on the trail. Eagle Mountain is still a highly recommended hike, but for those looking for some different trails to try that may not be as busy I recommend these.

The ***Devil Track Canyon*** trail follows the Superior Hiking Trail for 2.3 miles to a bridge that crosses the river at the bottom of the gorge. The trail winds along the top of the canyon, and though you often can't see the river, you can hear the roar of it below. For those who want to extend their hike, it's well worth the extra effort to hike another mile up to the Pincushion Mountain overlook. You'll have great views of Lake Superior, ample reward for the extra mileage. To get to the Devil Track Canyon hike take MN 61 northeast from Grand Marais to CR 58, turn left and go about a mile to a parking area for the Superior Hiking Trail.

Grand Portage State Park is located within the Ojibway-owned ***Grand Portage Indian Reservation***, and sits on the ***Pigeon River***, once home to ***Fort Charlotte***. This historic trail was called *Gichi Onigamiing* by American Indians, the Great Carrying Place, and was used for thousands of years as part of a cross-continent trade network before Europeans arrived. American Indians, and the voyageurs who came later, used the trail to avoid the High Falls on the Pigeon River to get to Lake Superior. The voyageurs called the trail the Grand Portage (from *portager*, which means "to carry") and would stop at Fort Charlotte, unload furs from the twenty-four-foot river canoes, and carry them to Lake Superior where they were loaded into the thirty-six-foot Montreal canoes for the trip east. The process was reversed for provisions and trade goods heading west to villages inland.

This rugged trail is 8.5 miles long, and makes for a long day for those who try to hike the entire round trip in a day. Old Highway 61 divides the trail into two sections, the shorter eastern part that goes to Lake Superior, and the longer western part that runs to the site of Fort Charlotte. The western section is a nine-mile round trip, and passes through a huge beaver pond swamp before reaching the Pigeon River. You won't pass any overlooks with spectacular views of the area, but you can't escape the feeling of hiking the same path used for thousands of years by American Indians and voyageurs. This is also moose country, and though you may not see one of these magnificent animals, you will likely see plenty of hoofprints in the trail. I can't guarantee you won't see other people on either section of the Grand Portage, but it's safe to say you won't see many, especially on the western section.

a wayside parking area with a dramatic view of Grand Portage's large natural harbor and the *Susie Island chain* beyond. On a clear day you can also see Michigan's Isle Royale National Park in the hazy distance. Rising up from the shore is a steep escarpment of hills, over which hardy voyageurs during the latter part of the eighteenth century carried their heavy birchbark canoes and many tons of animal pelts tied in ninety-pound bundles.

The white-cedar stockade and log buildings at *Grand Portage National Monument* have been painstakingly reconstructed by the National Park Service to preserve the spirit of this hub of the fur trade. Costumed guides and such special events as the annual Rendezvous and Powwow in mid-Aug give visitors a vivid impression of the lifestyle that reigned here from 1784 to 1803, when the North West Company used the settlement as the headquarters of its fur trade empire. Each summer hundreds of voyageurs, portaging their canoes and bearing backbreaking loads of furs from their wintering posts in the Canadian Northwest, hiked down the nine-mile Grand Portage Trail. They were met at the stockade by their counterparts, who had traveled by even larger birchbark freight canoes across the Great Lakes from Montreal with heavy supplies of trade goods. For several weeks in midsummer, the two groups exchanged their cargoes and, with the help of local Ojibway, celebrated one of the biggest parties on the frontier. Leaving enough time to return safely to their respective wintering posts, the two groups then loaded up their canoes for the long trip home. The monument, which is well marked along US 61, is open daily mid-May to mid-Oct; a small fee is charged. For information on special programs, call (218) 475-0123.

The dock in front of the Grand Portage monument welcomes ships from the open lake, just as it did hundreds of years ago. Throughout summer it is also the dock site of the passenger ferry *Wenonah,* which departs daily for the nearest end of Michigan's *Isle Royale National Park*, twenty-two miles off

Something Different in the Arrowhead

Arrowhead offers much in the way of traditional recreation: swimming, boating, and other lake-based activities in the summer and skiing and snowmobiling in the winter. But for something different try a sightseeing trip to view the ice-coated rocks along Lake Superior, or stop at Lutsen Mountains and take a gondola ride to the top of Moose Mountain for a spectacular view of the big lake. If you want to get active, try a dogsledding trip or a lodge-to-lodge ski excursion along the Gunflint Trail, or spend a night or two in a backcountry yurt. It gets brisk during an Arrowhead winter, but you won't have to fight off mosquitoes or hordes of other travelers.

shore; round-trip voyages on this ferry last most of the day and are expensive. Those wishing to circumnavigate this largest island in the largest lake in the world can book passage on the *Voyageur*, which departs every other day from a landing at the northeast end of the harbor. For more information about these excursions, call (218) 600-0765 May through Oct or check out isleroyaleboats .com.

You'll understand why the voyageurs preferred a nine-mile hike through the mosquito-infested woods to a canoe trip down the Pigeon River, which forms the Minnesota–Ontario border, if you pay a visit to ***Grand Portage State Park***. This newest of Minnesota's state parks provides parking and an access trail to 120-foot High Falls on the Pigeon River, Minnesota's highest waterfall. To find it follow MN 61 almost to its terminus at the US Customs station, where there is a small parking lot on the north side of the road.

Like the voyageurs before them, the loggers who worked the Pigeon River Valley around the turn of the twentieth century were also intimidated by High Falls. Through the mist you can see the remains of a flume that carried their logs past the waterfall without the logs being turned into splinters. Still, the river's many violent rapids were so rough that an especially low grade of lumber was developed to market boards made from Pigeon River logs.

Places to Stay in the Arrowhead Region

AITKIN

40 Club Inn
960 Second St. Northwest
(218) 927-2903
fortyclubinn.com

Ripple River Motel
701 Minnesota Ave. South
(218) 927-3734
ripplerivermotel.com

DULUTH

Comfort Suites
408 Canal Park Dr.
(218) 727-1378
liftbridgelodge.com

Hampton Inn
310 Canal Park Dr.
(218) 720-3000
hilton.com

Inn on Gitche Gumee
8517 Congdon Blvd.
(507) 273-3995
innongitchegumee.org

ELY

Adventure Inn
1145 East Sheridan St.
(218) 365-3140
adventureinn-ely.com

Grand Ely Lodge Resort
400 North Pioneer Rd.
(218) 365-6565
grandelylodge.com

**Northwoods Inn
and Suites**
1605 East Sheridan St.
(218) 365-2873
nwisuites.com

GRAND MARAIS

Anderson's Cabins
two miles north of Grand
Marais on Lake Superior
(218) 387-1814
andersonscabins.com

Aspen Lodge
208 Hwy. 61 East
(218) 387-2500
gmhotel.net

**Best Western
Superior Inn**
108 East Hwy. 61
(218) 387-2240
bestwestern.com

East Bay Suites
21 Wisconsin St.
(800) 414-2807
odysseyresorts.com

**MacArthur House
Bed and Breakfast**
520 West Second St.
(218) 260-6390
macarthurhouse.net

GRAND RAPIDS

AmericInn
1812 South Pokegama
Ave.
(218) 212-1842
wyndhamhotels.com

**Green Heron Bed
& Breakfast**
2810 Meyers Bay Rd.
(218) 999-5795
greenheronbandb.com

Pokegama Lake Resort
20648 Crystal Springs Rd.
(218) 301-0428
pokegamalakeresort.com

Timberlake Lodge Hotel
144 Southeast Seventeenth
St.
(218) 326-2600
timberlakelodgehotel.com

HIBBING/EVELETH/
VIRGINIA

Quality Inn and Suites
502 Chestnut St.
Virginia
(218) 749-1000
choicehotels.com

Hampton Inn Hibbing
4225 Ninth Ave. West
(218) 262-0000
hilton.com

**Green Gate
Guest Houses**
5748 Giants Ridge Rd.
Biwabik
(218) 290-2607
greengateguesthouses.com

**Country Inn of
Hoyt Lakes**
99 Kennedy Memorial Dr.
Hoyt Lakes
(218) 225-3555
Hinckley

**Dakota Lodge
Bed & Breakfast**
MN 48
(320) 384-6052

Days Inn
104 Grindstone Ct.
(320) 384-7751
wyndhamhotels.com

Americas Best Value Inn
325 Fire Monument Rd.
(320) 384-6112
redlion.com

**Woodland Trails
Bed & Breakfast**
40361 Grace Lake Rd.
(612) 590-7330
woodlandtrails.net

INTERNATIONAL FALLS/
RANIER

AmericInn Hotel & Suites
2500 Keenan Dr.
International Falls
(218) 209-2487
wyndhamhotels.com

**Cobblestone Hotel
and Suites**
1 Memorial Dr.
(218) 324-4660
staycobblestone.com

Island View Lodge
1817 Hwy. 11 East
International Falls
(218) 286-3511
gotorainylake.com

**Rainy Lake Inn and
Suites at Tara's Wharf**
2065 Spruce St. Landing
Ranier
(218) 286-5699
taraswharf.com

MCGREGOR

Crossroads Hotel
403 Meadow Dr.
(218) 768-7378

MORA

AmericInn Lodge & Suites
1877 Frontage Rd.
(320) 679-5700
wyndhamhotels.com

TWO HARBORS

AmericInn
1088 Hwy. 61
(218) 834-3000
wyndhamhotels.com

Country Inn
1204 Seventh Ave.
(218) 834-5557
countryinntwoharbors.com

Grand Superior Lodge
2826 Hwy. 61
(218) 834-3796
odysseyresorts.com

**Lighthouse Bed
& Breakfast**
One Lighthouse Point
(218) 834-4898
lighthousebb.org

**Northern Rail
Traincar Inn**
1730 County Hwy. 3
(877) 834-0955
northernrail.net

Places to Eat in the Arrowhead Region

AITKIN

Smokey Jake's BBQ
(American)
12 Second St.
(218) 928-8100
smokeyjakesbbq.com

The Beanery
(coffee and sandwiches)
301 Minnesota Ave. North
(218) 927-7811

The Landing
(American)
145 Southgate Dr.
(218) 927-9998
the-landing-aitkin.edan.io

Roadside Restaurant
(homemade soups and
baked goods)
306 Second St. Northeast
(218) 927-2113

Rosallini's
(pizza, pasta)
119 Minnesota Ave. North
(218) 927-6412
rosallinispizzas.com

DULUTH

**At Sara's Table
Chester Creek Cafe**
(coffee, American)
1902 East Eighth St.
(218) 724-6811
astccc.net

Fitgers Brewhouse
(American)
600 East Superior St.
(218) 279-2739
fitgersbrewhouse.com

Grandma's
(American)
522 Lake Ave. South
(218) 727-4192
grandmasrestaurants.com

Hanabi Japanese Cuisine
110 North First Ave. West
(218) 464-4412
hanabiduluth.com

Lake Avenue Restaurant
(eclectic)
394 Lake Ave. South
(218) 722-2355
lakeaveduluth.com

**Little Angie's
Cantina & Grill**
(Southwest, American)
11 East Buchanan St.
(218) 727-6117
littleangies.com

New Scenic Cafe
(international)
5461 North Shore Dr.
(218) 525-6274
newsceniccafe.com

Old Chicago Pizza
327 Lake Ave. South
(218) 409-8830
oldchicago.com

Pizza Luce
11 East Superior St.
(218) 727-7400
pizzaluce.com

Portland Malt Shop
(ice cream—seasonal)
716 East Superior St.
portlandmaltshoppe.com

Va Bene Caffe
(Italian)
734 East Superior St.
(218) 722-1518
vabenecaffe.com

Love Creamery
small batch ice cream
1908 West Superior St.
(218) 576-5639
lovecreamery.com

ELY

**Boathouse Brewpub
and Restaurant**
(American)
47 East Sheridan
(218) 365-4301
boathousebrewpub.com

Burntside Lodge
(American)
2755 Burntside Lodge Rd.
(218) 365-3894
burntside.com

Ely Steakhouse
(American)
216 East Sheridan
(218) 365-7412
elysteakhouse.com

Evergreen Restaurant
(American)
400 North Pioneer Rd.
(218) 365-6875
grandelylodge.com

**Gator's Grilled
Cheese Emporium**
955 East Sheridan St.
(218) 365-7348

**Northern Grounds
(coffee, etc.)**
2 West Sheridan St.
(218) 365-6160
thenortherngrounds.com

Sir G's
(Italian)
520 East Sheridan
(218) 365-3688

GRAND MARAIS

Angry Trout
(eclectic)
408 MN 61
(218) 387-1265
angrytroutcafe.com

**Birch Terrace
Restaurant**
(American)
601 MN 61
(218) 387-2215

Blue Water Cafe
(American)
20 West Wisconsin St.
(218) 387-1597
bluewatercafe.com

**Cascade Lodge
& Restaurant**
(American)
MN 61 (nine miles
south of Grand Marais)
(218) 387-1112
cascadelodgemn.com

Hungry Hippie Tacos
15 West Hwy. 61
(218) 387-3382
hungryhippietacos.com

**Java Moose
Espresso Café**
218 West Hwy. 61
(218) 387-9400
javamoosegrandmarais
.com

My Sister's Place
(American)
401 East Hwy. 61
(218) 387-1915
mysistersplacerestaurant
.com

Sven and Ole's Pizza
9 West Wisconsin St.
(218) 387-1713

World's Best Donuts
10 East Wisconsin St.
(218) 387-1345
worldsbestdonutsmn.com

GRAND RAPIDS

Dragonfly Coffee
201 Northwest Fourth St.
(218) 999-5771

Bixby's Cafe
(soup and sandwiches)
400 River Rd.
(218) 999-4230
grbixbys.com

**Brewed Awakenings
Coffeehouse**
24 Northeast Fourth St.
(218) 327-1088

Dotties Hometown Cafe
(American)
324 Northeast Fourth St.
(218) 327-1400

El Potro
(Mexican)
508 South Pokegama Ave.
(218) 326-6275
elpotromexicanrestaurant
.business.site

New China Restaurant
214 Northwest First Ave.
(218) 327-1455

Pasties Plus
1407 Northwest Fourth St.
(218) 398-2994

Sammy's Pizza
802 South Pokegama Ave.
(218) 326-8551
sammyspizzagrandrapids
.com

17th Street Grill
(American)
144 Southeast Seventeenth
St.
(218) 326-2600
timberlakelodgehotel.com

HIBBING/EVELETH/
VIRGINIA

Copper Nickel Pub
(American)
111 Main St. North
Aurora
(218) 306-6149

**Grandma's Saloon
& Grill**
1302 Twelfth Ave. West
Virginia
(218) 749-1960
grandmasrestaurants.com

**The Hive Coffee
and Bakehouse**
103 Main St. North
Aurora
(218) 229-0001
thehiveaurora.com

La Cocina & Cantina
(Mexican)
407 Chestnut St.
Virginia
(218) 749-8226
lacocinacantina.com

SELECTED WEBSITES IN THE ARROWHEAD

Aitkin Area Information
(218) 927-2316
aitkin.com

Duluth Convention and Visitors Bureau
(218) 722-4011
visitduluth.com

Ely Chamber of Commerce
(218) 365-6123
ely.org

Grand Marais Area Tourism Association
(218) 387-2524
visitcookcounty.com

Visit Grand Rapids
(855) 944-7748
visitgrandrapids.com

Hinckley Convention and Visitors Bureau
(320) 384-0126
hinckleymn.com

International Falls Chamber of Commerce
(218) 283-9400
ifallschamber.com

Iron Range Tourism Bureau
(218) 749-8161
(Hibbing, Eveleth, etc.)
ironrange.org

Mora Area Chamber of Commerce
(320) 679-5792
moramn.com

Two Harbors Chamber of Commerce
(218) 834-2600
northshorevisitor.com

Natural Harvest Food Co-op & Coffee Bar
732 Fouth St. North
Virginia
(218) 741-4663
naturalharvest.coop

Rudy's Bar and Grill
116 Main St. North
Aurora
(218) 229-3983
rudysmn.com

Saigon Café
111 North Hwy. 135
Virginia
(218) 741-6465

Sammy's Pizza
106 East Howard St.
Hibbing
(218) 263-7574
sammyspizzahibbing.com

Whistling Bird Cafe & Bar
(Caribbean, pasta)
101 Broadway
Gilbert
(218) 741-5030
thewhistlingbird.com

HINCKLEY

Bogey's on Main
(American)
104 Main St. West
(320) 384-7855

Tobies
(American)
404 Fire Monument Rd.
(320) 384-6174
tobies.com

Whistle Stop Café
305 Old Hwy. 61 South
(320) 384-6106
whistlestopcafehinckley
.com

INTERNATIONAL FALLS

Chocolate Moose Restaurant Company
2501 Second Ave. West
(218) 283-8888
chocolatemooserestaurant
.com

Coffee Landing Café
444 Third St.
(218) 373-2233

Sammy's Pizza
301 Third Ave.
(218) 373-0190
sammyspizzaifalls.com

The Library
(American)
1323 Third St.
(218) 373-2739
thelibrary.delivery

Rose Garden Restaurant
(Chinese)
311 Fourth Ave.
(218) 283-4551

MCGREGOR

Fireside Inn
(American)
415 Country Meadow Dr.
(218) 768-3818

**The Blue Moose
on the Lake**
48493 Lily Ave.
(218) 426-3029

MORA

Downtown Deli
(bistro, coffee shop)
113 Southeast Railroad
Ave.
(320) 679-5555

Emma's Pizza
113 South Lake St.
(320) 679-9229

Freddies
(full menu)
810 Hwy. 65
(320) 679-2811
freddiesrestaurantmora.com

El Jalisco Grill and Bar
(Mexican)
30 North Union St.
(320) 679-5370
eljaliscogrillandbar.com

Sportsmen's Cafe
67 Hwy. 65
(320) 225-2233

TWO HARBORS

Blackwoods Grill & Bar
(American)
612 Seventh Ave.
(218) 834-3846
blackwoods.com

Cedar Coffee Company
1130 Eleventh St.
(218) 510-0160
cedarcoffeecompany.com

Do North Pizzeria
15 County Hwy. 20
(218) 834-3555
donorthpizza.com

Judy's Cafe
(home cooking, American)
623 Seventh Ave.
(218) 834-4802

Madeira Bistro
632 First Ave.
(218) 337-2103
madeira-bistro.com

**Vanilla Bean
Bakery & Cafe**
812 Seventh Ave.
(218) 834-3714
thevanillabean.com

Lilly's Asian Café
826 Seventh Ave.
(218) 834-4373
lillysasiancafe.kwickmenu
.com

Index